# LINCOLN'S ROAD
## TO WAR

## ALSO BY DAVID ALAN JOHNSON

*The City Ablaze*

*The London Blitz*

*V for Vengeance*

*Union: The Archives Photographs Series*

*The Battle of Britain: The American Factor*

*Germany's Spies and Saboteurs*

*Righteous Deception: German Officers against Hitler*

*Betrayal: The True Story of J. Edgar Hoover and the Nazi Saboteurs*

*Decided on the Battlefield: Lincoln, Grant,
Sherman, and the Election of 1864*

*Union Revisited*

*Battle of Wills: Robert E. Lee, Ulysses S. Grant,
and the Last Year of the Civil War*

*Yanks in the RAF*

*The Last Weeks of Abraham Lincoln*

*Admiral Canaris: How Hitler's Chief of Intelligence Betrayed the Nazis*

DAVID ALAN JOHNSON

# LINCOLN'S ROAD = TO = WAR

★ ★ ★ ★ ★ ★

## A DAY-BY-DAY ACCOUNT
### *of the* FIRST 60 DAYS *of*
### ABRAHAM LINCOLN'S PRESIDENCY

LP
LYONS
PRESS

*Essex, Connecticut*

*To Laura, thanks again for everything.*

**LYONS PRESS**

An imprint of The Globe Pequot Publishing Group, Inc.
64 South Main St.
Essex, CT 06426
www.GlobePequot.com

British Library Cataloguing in Publication Information Available

Library of Congress Cataloging-in-Publication Data Available
ISBN 9781493092024 (cloth) | ISBN 9781493092031 (epub)

# CONTENTS

# CONTENTS

# INTRODUCTION

The first two months after the inauguration of Abraham Lincoln, between March 4 and May 3, 1861, mark one of the most significant periods in American history. The antagonism between North and South, which had been intensifying since Lincoln's election as president in November 1860, worsened when the president-elect was sworn into office. Just over a month after the inauguration, feelings between the two sides deteriorated to the point where any sort of reconciliation became impossible. During the early morning hours of April 12, rebel artillery opened fire on Fort Sumter, situated on a man-made island in the entrance to Charleston Harbor, South Carolina. This was immediately followed by President Lincoln's call for seventy-five thousand volunteers from state militias, along with his order to blockade all Southern ports. The first full-scale battle of what had finally developed into a civil war, the Battle of Bull Run/Manassas, took place on July 21, 1861.

These early weeks of Abraham Lincoln's administration were pivotal to the following four years of his presidency. Between his inauguration and the bombardment of Fort Sumter, Lincoln evolved from an inexperienced, newly installed president trying desperately to avoid a war, to a reluctant commander in chief resolved to defend Fort Sumter against rebel aggression, and finally to a war president determined to see the fighting through to the end and to restore the Union. Abraham Lincoln was completely unprepared to deal with the conflicts and emergencies that dominated the first few weeks of his presidency, and he knew just how unprepared he was—he would later remark that he did not control events as much as the events controlled him. But by the third week of April, President Lincoln was prepared to use all of his resources to direct the course of the war, although he realized that he still had a great deal to learn.

Carl Sandburg wrote that the election of Abraham Lincoln sent a signal throughout the country. His inauguration amplified that signal. To the North, the inauguration promised a time of prosperity: for building railroads; for establishing homesteads on the western frontiers. But to residents of the Southern states, Abraham Lincoln's presidency signaled a threat to their very way of life, which included prohibiting the institution of slavery. In the North, Lincoln was often described as a man of the people, although his political colleagues did not always agree with him. In the South, the prevailing opinion of Abraham Lincoln was almost unanimously negative. Newspapers in Southern cities called him, among other things, a lunatic, a radical abolitionist, and a tyrant. By the end of 1860, a secession movement had begun and was gaining momentum across the South—South Carolina voted to secede from the Union on December 20, 1860. Several other states soon followed. The United States was dividing into two separate sections: an alarmed North and an increasingly hostile South. No one in the North, including the new president, knew exactly what to do about the growing crisis.

One of President Lincoln's main difficulties was that he did not take the threat of war seriously. In mid-February, the president-elect told a gathering in Cleveland, Ohio, that the crisis between North and South was an artificial crisis. But the fort's commander, Major Robert Anderson, had serious doubts as to whether or not he could keep from surrendering to the South Carolina militia. Major Anderson reported that his supplies were running out, and that he would require at least seventy thousand men to reinforce the garrison. This was an impossible request—at the time, the entire US Army consisted of about sixteen thousand men. The majority of these troops were stationed at frontier garrisons in the West. While President Lincoln was downplaying the emergency, and doing his best to prevent war, Confederate president Jefferson Davis informed a crowd in Stevenson, Alabama that he hoped for peace but was prepared for war.

In his inauguration address on March 4, 1861, President Lincoln did his best to be reconciliatory, advising Southern secessionists that there would be no war unless they were the aggressors. But he also made it clear that the Union was indivisible, and that secession meant anarchy. The Union would remain intact. Lincoln assured the Southern states that he bore them no ill will, but also that he would not tolerate secession. The very end of his thirty-minute speech is the most well-known and best remembered part of it, and is also the most conciliatory. "The mystic chords of memory" would "swell the chorus of the Union" when touched again "by the better angels of our nature."

The president's first days in office were filled with stress and anxiety. He insisted upon seeing everyone who came to the White House in search of a job or some sort of appointment. His close associates warned him that he was wearing himself out, but President Lincoln ignored all warnings and continued to talk to any and all job seekers. But there were other, more pressing worries. Lincoln was fully aware that he did not have either the executive or the military experience that he would need to see him through the coming crisis, which was the main source of his anxieties. He was totally unprepared to carry out the duties of his elected office. Henry Adams, the son of the American ambassador to Britain, admitted that he had never seen anyone so in need of education as the newly sworn-in president.

The most difficult situation for the president, the state of affairs that gave him the most anxiety, was the crisis at Fort Sumter. Another federal installation, Fort Pickens outside Pensacola, Florida, was also under threat, but Fort Sumter was the main point of contention. President Lincoln conferred with members of his cabinet, as well as with senior army and navy officers, over what should be done about the emergency. His secretary of state, William H. Seward, advised him not to send reinforcements to the fort; Seward was afraid this would trigger an open conflict. The postmaster general, Montgomery Blair, argued that surrendering Sumter would only encourage secessionists, which would also precipitate a war. General Winfield Scott, the commander in chief of the army, thought reinforcing the fort would not be feasible, because it would take six months. At the end of March, after listening to all sides and opinions,

President Lincoln decided to resupply Fort Sumter. This was his first real decision as commander in chief.

Lincoln's decision was based as much on his own personality and emotional makeup as it was on political and military considerations. He had a strong will and personality, both of which allowed him to make difficult decisions. Most of his cabinet advised him to surrender the fort; only two members were in favor of sending supplies. But President Lincoln did not have the temperament or disposition to sidestep a crisis. He did not want war, but he was not going to surrender a government military installation to avoid one.

Still hoping to avoid war, but also convinced that failing to resupply Fort Sumter would signal his acceptance of secession, President Lincoln sent an old friend to South Carolina to determine if the residents of Charleston still had any pro-Union sentiments. The man Lincoln sent, Stephen Hurlbut, grew up in Charleston and still had relatives living there. When Stephen Hurlbut returned to Washington after his fact-finding visit, he reported that all feelings of national patriotism had disappeared; the city was solidly in favor of Southern independence. The secession crisis showed no signs of abating. If anything, bad feeling against the North was on the increase. Many people were of the opinion that war was just what was needed to unify the South.

Besides the crisis over Fort Sumter and the problem with secession, President Lincoln was also having more than his share of difficulties with members of his cabinet. One of his main sources of irritation was Secretary of State William H. Seward. Secretary Seward had many years of experience in government, including two terms as US senator, and was exasperated by the president's inexperience and seeming lack of leadership. At the end of March, Secretary Seward sent a note to Lincoln; the note reprimanded the president for his lack of any sort of policy, either foreign or domestic. President Lincoln was not happy with Seward's message, and wrote an angry reply. But he realized that his response would do more harm than good, and decided not to send it. He did not want to alienate Seward; he knew that he would have to rely upon the knowledge and experience of his secretary of state in the near future, and did not want to make an enemy. Instead, he spoke with Seward in person, which avoided a confrontation. Lincoln may have been a novice in matters of statesmanship, but he was an expert in diplomacy and in dealing with people—qualities that would serve him well during the next four years.

Sometimes, President Lincoln's attempts at reconciliation had the opposite effect. On April 6, he notified the governor of South Carolina, Francis W. Pickens, that he intended to resupply Fort Sumter. In his message, the president said that he was sending provisions only—no arms, ammunition, or troops would be sent. It was an attempt to ease tensions, to let the governor know in advance that only food and other basic necessities would be delivered to the fort, and that there was no threat intended. But Governor Pickens notified Confederate president Jefferson Davis of Lincoln's message. President Davis did not see anything conciliatory about Lincoln's communication or his intentions. As far as President Davis was concerned, Lincoln's communiqué was nothing less than a direct threat. At noon on April 11, a message was sent to Major Anderson at Fort Sumter—a demand to surrender the fort. Major Anderson politely refused.

Major Robert Anderson, Fort Sumter's commanding officer, had serious doubts as to whether or not he could successfully defend the fort.

At 4:30 a.m. on April 12, Charleston's heavy artillery, commanded by Confederate general Pierre G. T. Beauregard, opened fire on Fort Sumter. After a thirty-four-hour bombardment, Major Anderson lowered the US flag and turned the fort over to the Confederates.

At 4:30 a.m. on April 12, Charleston's heavy artillery, commanded by Confederate general Pierre G. T. Beauregard, opened fire on Fort Sumter. After a thirty-four-hour bombardment, Major Anderson lowered the US flag, turned the fort over to the Confederates, and departed for New York by steamer with his men. No one on either side was killed in the bombardment.

President Lincoln could now state that the war had been started by Southern secessionists. South Carolina was the aggressor—the state had attacked a US installation that was running low on supplies and would not allow the fort's garrison to receive vitally needed food and provisions. The attack on Fort Sumter unified the North; it ended all the arguments over whether the fort should be reinforced, or if Southern states should be allowed to secede. Patriotic demonstrations were held in cities throughout the North; thousands of people waved flags and shouted that Jefferson Davis should be hanged. Also, thousands of young men north of the Mason-Dixon Line volunteered to join their state militias, hurrying to get into the war before it ended—everyone predicted that the fighting would be over within ninety days, and no one wanted to miss it.

The war that President Lincoln tried to avoid had begun. He called for seventy-five thousand state militia volunteers to reinforce the army. His opponent in the recent presidential election, Stephen A. Douglas, supported the president; he told Lincoln that he would have called for two hundred thousand volunteers. Lincoln admitted that the bombardment of Fort Sumter did him, as well as the country, a service. The North was now united behind him. But after Fort Sumter, the president now had a different set of problems to deal with—the problems of a war president, which would severely test his abilities as a head of state. On April 19, in an attempt to isolate all of the seceded states, he ordered a blockade of all Southern ports.

One of President Lincoln's primary worries concerned the officer corps of the US Army—about one-third of all officers resigned their commissions to join the Confederate forces. On April 18, the day after Virginia seceded from the Union, Colonel Robert E. Lee announced his decision to resign his commission and offer his services to Virginia. President Lincoln would be going to war with an army of undertrained volunteers led by officers with no combat experience. He was preparing for a protracted and bitter war, while hoping for a relatively short conflict.

All hopes for any sort of quick war and easy victory ended on July 21, 1861, at Manassas, Virginia, where Union and Confederate forces faced each other in the war's first major battle. Early fighting favored the

Union troops. Spectators who had come to watch the battle were certain that the North would win. But the tide turned against the Union when fresh Confederate troops arrived, surprising the Union forces. The Battle of Bull Run / Manassas turned into a rout as Northern soldiers broke ranks and ran from the field. In Washington, President Lincoln was distraught and agitated when he received news that the battle was lost. He determined to find out exactly why the fighting had ended in disaster for the federal troops. In the coming weeks, he would try to find the general who would reorganize the army, raise morale, and turn a group of green recruits into a well-trained body of soldiers for the coming war. During the next four years, Lincoln's tenure as president would be defined by the war.

# THE MOST WIDELY ANTICIPATED SPEECH

President-elect Abraham Lincoln went over his speech for the dozenth time that morning. After reading and rereading it silently to himself, he decided to read it out loud to his wife Mary as well as to his sons. He was all too aware that his inaugural address was the most important speech of his political career to date, and he wanted to make sure that it gave the impression he intended. The address defined his position on both slavery and secession, the two most heated topics of the hour, as well as on the supremacy of the federal government and the US Constitution.

The address was the most widely anticipated speech in recent years—made by any politician. News reporters throughout the North and the South were standing by to take note of Lincoln's words, and then to send them off to their readers by telegram. Northerners hoped that the speech would give them assurances that the new president intended to keep the Union intact. Southerners waited to see what Lincoln had to say about the abolition of slavery and the rights of the slaveholding states.

From the window of his suite at Willard's Hotel, the most fashionable hotel in Washington, the president-elect could see and hear the crowds in the street below. Washington was overrun with tourists who had come to town to see the new president sworn in. Now that the day had arrived, it seemed that there were even more people than before. Every hotel, including Willard's, was filled to capacity and beyond; all the ballrooms, reception rooms, hallways, and corridors were crammed with beds and cots to accommodate the hordes of visitors—at top prices.

But along with the multitude of sightseers who had come to Washington in a holiday mood, the city also had its share of malcontents and troublemakers—there had been rumors of assassination attempts against the new president. Soldiers stood guard on the lookout for trouble; mounted cavalrymen patrolled the streets, and riflemen had been strategically placed on rooftops throughout the city. There were those among Washington's visitors who hated Lincoln and wanted to see him dead. Underneath the cheerfulness of inauguration day and all of its festivities, there was an undercurrent of foreboding. The country was on the brink of civil war. No one was more aware of this than Abraham Lincoln.

Because he realized the significance of his inauguration address, as well as how thoroughly it would be scrutinized by readers, North and South, Lincoln began working on it more than a month before inauguration day. "Late in January, Mr. Lincoln informed me that he was ready to begin the preparation of his address," Lincoln's law partner, William H. Herndon, would recall many years later. According to Herndon, Lincoln did not own very many books: "He never seemed to care to own or collect books." But since Herndon had "a very respectable collection" of books himself, Herndon gave the president-elect the run of his own library.[1]

Lincoln only consulted four books from Herndon's collection. One was a volume that included the US Constitution. The other three contained Andrew Jackson's "Proclamation on Nullification" from 1832; Daniel Webster's speech of 1830, which closed with "Liberty and Union, now and forever, one and inseparable;"[2] and Henry Clay's speech supporting the Compromise of 1850. The 1850 compromise was actually five separate bills that had been passed by Congress in September 1850, bills that were designed to settle a conflict between slave and free states that had been acquired in the Mexican War.

Andrew Jackson's proclamation was of special interest to Lincoln—it had been issued in 1832, in reaction to South Carolina's threat to secede from the Union. A South Carolina convention declared a tariff, which had been signed into law in July 1832, to be null and void—according to the convention, the state had the right to ignore, or "nullify," any federal law that was not in its best interests. The convention went on to warn that any attempt by the federal government to enforce that tariff would result in the state withdrawing from the Union. One of the more outspoken supporters of the nullification and secession declaration was South Carolina senator John C. Calhoun. Senator Calhoun declared that Congress did not have the authority to pass such a tariff. But President Jackson declared that nullification was treason, and promised to hang John C. Calhoun if South Carolina carried out its threat to secede.

In his response, President Jackson informed the citizens of South Carolina, "The Constitution . . . forms a *government*, not a league. . . . To say that any State may at pleasure secede from the Union is to say that the United States is not a nation." South Carolina's right-of-secession claim was denied. Andrew Jackson's proclamation had a special interest and relevance for Abraham Lincoln twenty-nine years later; he was having his own problems with South Carolina and secession.[3] But in 1832, South Carolina stood alone in its threat to leave the Union. In March 1861, six other states had already formally seceded from the United States, and several others were threatening to join South Carolina.

Lincoln began working on his inaugural speech "in a room upstairs over a store across the street from the State House," according to William Herndon.[4] When he had finished what he considered to be an acceptable draft of the address, he had it set in type by a printer. Copies of the printed version were sent to friends and acquaintances for their comments and suggestions. Among those who received a printed copy was Lincoln's old friend and political supporter, Orville Browning. After going over the speech, Orville Browning came to the conclusion that Lincoln was much too aggressive in his approach to the Southern states. For one thing, Lincoln threatened to reclaim federal installations, including Fort Moultrie and Castle Pinckney in Charleston Harbor, close by Fort Sumter. Browning advised that South Carolina would react with violence to this threat and persuaded Lincoln to eliminate this passage.

Other friends and supporters who read the printed draft of the inaugural address included Francis P. Blair, one of Lincoln's political advisors, and David Davis, a senator from Illinois and Lincoln's campaign manager during the 1860 presidential campaign. But probably the most influential of those who read the speech was William H. Seward, Lincoln's secretary of state designate. Along with Orville Browning, Seward also thought that Lincoln's general tone was much too warlike. In the original text, Lincoln said that he would reclaim all properties that had been taken over by the Southern states. To Secretary Seward, this sounded ominously like a threat to invade, which was exactly what he was trying to avoid. He suggested that the language be toned down. Secretary Seward spent several hours editing the draft, doing his best to defuse the language and make the overall message of the speech as conciliatory as possible.

At noon, outgoing President James Buchanan arrived at Willard's Hotel to accompany the president-elect to the inauguration. Lincoln took a seat in a four-seated open carriage, sitting just opposite President Buchanan. The other two seats were occupied by Senator Edward Baker of Oregon and Senator James Pearce of Maryland. President-elect Lincoln had originally been slated to ride in a closed carriage, but he opted for an open vehicle so that he could be seen by more people in the crowd. Because so many soldiers surrounded the carriage to protect Lincoln from assassins, the president-elect was nearly hidden from sight despite his intentions. The ride to the Capitol was uneventful.

President James Buchanan felt absolutely no sadness or regret over leaving the White House. His four years as president had been anything but a happy experience for him. The problems of secession and slavery had plagued his presidency, but he had not been able to do anything about solving either one of them. Even though he firmly believed that secession was a blatant violation of the Constitution, he also thought that he did not have either the right or the authority to block the Southern states from leaving the Union. Some cynics claimed that President Buchanan's only real ambition was to delay the outbreak of civil war until he left office. "If you are as happy in entering the White House as I am in returning to Wheatland," he told Lincoln, "you are a happy man."[5] He could not wait to get out of Washington and back to Wheatland, his estate in Pennsylvania, and leave all the problems of the looming civil war to the new president.

President James Buchanan felt absolutely no sadness or regret over leaving the White House. Some cynics claimed that President Buchanan's only real ambition was to delay the outbreak of civil war until he left office.

The open carriage made its way from Willard's Hotel to the Capitol, accompanied by marching bands, military formations, colorful horse-drawn floats, and delegations from all the states that had not left the Union. The California delegation was led by a carriage that carried the slogan, "California True to the Union." The one hundred members of the Virginia delegation carried the US flag.[6] But the thousands of spectators along the route had only one thing on their mind—to catch a glimpse of the president-elect. When Lincoln and his party arrived at the Capitol's East Portico, the crowd of onlookers burst into a scattering of applause and cheers. Some of the spectators remarked that attendance at this inauguration was more sparce than during previous ceremonies, mainly because there had been so much talk of rioting in the streets and possible assassination attempts.

Lincoln and the others walked to the Capitol entrance, a distance of about two hundred feet, between two wooden barricades that had been installed to protect the president-elect from snipers. Once inside the building, the group made its way toward the Senate chamber, which had been searched for a suspected bomb earlier that morning. Supreme Court justices, senators, members of the House of Representatives, and members of the diplomatic corps, all took their seats in their appointed places. Mrs. Lincoln and her party sat in the diplomatic gallery. The outgoing vice president, John Breckinridge of Kentucky, gave a short farewell address, and the incoming vice president, Hannibal Hamlin, began his inauguration address.

Hamlin's inaugural speech was short and not very remarkable. Most newspapers did not even bother to print excerpts from it; some did not even mention it. After Vice President Hamlin had been sworn in by Senator Breckinridge, president-elect Lincoln and all of the other notables filed out of the Senate Chamber. They proceeded to a large platform in front of the Eastern Portico. "A square platform had been built out from the steps of the eastern portico, with benches for distinguished spectators on three sides," William Herndon would write.[7] "A rickety table had been provided for the president," another spectator pointed out, "on which he could hardly find room for his hat."[8]

Herndon was not at all impressed by the president-elect's appearance. Lincoln came to his inauguration sporting "[a] crop of whiskers, of the blacking-brush variety," which were "stiff and ungraceful" and which did not do anything to improve his face—which was "never handsome to begin with," Herndon ungraciously remarked. Also, Lincoln had dressed in an uncomfortable-looking suit of "brand-new clothes," which made him look even more awkward. Everything he wore was black, including "a glossy hat evidently just out of the box." To complete the picture, he also carried "a huge ebony cane, with a gold head the size of an egg." Because of his stiff new suit and his scruffy beard, Herndon could not help but feel sorry for his law partner—he "looked so miserably uncomfortable that I could not help pitying him."[9]

The president-elect was introduced to the crowd of between twenty thousand and thirty thousand, depending upon which source is consulted, by Senator Baker. Following his friend's brief remarks, Lincoln stood up and walked toward the rostrum with his ebony cane and his hat in his hand. "Reaching the platform, his discomfort was visibly increased by not knowing what to do with hat and cane," William Herndon recalled, "so he stood there, a target for ten thousand eyes, holding cane in one hand and hat in the other, the very picture of helpless embarrassment."[10] He managed to find a place next to the rostrum for his cane, but the table was too small for his hat. Fortunately, Stephen Douglas came to Lincoln's rescue; he took the hat and held it throughout the ceremony.[11]

With his hands free after an awkward minute, Lincoln took a pair of steel-rimmed glasses from his pocket and placed them deliberately on his nose. From another pocket, he then produced a copy of his carefully edited inauguration speech and began reading it in a strong, high-pitched voice. William Herndon, who was fairly close to Lincoln, thought that the president-elect "read his inaugural address in a clear and distinct voice."[12] He began in a conventional manner, informing his listeners, and the country at large: "In compliance with a custom as old as the government itself, I appear before you to address you briefly" before taking the oath of office.[13]

Following this short introduction, the president-elect did his best to assure "the people of the Southern States" that he had no intention of endangering "their property, and their peace, and personal security," and neither did the Republican administration. But he also wanted to make it clear that "the central idea of secession is the essence of anarchy," which would not be tolerated. In another attempt at reassuring the slave-holding states, Lincoln made a point of declaring, "I have no purpose, directly or indirectly, to interfere with the institution of slavery in the States where it exists. I believe that I have no lawful right to do so, and I have no inclination to do so."

As far as the controversy over fugitive slaves was concerned, Lincoln declared that he was in favor of returning all runaways to their rightful owners—all fugitives should be "delivered up" to their owners. The only real difficulty in the fugitive law, as least as far as Lincoln was concerned, was whether or not it should be "enforced by national or state authority," but this was only a very minor point. "If the slave is to be surrendered, it can be of but little consequence to him, or to others, by which authority it is done."

After addressing the issue of slavery, and stating his policy to leave slavery alone in the states where it already existed, the president-elect next spoke about the matter of secession. He was quite direct and straightforward regarding this subject: "no State, upon its own mere motion, can lawfully get out of the Union . . . I shall take care, as the Constitution itself expressly enjoins upon me, that the laws of the Union be faithfully executed in all the States." But even after making this point, Lincoln went on to give his assurances that "there needs to be no bloodshed or violence; and there shall be none, unless it be forced upon the national authority." Lincoln wanted to make it very clear that he did not intend to use force or coercion to exercise his powers as president. "The power confided to me will be used to hold, occupy, and possess the property and places belonging to the government, and to collect the duties and imposts; but beyond what may be necessary for these objects, there will be no invasion—no using of force against or among the people anywhere."

The audience listened "attentively" to the president-elect's message, including reporters from the many newspapers who would be hurrying to send their copy back home, by telegraph or by courier, as soon as the speech ended. William Herndon thought "the closest listener" was Stephen Douglas. Senator Douglas "leaned forward as if to catch every word, nodding his head emphatically at those passages which most pleased him."[14] All the reporters listened, as well, and wrote down every word. According to the *New York Herald*, "there was much cheering, especially at any allusion to the Union."[15]

The president-elect was about three-quarters of the way through his speech at this point, and continued in the same conciliatory tone. "This country, with its institutions, belongs to the people who inhabit it," he said. "Whenever they shall grow weary of the existing Government, they can exercise their *constitutional* right of amending it, or their *revolutionary* right to dismember or overthrow it." Still trying his best to play the role of peacemaker, Lincoln added, "My countrymen, one and all, think calmly and *well*, upon this whole subject.... Intelligence, patriotism, Christianity, and a firm reliance on Him, who has never yet forsaken this favored land, are still competent to adjust, in the best way, all our present difficulty."

Nearing the end of his address, Lincoln spoke to the residents of the Southern states directly. "In *your* hands, my dissatisfied fellow countrymen, and not in *mine*, is the momentous issue of civil war. The government will not assail *you*. ["Unless you *first* assail *it*" had originally been part of the sentence, but was deleted.] You can have no conflict without being yourselves the aggressors." He went on to remind the Southern residents, "*You* have no oath registered in Heaven to destroy the government, while *I* shall have the most solemn one to 'preserve, protect, and defend it.'"

The final section of the inaugural address is probably the most eloquent, and is certainly the best remembered part: "I am loath to close. We are not enemies, but friends. We must not be enemies. Though passion may have strained, it must not break our bonds of affection. The mystic chords of memory, stretching from every battle-field, and patriot grave, to every living heart and hearth-stone, all over this broad land, will yet swell the chorus of the Union, when again touched, as surely they will be, by the better angels of our nature."

When the president-elect finished delivering his speech, a battery of artillery startled the public by firing an ear-shattering salute. The crowd in front of the Capitol burst into long and enthusiastic cheering after the noise and cannon smoke drifted away, but it was not the usual cheering that follows a political address. A reporter from a New York newspaper who witnessed the delivery of the address remarked, "All seemed to be moved with the profound conviction that their own fate and that of the country depended on the developments of that memorable hour."[16] Like Lincoln himself, the crowd—including those who lived south of the Mason-Dixon Line—realized that the address had been one of the most important speeches of their lives.

After the cheering died down, eighty-four-year-old chief justice Roger B. Taney came forward to administer the oath of office. Justice Taney's "black robes, attenuated figure, and cadaverous countenance reminded me of a galvanized corpse," William Herndon wrote.[17] The chief justice produced a Bible, a small burgundy book that became known as the Lincoln Bible. Abraham Lincoln placed his left hand on it, raised his right hand, and solemnly swore to execute the office of president and to preserve, protect, and defend the Constitution of the United States. After taking the oath, he leaned forward and kissed the Bible. Abraham Lincoln was now the sixteenth president of the United States.

Now that the inauguration ceremony was finally over, and all of its formalities had been carried out, the newly installed president was escorted back to the Senate chamber, through the Capitol Building, and outside to his open carriage. Former president James Buchanan accompanied him in his walk through the building and rode with him back to the White House. The two made an odd-looking pair: the heavy-set and aged Buchanan and the tall, thin, and relatively young-looking Lincoln. But because of the strict security measures taken to guard President Lincoln, the cheering crowd along the route to the White House was not able to get much more than a glimpse of the two men as they passed by; the carriage was surrounded by soldiers.

According to the *New York Herald*, "Mr. Buchanan accompanied Mr. Lincoln to the main hall" of the White House, "and there he took his farewell leave of him, expressing the hope, in cordial terms, that his administration might prove a happy and prosperous one."[18] The former president left Washington on the following day for his estate at Wheatland, outside Lancaster, Pennsylvania, where he would live out the last seven years of his life.

President Lincoln's day was not over yet. Before he could attend his inaugural ball that evening, he had to deal with a problem involving his newly formed cabinet. Specifically, the difficulty centered around his designated secretary of state, William H. Seward.

Lincoln had asked Seward to join his cabinet as secretary of state in December 1860. In his note dated December 8, he told Seward, "I now offer you the place, in the hope that you will accept it, and with the belief that your position in the public eye, your integrity, ability, learning, and great experience, all combine to render it an appointment preeminently fit to be made."[19] This was not just empty flattery on

Secretary of State William H. Seward. Lincoln realized that he would require someone with Seward's ability and "great experience" to counsel and advise him, especially during the early days of his presidency.

Lincoln's part. Lincoln realized that he would require someone with Seward's ability and "great experience" to counsel and advise him, especially during the early days of his presidency.

William Henry Seward had spent most of his adult life in public office. He had been a member of the New York Assembly, had served a term as governor of New York, and had served two terms as US senator. President Lincoln, on the other hand, had a very limited career in elected office—eight years in the Illinois legislature and one term, two years, in the US House of Representatives. He had absolutely no experience at all in the field of diplomacy or foreign relations; Seward had spent four years on the Senate Foreign Relations Committee. William Seward seemed the perfect candidate as Lincoln's secretary of state.

But President Lincoln had named an adversary of William Seward, Salmon P. Chase, as his secretary of the treasury, which led to a disagreement between Lincoln and Seward. Seward did not want Chase to be a member of the president's cabinet. Although the two were basically on civil terms, they sharply differed on the subject of secession. Salmon Chase was, in the words of one writer, "viewed as the leader of the hard-line Republicans, those who would not compromise with the South,"[20] while Seward prided himself on being a moderate who took a more appeasing and conciliatory position on secession. As far as Seward was concerned, Salmon Chase was doing his best to start a war, while he thought of himself as doing his best to save the Union. He was not at all happy about Lincoln's appointing Salmon Chase to a cabinet position.

Seward was unhappy enough about Chase's appointment to withdraw his own name from consideration as secretary of state. In a note dated March 4, he told President Lincoln, "Circumstances which have occurred since I expressed to you in December last my willingness to accept the office of Secretary of State seem to me to render it my duty to ask leave to withdraw that consent."[21] Lincoln read the note, but had no intention of accepting Seward's retraction, especially not for any self-serving political reasons. Shortly before leaving Willard's Hotel for his inauguration, he sent a reply asking Seward to reconsider withdrawing his name: "I feel constrained to beg that you will countermand the withdrawal," he said, and continued in the same tone. "The public interest, I think, demands that you should; and my personal feelings are deeply inclined in the same direction." He ended with this request: "Please consider, and answer by 9 o'clock, A.M. to-morrow."[22]

But Seward did not wait until the next morning; he met with the president that afternoon, shortly after the inauguration ceremony ended. By that time, he had already decided to accept the post of secretary of state. His change of mind had been engineered by Lincoln himself. The opportunity of bringing about Seward's reversal of decision had fallen into Lincoln's lap unexpectedly; he immediately seized the chance.

Sometime after the election, a group of New York businessmen, who were also friends and supporters of Seward, "descended upon the president-elect" to protest the selection of Salmon Chase as treasury secretary. They emphatically did not want Chase as a member of Lincoln's cabinet. They argued that Chase's hard-line attitude toward the South, as well as his commitment to free trade, "would further injure business prospects." The group also insisted that Seward and Chase would never be able to work together as cabinet members because of their differences.[23]

Lincoln listened carefully to what the men had to say, agreed that the members of his cabinet should have the same basic point of view, and proceeded to show them two lists that he had drawn up. One of the lists had the names of his preferred cabinet members, which included both Chase and Seward. The second one, "a poorer one," named William L. Dayton as secretary of state and William H. Seward as ambassador to Great Britain. William Lewis Dayton from New Jersey did have a record in public service. He spent six years in the New Jersey legislature, four years as New Jersey attorney general, and three years in the US Senate. But he did not have anything approaching Seward's understanding of diplomacy or foreign relations.[24]

When they heard what Lincoln had to say about his possible cabinet choices, "the stunned delegation shuffled out" of the room; this was obviously not the response they had been expecting. Lincoln also spoke about his intentions regarding Chase and Seward with one of his advisors, Norman B. Judd. Judd had been instrumental in securing the Republican nomination as president for Lincoln in 1860 and had assisted Lincoln during the presidential campaign. Lincoln could be certain that either Judd or one of the members of the New York delegation would report back to Seward about the two lists. He also knew that Seward would much rather serve on his cabinet as secretary of state, even with Salmon Chase as secretary of the treasury, than be sent off to England as US ambassador.[25] When Lincoln sent his note asking Seward to "countermand the withdrawal," he could be fairly certain that Seward would comply with his request.

President Lincoln had read his man; Seward did agree to serve as secretary of state, just as the president had thought. Seward was genuinely concerned with the immediate future of the United States, which he called a "distracted country," and declared that he "did not dare to go home, or to England, and leave the country to chance."[26] He also did not want to leave the country to Abraham Lincoln. As far as Secretary Seward was concerned, the new president did not have either the intellect or the judgment to be an effective head of state—he once referred to Lincoln as a "little Illinois lawyer"[27]—and was convinced that Lincoln would be needing every bit of Seward's help if he hoped to succeed as president. It would take some time before Secretary Seward discovered that President Lincoln was a lot sharper than he supposed.

Later that day, the president's first dinner at the White House was interrupted by a group of well-wishers from New York. The *New York Times* said that the callers numbered "at least five hundred." Lincoln stepped outside to give the visitors a friendly informal speech. He thanked everyone for coming, noted that they all appeared to be happy, and hoped that his inauguration speech—"the public expression which I have this day given"—was a contributing factor to their good cheer. He went on to remark that he hoped "the loyal citizens of every State, and of every section, shall have no cause to feel any other sentiment," and apologized for the brevity of his remarks. After saying his farewells, Lincoln went back to "rejoin those who await my return" at the dinner table.[28] It was an affable speech, typical of Abraham Lincoln in its informality.

The last activity of President Lincoln's long day was the inaugural ball, which was renamed the "Union ball" because of the secession crisis. It was held in a temporary building on Judiciary Square, behind Washington Town Hall. The building was made of yellow pine and divided into two separate rooms: a dining area and a room for dancing. Even though the hall was temporary and looked very plain and bare from the outside, the interior was well lighted and beautifully decorated. "Much admiration was expressed at the handsome and tasteful manner in which the room was decorated, and the brilliancy of the light," according to one description of the two rooms. "The crowd was not excessive, and yet the immense ball room was well filled with ladies and gentlemen, who kept the dancing up till 4 o'clock this morning."[29]

Dancing began at ten o'clock. President Lincoln and his wife arrived about an hour later. The forty-five-piece band announced their entrance by interrupting the dance music with the brassy "Hail to the Chief." The president wore a new suit and a pair of white kid gloves for the occasion, and he appeared uncomfortable and slightly embarrassed. But Mrs. Lincoln seemed to be right at home. She wore a blue gown and a large blue feather in her hair, and danced at least one of her dances with Senator Stephen Douglas, who had been her husband's opponent in last November's election, and had also been his rival for Mary's hand in marriage years ago in Springfield, Illinois. She refused Stephen Douglas by telling him, "I can't consent to be your wife. I shall become Mrs. President, or I am the victim of false prophets, but it won't be as Mrs. Douglas."[30] As things turned out, she guessed correctly in her choice of husband. At the Union ball, she was certainly enjoying her new role as "Mrs. President." Many friends and acquaintances remarked that this was the happiest night of her life.

Mary Lincoln spent much of the night dancing—waltzes, mazurkas, polkas—and generally enjoyed herself. From most accounts of those who attended the ball, the president spent most of the night shaking hands—with friends, acquaintances, politicians, and hangers-on. One newspaper account noted that he "held quite a levee, and was introduced to a great many notable personages who were present."[31] Among the notables were Vice President Hamlin and Secretary of State Seward. He also took part in the festivities, but it was fairly evident that his mind was elsewhere. A good many others in attendance shared his anxiety; one of the reporters covering the event observed that the inaugural celebration was "a somewhat melancholy affair, abounding in fears and forebodings of coming evil." It was also noted that the number of army and naval officers in uniform was "remarkably small"—many had already left the Union forces and had gone South with their states. "So many have resigned, you know," an older woman pointed out.[32]

After about two hours, President Lincoln decided to call it a night and retire to the White House. Mary elected to stay at the ball and enjoy the music and the dancing, which continued until the early morning hours. The president wanted to be fully rested for his first full day in office. His wife could afford to remain at the party, but he left at about 1:00 a.m., which was late enough. In the morning, all the woes that President Buchanan had been able to walk away from, especially the growing problem of secession and the increasing anger of the Southern states, would be waiting for him.

Seven states had already left the Union—South Carolina (December 20, 1860), Mississippi (January 9, 1861), Florida (January 10, 1861), Alabama (January 11, 1861), Georgia (January 19, 1861), Louisiana (January 26, 1861), and Texas (February 1, 1861)—and several others, including Virginia, were threatening to leave. President Lincoln was fully aware that he had his work cut out for him. Henry Adams, the son of Lincoln's ambassador to Great Britain, sarcastically described the president's situation: "the new president and his chief advisors in Washington decided that, before they could administer the Government, they must make sure of a government to administer."[33]

# CRISIS ON THE FIRST DAY

For all of the time and effort that Orville Browning, William Seward, Abraham Lincoln, and all the others spent in editing the inaugural address, changing the tone and the wording of the speech to make it more conciliatory, they might just as well not have bothered. Throughout the South, the reaction to the president's speech was almost unanimously hostile. Newspaper editors south of the Mason-Dixon Line attacked the president's address, his attitude toward the South, and sometimes President Lincoln himself. The *Richmond Enquirer* began its editorial with the headline: "THE DECLARATION OF WAR." The article went on in the same angry manner: "Mr. Lincoln's Inaugural Address is before our readers—couched in the cool, unimpassioned, deliberate language of the fanatic, with the purpose of pursuing the promptings of fanaticism even to the dismemberment of the Government with the horrors of civil war."[1]

Other Southern newspapers were just as antagonistic. The *Charleston Mercury* declared Lincoln's inauguration address to be nothing less than "the tocsin of battle," and ridiculed the president, as well, calling him an "Ourang-Outang."[2] Wilmington, North Carolina's *Wilmington Herald* said, "There is no mitigation of Lincoln's fanaticism in this inaugural address, and, painful as it may be to the American people, they might as well open their eyes to the solemn fact that war is inevitable."[3] The *Richmond Enquirer's* editorial spoke for most of the South, declaring: "The question, 'where shall Virginia go?' is answered by Mr. Lincoln. 'She must go *to war.*'"[4] Southern newspapers made it more than evident that the slave states did not want to be either soothed or pacified. The seven states that had already seceded had no intention of rejoining the Union peaceably; they were more than prepared to fight for their independence. No amount of persuasion or coercion would change their mind.

All news editors, North and South, were surprised by the sheer number of papers that were sold on March 5; everybody wanted to read the speech, or even excerpts of it, and bought newspapers in record numbers that day. "Thousands upon thousands were waiting eagerly for them, and probably not less than a hundred thousand were sold during the afternoon," a *New York Times* editorial observed. Unlike Southern reporters, writers on the *Times* took a favorable view of President Lincoln's speech. "It was universally regarded as a document of precisely the right stamp," the *New York Times* thought, "firm in support of the Government, and highly conciliatory towards all who have been led to entertain unjust and unfounded apprehensions of the character and purposes of the incoming Administration."[5]

President Lincoln was probably unaware of what the *Charleston Mercury*, or any other Southern news editor, had to say about his looks and appearance; he was not usually fazed by personal attacks. And the aggressive reaction to his inaugural address would have disappointed more than surprised him. But he was completely taken aback by a letter he found on his desk on Tuesday morning, the beginning of his first full day as president. The four-page message was from outgoing secretary of war Joseph Holt, who was still serving as a sort of acting secretary of war. He held the post in James Buchanan's cabinet. President Lincoln's appointee, Simon Cameron, had not yet been approved by the Senate. In his report, Joseph Holt passed along information from the commander of Fort Sumter, Major Robert Anderson, concerning the deteriorating situation at the fort. According to Major Anderson, the situation was already bad and looked to be getting worse.

Fort Sumter had been a bone of contention between South Carolina and the federal government ever since December 20, 1860, when the state seceded from the Union. It guarded the entrance to Charleston Harbor, but residents of Charleston considered the fort and its garrison of federal soldiers to be an open insult. Major Anderson reported that rebel artillery batteries had been installed all around the fort. The batteries at Fort Johnson, Fort Moultrie, and Castle Pinckney, each within artillery range of Fort Sumter, had been federal installations. Now that they had been taken over by rebel units, their big guns were turned against Sumter and its eighty-man garrison.

Joseph Holt's letter contained nothing but bad news for the president—in it, Major Anderson expressed serious doubts over whether he would be able to keep Fort Sumter from being captured. The major was running low on rations and supplies, Holt reported, and went on to say that Sumter would need a force of not less than twenty thousand "good and well-disciplined men" to defend the fort: "The declaration now made by the Major, that he would not be willing to risk his reputation on an attempt to throw reinforcements into Charleston Harbor and with a view of holding possession of the same with a force of less than twenty thousand good and well-disciplined men, takes the Department by surprise as his previous correspondence contains no such estimation."[6] If Joseph Holt was surprised to learn that Fort Sumter was in such a dangerous position—surrounded by hostile artillery, undermanned, and low on supplies—President Lincoln was beyond being surprised. He was nearly in a state of shock.

The president's first reaction was to question the loyalty of Major Robert Anderson—the major was originally from Kentucky and married to Elizabeth Bayard Anderson, who was born in Georgia—but his suspicions were completely unfounded. Major Anderson remained loyal to the Union. But President Lincoln's main concern was his own lack of experience—he was almost painfully aware that he knew next to nothing about the office of the president and the duties that went with it. He would have been forced to agree with a less-than-generous statement made by Charles Francis Adams regarding his shortcomings. Charles Francis Adams was the father of Henry Adams, Lincoln's ambassador to Great Britain, and could be just as blunt as his sharp witted son when the spirit moved him. "It is plain . . . that he has nothing of purpose or system in his head, and that he is open to all sorts of influences except elevated ideas of his duty," the elder Adams wrote in his diary. "He is ignorant, and must have help."[7] The newly sworn-in president might have flinched at the roughness of these remarks, but he also would have seen the truth in them.

President Lincoln did not need any comments regarding his inexperience, no matter how accurate or well intentioned they might have been. What he desperately needed was some sound advice regarding the Sumter crisis, and how to solve it. And the most qualified person to give such advice, in the opinion of Abraham Lincoln and just about everyone else in the country, was General Winfield Scott. General Scott was general in chief of the army and, in the words of a contemporary, the old general "happened to be the only military figure that looked equal to the crisis."[8] He was a hero of the Mexican War of 1846–1848, and conducted a brilliant campaign against Mexican general Santa Anna. After outmaneuvering and outwitting a much larger enemy force for six months, which ended in the capture of Mexico City, General Scott was named the greatest living general by the Duke of Wellington. President Lincoln summoned the general to the White House to discuss Major Anderson's views on the defense of Fort Sumter.

When the general arrived at the White House, President Lincoln handed him Joseph Holt's report and asked for his opinion of Major Anderson's remarks. Following a short conversation, General Scott left the president and took Joseph Holt's report with him to read at home. President Lincoln turned his attention to other matters.

At around noon, the Senate approved President Lincoln's cabinet appointees: Edward Bates, attorney general; Montgomery Blair, postmaster general; Simon Cameron, secretary of war; Salmon P. Chase, secretary of the treasury; William H. Seward, secretary of state; Caleb B. Smith, secretary of the interior; and Gideon Welles, secretary of the navy. Four of the seven appointees—Blair, Cameron, Chase, and Welles— were Democrats; three—Bates, Seward, and Smith—were Republicans. The president did not seem all that concerned with the four-to-three Democratic majority. He explained that his influence would more than even out any imbalance.

President Lincoln met with delegations from several states that after-noon, and greeted each delegation with a short speech. In his address to the Pennsylvania group, he started out by thanking everyone for their support in "the late election," and hoped for the continuation of that support. The president then went on to make his main point about, as he put it, "a President and a Government." The address was not just a nice political talk to a group of fellow Republicans; the primary message was actually about avoiding a war with the Southern states: "while we exercise our opinion . . . others have also rights to the exercise of their opinions, and we should endeavor to allow these rights, and act in such a manner as to create no bad feeling." A moment later, he followed up this point by saying, "We must remember that the people of all the States are entitled to all the privileges and immunities of the citizens of the several States." Although the speech was delivered to residents of Pennsylvania, it was really intended for consumption by the Southern press and its readers. Lincoln knew that news editors south of the Mason-Dixon Line would print his remarks on their front pages, and that his message of reconciliation would be read from Virginia to Texas.[9]

The president also spoke to a group of delegates from Massachusetts. Just as he had done in his remarks to the Pennsylvania delegation, Lincoln began by thanking the representatives from "the Old Bay State" for their confidence and their support. "I am thankful for the expressions of those who have voted with us," he said. But in the very next sentence, the president revealed what was really on his mind. "As President, in the administration of the Government, I hope to be man enough not to know one citizen of the United States from another, [cries of "Good!"] nor one section from another."[10]

President Lincoln used the same technique when he addressed the delegates of "my own home state of Illinois," a delegation that numbered "several hundred." He thanked everyone for their backing, and then went on to talk about reconciling any sectional differences with the Southern states. He even went so far as to use the word *Confederacy* in describing the United States: "I have to request of you, which I think I need hardly do, either, that you will sustain me in trying to do ample and full justice to all the people of the different sections of this great Confederacy."[11] The president was clearly using every possible opportunity to circulate his message of reconciliation. He could only hope that he was getting through to the angry and resentful citizens of the South.

During the evening hours, President Lincoln received General Winfield Scott's reply regarding the ongoing Fort Sumter crisis. The message was not delivered by the general himself, but by Secretary of State Seward. The aged general had probably retired for the night and had asked Secretary Seward to take it over to the White House in his place. If the president was expecting good news from his general in chief, or even any sort of encouragement, he was very quickly disappointed.

General Scott came right to the point: he recommended surrendering Fort Sumter and evacuating its garrison. Three or four weeks earlier, it might have been possible to reinforce Major Anderson, but now, in his opinion, it was far too late. He saw "no alternative but "a surrender." In a rambling response, General Scott advised President Lincoln, "we cannot send the third of the men (regulars) in several weeks months, necessary to give them relief beyond a few weeks, if for a day. Evacuation seems almost inevitable . . . if, indeed, the worn out garrison be not assaulted & carried in the present week."[12]

President Lincoln read General Scott's reply with alarm. Only the day before, he had announced that he would "hold, occupy, and possess the property and places belonging to the government."[13] This promise had been printed on every front page of every newspaper throughout the country. Now his chief military consultant was advising him that Fort Sumter could not possibly be held. General Scott also stated that it would be impossible to send even one-third of the twenty thousand men Major Anderson was requesting. The entire United States Army consisted of about sixteen thousand men. Most of these troops were stationed at western frontier outposts, hundreds of miles from Fort Sumter. Major Anderson's call for twenty thousand trained soldiers was an impossible request.

Actually, the situation was even worse than General Scott was admitting. Roughly two weeks before he was elected president, Lincoln had received a note from a captain of artillery named George Whitfield Hazzard on October 21, 1860, on the subject of the overwhelming number of Southern officers in the US Army. According to Captain Hazzard, "So long has southern influence and southern patronage controlled our army that I know only one officer of any rank in it who is not an avowed admirer of the peculiar institution." That officer was Colonel Edwin V. Sumner, who was a cousin of US senator Charles Sumner of Massachusetts. "The command of the army and of the military geographical departments of Texas Utah and New Mexico is conferred on Virginians," Captain Hazzard went on: "Every military Bureau is presided over by a Virginian or the husband of a Virginia wife. The Colonels of four of our five mounted regiments are Southerners; the Adjutant General is brother in law of Senator Mason of Virginia; the Act'g Com. Genl. the Surgeon General, the Judge Advocate General and his assistant, and the Qr. Mr. General all Virginians. The grossest favoritism has been practised to secure this result." He ended the letter by telling Lincoln, "This letter is written without consultation with any living soul. I send it to you because I think you ought to possess the knowledge I have attempted to convey."[14] If the captain was to be believed, the entire officer corps of the US Army was infested by disloyal, pro-Confederate officers. President Lincoln would learn the truth of Captain Hazzard's observations for himself within the next few months.

The newly installed president's distressed state of mind was not helped any by his secretary of state, who believed that the secession crisis was only a passing phase. In a conversation with British reporter William H. Russell, Secretary of State Seward declared that the seceded Southern states would soon get over their desire to leave the Union. "When the Southern States see that we mean them no wrong—that we intend no violence to persons, rights, or things—that the Federal Government seeks only to fulfil obligations imposed on it in respect to the national property, they will see their mistake, and one after another they will come back into the union." Secretary Seward went on to predict that Secession would be over in three months.[15]

President Lincoln had agreed with this point of view only a short time before. On February 15, just two and a half weeks earlier, the president-elect told an audience in Cleveland that there was no such thing as a secession crisis. "The crisis, as it is called, is altogether an artificial crisis. In all parts of the nation there are differences of opinion and politics," he said. A minute later, he repeated himself to emphasize his point. "As I said before, this crisis is all artificial. It has no foundation in facts."[16] Now, only a day after his inauguration, he was told that there was no alternative to surrendering Fort Sumter and that the majority of officers throughout the entire US Army were pro-Confederate and probably could not be depended upon in a crisis.

Major Anderson's warning regarding Fort Sumter came as a profound shock—it let the president know, in no uncertain terms, that the crisis was anything but artificial. He realized that he would be needing the counsel of his senior advisors to get through the emergency. But President Lincoln was not getting very much in the way of support or guidance from either his leading military advisor or from the most prominent member of his cabinet, the two people he was counting upon the most. General Scott recommended the outright surrender of Fort Sumter, on the grounds that it could not possibly be held, and Secretary of State Seward held the opinion that the secession crisis was not real, or at least was not permanent.

The Fort Sumter dilemma gave President Lincoln headaches, insomnia, and what has been described as the "hypo," a period of debilitating depression and melancholy. The president would later tell Senator Orville Hickman Browning of Illinois, "of all the trials I have had since I came here, none begin to compare with those I had between the inauguration and the fall of Fort Sumpter. They were so great that could I have anticipated them, I would not have believed it possible to survive them."[17] This mood of unhappiness and despair would continue for the next several weeks, not subsiding until the crisis finally ended.

# FIRST CABINET MEETING

Presient Lincoln's second full day in office started out with a series of short speeches to visiting political delegations. Groups of visitors from California, Indiana, Maine, Minnesota, Ohio, and Vermont paid their respects to the president at the White House. But apparently only one of the speeches, President Lincoln's reply to the Minnesota delegation, was covered by reporters; all the others were either lost or were not copied by the press.

After telling his audience that he did not have the time to make a speech, and cracking a joke that "the people up your way have very correct political views" that exactly coincided with his own, which generated a laugh, President Lincoln came to the main part of his comments. Because the citizens of Minnesota agreed with his political outlook, he went on to say, "I have no reason to doubt that they look upon the rights of their brethren further South, as being entirely equal to their own."[1] This was another attempt to assure the Southern states that he had no intention of interfering with them or with their way of life; the people of Mississippi had the same rights as the people of Minnesota.

The president's comments were printed in the *Cincinnati Daily Commercial*, and these may or may not have found their way to Richmond and points south. As soon as he finished his five-minute speech, "[t]he President then shook hands, and bowed himself out with less grace than Beau Brummel or Chesterfield"—he had delivered his remarks, and now had other matters to handle.[2]

One of the problems that had to be addressed immediately involved the appointment of Salmon P. Chase as the new secretary of the treasury. Secretary Chase had not been present in the Senate when the cabinet nominations were approved. He did not find out that he had been named as the new treasury secretary until he returned to the Senate and was informed by his colleagues. Lincoln had mentioned that he might name Chase to his cabinet during a meeting in January, but he never specifically offered him a position. When Lincoln sent Chase's nomination to the Senate, he neglected to mention it to Chase. The news came as a complete and unpleasant surprise; Chase was annoyed by the appointment and informed President Lincoln that he would not accept the post.

When the president was informed of Chase's decision, it was his turn to be surprised; he certainly was not expecting this reaction. In attempt to convince Chase to accept the job, President Lincoln explained that his refusal would make both of them look awkward, especially since Chase had been a rival for the Republican presidential nomination in 1860—to the public, this would look like political infighting and grudge holding, which could only hurt both of them. President Lincoln's argument was influential enough to convince Salmon P. Chase to change his mind. "I accept the post which you have tendered me," he wrote. "My distrust of my own judgment in this decision, and of my ability to perform adequately the duties about to devolve on me, is very great; but trusting to your indulgence and humbly invoking Divine favor and guidance, I will give my best endeavor to your service and our country's."[3] Chase also resigned his Senate seat; Senator Chase was now Secretary Chase. Once again, Lincoln had used his powers of persuasion to get what he wanted.

President Lincoln also had another, more routine, matter to resolve involving another member of his cabinet. He sent a brief note to Secretary of State Seward regarding two political supporters: "Will you please send me the blank nominations of Mr. Judd & Mr. Kreismann as spoken of by us?" Norman B. Judd had formally placed Abraham Lincoln's name in nomination as president during the 1860 Republican convention. Herman Kreismann was active among Republicans of German descent; his influence with German voters was important to the Republican Party. Lincoln rewarded both men by granting them diplomatic appointments—Judd was named minister to the Kingdom of Prussia; Kreismann would be secretary of the Prussian legation. The president was a firm believer in the old political maxim of rewarding friends for past services.[4]

While the president was occupied with speeches and political appointments, Mary Lincoln had a few things of her own to do. She decided to pay a visit to the Soldiers' Home, her first look at the house that would become the retreat and refuge for the Lincolns in the coming years. The building has been described as "a large, fine building, built of stone, in castellated style, about two miles and a half from Washington."[5] The visit was probably the result of a suggestion by former president James Buchanan, who used it as a retreat himself. Mary liked the building and the grounds, which were more secluded and relaxing than the White House. But she also discovered that nearly everything needed modernizing and renovating, and made up her mind that she would see to improving the premises herself.

Mary had already made the same decision concerning the White House—she quickly discovered that the interior of just about every room in the building was very much in need of refurbishing and redecorating. "The East Room has a faded, worn, untidy look, in spite of its frescoing and its glittering chandeliers," William O. Stoddard, who had been appointed the president's secretary, would later write. "Its paint and furniture require renewal; but so does almost everything else about the house, within and without."[6] The president himself was not very concerned with the appearance of their new home; his office was presentable enough, and that was good enough for him. But "presentable" was far from being good enough for Mary Lincoln. From what she had seen of the White House so far, everything needed a complete makeover—new carpets, new paint, new furniture, new curtains. Visitors often described the Executive Mansion as resembling a third-rate hotel. Mary decided that it should look like a manor house, or at least like the home of the nation's chief executive. She had been informed that every president—and his wife—received an allowance of $20,000 maintaining and improving the White House. As far as she was concerned, she would need every penny of that budget to give it the style and grandeur she had in mind.

President Lincoln's last official activity of the day was to attend his first cabinet meeting, which took place during the evening. The meeting was held in the president's office, which he often called "the shop," a large room that reflected his personality—casual to the point of being unkempt. "The room and its furnishing were as battered as its occupant in the early days of the war," according to one description. "Oilcloth covered the floor but nothing could cover the dilapidated state of the president's desk or the gloom that sometimes enveloped President Lincoln."[7] The furniture included an armchair, as well as an old mahogany desk that looked older than the White House itself. A large oak table was the focal point of the room; it was usually covered with books and clutter. But on this particular day, the books and the disorder had been cleared away to make room for the cabinet meeting. All of the members sat at the table, along with the president. Lincoln usually sat at the head of the table, sitting sideways to make room for his long legs.

Most accounts agree that nothing of consequence was discussed during the course of the session, not even the situation at Fort Sumter. Attorney General Edward Bates noted in his diary, "Prest. Lincolns first *Cabinet Council*—intended, I suppose, to be formal and introductory only—in fact, uninteresting."[8] Most newspapers did not mention the meeting, although Washington's *Star* gave thumbnail biographies of all the cabinet members. President Lincoln did not say very much; he was there to listen, not to talk. The meeting was not uninteresting to him; he was well aware that he had a great deal to learn. A crisis was looming, and he did not have much time to learn everything he needed to know— about his own duties as chief executive, about diplomacy, about directing the army and the navy, about everything connected with being a wartime president. By paying attention to those who had more knowledge and experience than he had, Lincoln hoped that he could absorb enough education to see him through his first weeks and months in the White House. At the end of that time, he trusted that his own experiences as president, his on the job training, would begin to take effect.

# MARCH 7, 1861, THURSDAY
## ENCOURAGING NEWS FROM VIRGINIA

**B**efore breakfast, President Lincoln rode on horseback out to the Soldiers' Home, which was already becoming a welcome source of relief from the tensions of the White House. Even getting away for a little while helped steady his nerves; he enjoyed the peace and serenity of the place, as well as the ride itself. But the outing was only a short diversion. The president was soon back at his desk, dealing with the daily office routine, putting up with an endless flow of job seekers, and reading communiqués regarding Fort Sumter.

When he returned to the White House, one of President Lincoln's activities was to send a note to Secretary of State Seward. He recently received a letter from the Portuguese minister, J.G de Figaniere é Moraô, and needed Secretary Seward to come to the White House to give him some advice. Senor Moraô sent his congratulations on the president's inauguration. Lincoln wanted to send a reply, and he needed Secretary Seward's help: "To whom the reply should be addressed—that is, by what title, or style." The president had no experience at all in dealing with foreign diplomats. He also requested that Secretary Seward bring Joseph Holt's message regarding Fort Sumter with him; he specifically wanted to read General Scott's remarks. "I wish to examine the General's opinion, which I have not yet done," he explained.[1]

After Secretary Seward paid his duty call and had left the White House, the president sent his response to the Portuguese minister later that day. The letter was addressed to "Mr. Figaniere and Gentlemen of the Diplomatic Body." It was a very formal and polite note, the sort of letter that is routinely sent to diplomats and foreign ministers. "Please accept my sincere thanks for your kind congratulations," the letter began,

LINCOLN'S ROAD TO WAR

and went on to say, "Allow me to express the hope that these friendly relations may remain undisturbed." The letter was signed by the president and duly sent off to the Portuguese ministry.[2]

As part of his office routine this Thursday, President Lincoln also wrote a "To whom it may concern" letter of recommendation. He did not need any help in composing this letter; he had written many of them during his career: "William Johnson, a colored boy, and bearer of this, has been with me about twelve months; and has been, so far, as I believe, honest, faithful, sober, industrious, and handy as a servant."[3]

When the Republicans won the White House in November, they also won the privilege of awarding thousands of jobs to their political friends and allies. All the positions that had been held by Democrats during the James Buchanan administration had suddenly become available now that Abraham Lincoln and his party had come to power—everything from federal marshals to assistant clerks. Anyone who had given their support to the Republican Party, donated money to Lincoln's campaign, or did anything to help Lincoln get elected felt entitled to receive a reward for their efforts. Most came looking for a job or an appointment, and descended upon the White House to collect their payments. The president felt duty-bound to talk to as many of these fortune hunters and job seekers as time allowed.

The interviewing of job seekers was an activity that frequently took up a major part of President Lincoln's working day, much to his annoyance as well as the annoyance of his advisors. John Nicolay complained that so many opportunists came to the White House to petition for work that there was hardly time to eat, sleep, or breathe. A senator remarked, "I have been to see him two or three times, but stayed but a few moments each time, as I was pained and disgusted with the ill-bred, ravenous crowd there was about him."[4]

They came all day long, beginning in the morning and continuing into the evening hours, giving the already overworked president additional stress and strain. Not everyone who came to see President Lincoln wanted a job. There were also reporters looking for an interview, politicians asking for a presidential endorsement, inventors promoting their ideas, businessmen petitioning for government contracts, and parents trying to secure commissions for their sons in the army, along with a variety of other self-centered and mercenary individuals. An official from New York recalled, "I had a long and memorable interview with the president. As I stepped from the crowd in his reception-room, he said to me: 'What do you want?' I answered: 'Nothing, Mr. President, I only came to pay my respects and bid you good-by, as I am leaving Washington.' 'It is such a luxury,' he then remarked, 'to find a man who does not want anything.'"[5]

President Lincoln received some encouraging news from the Virginia Secession Convention. The convention had gathered in Richmond to determine whether Virginia should withdraw from the United States and, on March 6, had agreed not to secede, at least for the time being. No action would be taken as long as Washington did not threaten military action to keep Virginia in the Union. The Special Committee on Secession reported that "in their opinion, there has been no movement of armed men by the Federal Government, indicating the purpose of attack or coercion."[6] This news came as a great relief to the president, even though it did not end his anxiety over Fort Sumter. If Virginia seceded, and Maryland followed its example, Washington, DC, would be completely surrounded by hostile states. There would be no way in or out of the capital except by way of the Potomac River, which was sure to be blocked by rebel forces. Virginia's decision might persuade a few other slave states to act with more coolness on the subject of secession, and might also help to defuse the growing tension between Northern and Southern states.

# IN A QUANDARY

The first week of March 1861 was a disturbing time, as well as a trying time, for the newly sworn-in president. Nothing was certain; everything seemed unsettled and on the verge of blowing up. The country was not at war, but it was not at peace, either. Some members of the cabinet wanted to reinforce Fort Sumter; others wanted to abandon it to the rebels. Virginia had just issued a conciliatory message regarding secession, but South Carolina announced that it was prepared for war. The *Charleston Courier* announced that General Pierre G. T. Beauregard, the commander of fortifications in Charleston Harbor, expressed "perfect confidence" that Fort Sumter could be bombarded into submission. "He says that it is only a question of time."[1] And the Confederate government in Montgomery, Alabama, declared that it was ready to go to war. An "informal communication" from Montgomery stated that if commissioners from the Confederate states were not received by the federal government, which meant recognizing the independence of the Confederacy, the commissioners "are instructed to retire and return at once to their government, where hostile relations will at once exist."[2] The best that the inexperienced president could do was hope for the best, and also hope that he would make all the right decisions to avoid a crisis.

But if Abraham Lincoln was uneasy and unsure of himself, Confederate president Jefferson Davis was filled with confidence. President Davis was convinced that South Carolina, Mississippi, and the other states that had left the Union had every right to secede. He used a quote from the *New York Herald* to support his idea that secession was sanctioned by the Declaration of Independence: "If the Declaration of Independence justified the secession from the British Empire of three million

Confederate president Jefferson Davis was convinced that South Carolina, Mississippi, and the other states that had left the Union had every right to secede.

of subjects in 1776, it was not seen why it would not justify the secession of five millions of Southerners from the Union in 1861."[3] The editor of the *Herald*, Horace Greeley, was in full agreement with President Davis, and he said as much in several editorials. President Davis quoted Horace Greeley again to justify withdrawal from the Federal Union, citing another *Herald* editorial: "if the cotton states wished to withdraw from the Union, they should be allowed to do so."[4]

A great many people in the North agreed with Horace Greeley, and saw nothing wrong in the Southern states' desire to leave the Union. The mayor of New York City did more than just share Horace Greeley's point of view regarding secession—he liked the idea so much that he suggested that his city be allowed to leave the Union as well. Mayor Fernando Wood sent a memo to the New York City Common Council on January 6, 1861, just over two weeks after South Carolina issued its Declaration of Secession. "It would seem that dissolution of the Federal Union is inevitable," he declared. "With our aggrieved brethren of the Slave States, we have friendly relations and a common sympathy." Mayor Wood went on to say, "When Disunion has become a fixed and certain fact, why may not New York disrupt the bands which bind her to a venal and corrupt master."[5] It was a declaration that might have come from South Carolina or any of the states that had elected to depart from the Union. The proposal eventually came to nothing, but the fact that it was even seriously considered—by the governing body of a Northern city— shows that the idea of secession was not universally offensive throughout the North, and was even welcomed by some civic leaders.

President Lincoln was in a quandary. The North was divided over whether the cotton states should be allowed to go in peace, to walk calmly away from the republic and form their own country, or whether secession should be challenged at the risk of war. Lincoln did not know what to do about the problem of secession, or about Fort Sumter— should he surrender or reinforce? He realized that he did not have either the knowledge or the experience to make these decisions, a predicament that left him anxious and depressed. But he was also aware that he was the only person who had the power to make such decisions. Lincoln would learn how to be a war president in the coming months, but in March 1861 he did not know what to do. He would have to deal with the growing crisis by himself, whether he was prepared or not.

The Lincolns' first official reception was held at the White House on Friday evening. Some newspapers called the gathering "President Lincoln's First Levee,"[6] although it was actually Mary Lincoln's reception, the first of very many. President Lincoln's assistant secretary called it the "first of the regular series of Friday evening public receptions at the White House."[7] The president did not seem to enjoy these parties very much, even though he did his best not to let his unhappiness show whenever he was compelled to attend one. But Mrs. Lincoln loved banquets and social gatherings—and the more elaborate, the more she loved them. She enjoyed being First Lady, and loved entertaining. "Mrs. Lincoln came to Washington with a distinct understanding of her social duties and with an energetic purpose to perform them."[8] Mary Lincoln very quickly acquired the reputation of being not only First Lady but also First Hostess; many in Washington thought that she was the most gracious White House hostess since Dolly Madison.

This first reception received mixed reviews. The most strident complaint against the gathering was that too many people had been invited, and that it was overcrowded. Guests said that it was a crush and a terrible squeeze. The room was filled with representatives and diplomats and public officials but, according to a reporter from the *Evening Star*, "In such a jam, it was impossible to tell who was there, and who wasn't."[9] The *New York Herald* said, "It was a monster gathering. The oldest frequenters of the Executive mansion declare that they do not recollect ever to have seen so many people pass through the House at any previous levee."[10] A crowd had been anticipated at Mrs. Lincoln's first social function, "but we suppose few expected quite a jam."[11]

Both the president and his wife did not appear to be upset or dismayed by the number of people who came to their reception. Reporters and guests remarked on how patiently they received their guests. According to most newspaper accounts, both Mr. and Mrs. Lincoln spent most of the time shaking hands. "Mr. Lincoln took the position usually occupied by the President at receptions, and, during the whole time, did not have a resting spell of one minute, but shook hands continually," the *New York Herald*'s reporter noted. The writer went on to say, "Mrs. Lincoln bore the fatigue of the two-and-a-half hour siege with great patience."[12] At one point, the president noticed "a gentleman passing him of such towering proportions" that he stopped the unknown guest, "saying that he allowed no one taller than himself to pass him unchallenged." Lincoln has to admit himself "beaten in height" by six-foot, seven-inch Mr. Hatcher of

Loudon County, Virginia. It turned out to be a moment of levity in an otherwise wearing evening.[13]

At 10:30 p.m., President Lincoln decided to call it a night. "The universal impression is, that Old Abe's first public reception at the White House has been a triumphant success," declared one source.[14] He made one more turn around the room before retiring to his "private apartments." Mary Lincoln "remained for some time longer."[15] The president had another long day ahead of him, which would include a cabinet meeting to discuss Fort Sumter. Mary enjoyed the reception, but her husband was too tense and preoccupied to appreciate it.

MARCH 9, 1861, SATURDAY

# A TENSE CABINET MEETING

O n Saturday, President Lincoln met with delegates from Oregon, which started out to be a routine meeting but became something of an embarrassment to the president. The gathering began agreeably enough. "A gentleman of the party" mentioned that "Oregon was a large State, and would soon wield a powerful influence upon the affairs of Government."

The president was quick to agree. "Oh, yes," he said, "it's rather larger than Maryland and Rhode Island, which a man can hurry across in a few hours."

Another member of the delegation had a quick comeback to Lincoln's remark. He said that "they had heard of a man who was not long getting across one of those States."[1] This was a pointed reference to the president's secret, and embarrassing, train journey from Philadelphia to Washington on the night of February 22. The journey in question was deliberately kept secret because the Pinkerton Detectives had been warned that assassins were planning to murder the president as he changed trains in Baltimore. Baltimore was intensely pro-Confederate and anti-Lincoln; the threat was treated seriously. Precautions were taken to protect the president from any assassins by whisking him across the city under a disguise.

The president-elect traveled incognito, with no fanfare and no advance publicity. He wore a soft felt hat instead of his usual stovepipe, and wore either a shawl or an overcoat to cover his shoulders—several versions of this story have been told over the years. "Then I put on the soft hat and joined my friends without being recognized by strangers, for I was not the same man," Lincoln later recalled.[2] When the train reached

**45**

Baltimore, he left the station accompanied by Allan Pinkerton and his former law partner Ward Hill Lamon. The three of them traveled across Baltimore, the distance of about a mile, to the Camden Street Station and the Baltimore & Ohio train to Washington. No one recognized the president-elect, and there was no trouble or disturbance. After his arrival in Washington, Lincoln was driven by carriage to Willard's Hotel.

But this was not the end of the incident. A news reporter, Joseph Howard of the *New York Times*, heard about the story and decided to exaggerate it. He telegraphed his home office in New York that the president-elect's disguise was a lot more elaborate than just a felt hat and a long overcoat. In the new and embellished story, the felt hat became a Scottish-plaid cap; the overcoat was transformed into a military cloak. Other newspapers claimed that Lincoln wore a tam o' shanter and kilts. The episode became a source of humiliation to Lincoln. Newspaper accounts made him not only look ridiculous but also cowardly. Democrats ridiculed him for entering Washington like a thief in the night.

President Lincoln was not happy about the delegate's cutting remark, although he did his best not to let it show. He reacted to the quip "with a comical twist of his face" and said to the gathering, "Gentlemen, if you please we won't say anything more on that subject." No one else mentioned the obviously awkward topic again; it was unceremoniously "drapped."[3]

The president also had his share of routine chores to carry out. He had a conversation with the secretary of the navy, Gideon Welles, a meeting that lasted about thirty minutes. No mention of this meeting was made in Secretary Welles' diary. President Lincoln also sent a short note to Attorney General Edward Bates: "Please let Senator [Benjamin F.] Wade name the man to be District Attorney for the Northern District of Ohio;"[4] "The man" in question was Robert F. Paine of Cleveland. He also notified Secretary of State Seward to give "a full interview" to the appointed US minister to Spain, Carl Schurz.[5] But the president's main activity for the day was that evening's scheduled cabinet meeting. Attorney General Bates made this entry in his diary: "*Mar. 9. Saturday night. A Cabinet Council upon the State of the Country.*"[6]

In his diary, Secretary of the Navy Gideon Welles made a good many keen observations regarding his fellow cabinet members during the Fort Sumter crisis.

The "State of the Country" in March 1861 meant the state of Fort Sumter, which was the pressing topic of discussion. The cabinet had assembled to hear what General Winfield Scott had to say about Fort Sumter: should it be reinforced or abandoned? General Scott was considered the country's leading expert on all matters military; his opinion was much anticipated by all the cabinet members present.

What General Scott had to say took everyone but the president by surprise—there could be no possibility of keeping the fort from being captured by the rebels, and, therefore, it should be given up. "I was astonished to be informed that Fort Sumter, in Charleston Harbor, *must* be evacuated," Attorney General Bates wrote.[7] President Lincoln was the only person in the room who was not surprised—he had already heard what his general in chief had to say on the subject of Fort Sumter.

General Scott went on to list the reasons behind his recommendation to abandon Fort Sumter; he laid everything right on the line. The fort's garrison only had enough bread and rice on hand to last about twenty-six days, and only enough salted meat for forty-eight days. The general did not believe that Fort Sumter could possibly be relieved or reinforced within that period of time. It would take "many months" to carry out this operation, which would require a flotilla of warships, countless troop transports, and five thousand US Army troops along with twenty thousand volunteers. And the expedition would require an act of Congress before any sort of activity could even be considered.

President Lincoln was disturbed by what General Scott had to say, even though he had already heard much of it before, but he was not altogether convinced. Senior officers in the armed services were not convinced, either, and were not in complete agreement with the aging general. They could not even agree among themselves over whether Fort Sumter should be evacuated. "The *army* officers think destruction almost inevitable, where the *navy* officers think the damage but slight," Attorney General Bates wrote. "The one believes that Sumter cannot be relieved—or even provisioned—without an army of 20,000 men and a bloody battle: The other (the naval) believes that with light, rapid vessels, they can cross *the bar* at high tide of a dark night, run the enemy's forts (Moultrie and Cummings' Point) and reach Sumter with little risk."[8]

The members of President Lincoln's cabinet could not agree about Fort Sumter, either, much to the president's anxiety. Montgomery Blair and Salmon Chase were both in favor of holding the fort; all the other members, including Secretary of State Seward, wanted to hand it over to the rebels. Secretary Seward was especially emphatic in voicing his point of view. Gideon Welles made this pointed observation: "Mr. Seward opposed any and every scheme to reinforce Sumter."[9] The president was all too aware that he would be forced to make a fortify-or-evacuate decision and

Fort Sumter on August 23, 1863. Fort Sumter was already being threatened by South Carolina secessionists when Lincoln took the oath of office. During the first weeks after President Lincoln's inauguration, members of his cabinet could not agree about Fort Sumter—should it be abandoned or defended?

would probably be called upon to make that decision very soon. But none of his advisors, including high-ranking army and navy officers, could bring themselves to reach any consensus regarding what should be done.

President Lincoln desperately needed advice but could not get anything from his experts and advisors except contradictions. The Sumter crisis was putting him under a great deal of mental strain; because of the emergency, he suffered from severe headaches and was having trouble sleeping. The situation in South Carolina was already bad and looked to be getting worse. And the situation in Washington looked to be just as hopeless and offered no encouragement for the president.

"A strange state of things existed at that time in Washington. The atmosphere was thick with treason." Gideon Welles made this comment about the early days of Lincoln's presidency in his diary. "Democrats to a large extent sympathized with the Rebels more than with the Administration, which they opposed," he went on to explain, and also pointed out that "[t]he Republicans, on the other hand, were scarcely less partisan and unreasonable." Everyone was so wrapped up with their own self-interests that they did not seem to know or care about the secession crisis. "Neither party appeared to be apprehensive of or to realize the gathering storm," Secretary Welles noted with some exasperation. "There was a general belief, indulged in by most persons, that an adjustment would in some way be brought about, without any extensive resort to extreme measures."[10]

President Lincoln was just as exasperated as Secretary Welles. He sent a letter off to General Winfield Scott, asking the general to explain, in writing, exactly why he thought that Fort Sumter should be abandoned. Maybe seeing General Scott's reasons on paper would help him understand the situation, as well as the general's rationale, more clearly. The president asked General Scott three straightforward questions:

1st To what point of time can Major Anderson maintain his position at Fort Sumpter, without fresh supplies or reinforcement?

2d. Can you, with all the means now in your control, supply or re-inforce Fort Sumpter within that time?

3d If not, what amount of means and of what description, in addition to that already at your control, would enable you to supply and reinforce that fortress within the time?

After listing his queries, President Lincoln made one more request: "Please answer these, adding such statements, information, and counsel as your great skill and experience may suggest." Possibly the old general would be able to offer some positive advice for solving the Sumter dilemma. Lincoln was well aware that he needed all the advice he could get.[11]

President Lincoln also drafted a second note to General Scott, regarding "the maintenance of all the places within the military department of the United States." The note was signed by the secretary of war, Simon Cameron, but it was written by the president. Lincoln wanted General Scott "to exercise all possible vigilance" concerning these "places." He was referring not only to Fort Sumter but also to Fort Pickens in Pensacola Bay, Florida. Fort Pickens was also garrisoned by Union troops, but Pickens was not nearly as controversial as Fort Sumter—the Florida coast was not Charleston, South Carolina. Fort Pickens would be less of a flash point for civil war if its garrison was fortified by fresh troops. Secretary of State Seward supported the idea of defending Fort Pickens while surrendering Fort Sumter, which he thought would defuse the possibility of war. As far as Seward was concerned, this would be an even swap—the rebels would receive Fort Sumter without a fight, while the federal government would retain Fort Pickens. But in his short note to General Scott, President Lincoln made it clear that he intended to keep "all the places" in the hands of the US government, meaning both Fort Sumter and Fort Pickens.[12] Only five days before, during his inauguration address, he had promised to "hold, occupy, and possess" all government installations.[13] He intended to keep his promise.

# A RARE DAY OF PEACE AND QUIET

The first Sabbath after his inauguration turned out to be a day of relaxation for President Lincoln. He did have a meeting with Truman Smith, a political acquaintance and a former senator from Connecticut, at eight o'clock that evening, but nothing else of any importance seems to have taken place. No letters or telegrams were sent, and no other appointments were kept apart from his meeting with Truman Smith. It was a rare day of peace and quiet for the new president.

The only activity of any note was a visit to church that morning. "The first Sunday in the White House the family attended the New York Avenue Presbyterian Church, the Reverend Doctor Phineas D. Gurley, pastor," one of Lincoln's biographers stated.[1] The only reason that this is worthy of mention at all is because President Lincoln rarely set foot inside any church and, as he stated himself, was "not a member of any Christian Church."[2]

But even though he never belonged to any particular denomination, Lincoln visited a variety of churches over the years. He attended the local Baptist church with his parents in Pigeon Creek, Indiana, but never became a Baptist. In 1842, he married Mary Todd in an Episcopal church. After moving to Springfield, Illinois, Mr. and Mrs. Lincoln sporadically attended the Presbyterian church at the corner of Third and Washington Streets. From time to time, he also attended Unitarian and Episcopal churches. After he became president, he would occasionally spend part of Sunday morning at St. John's Episcopal Church, on Lafayette Square, Washington, although he was anything but a regular visitor on Sunday morning.

But even though he wanted nothing to do with the sectarian quarrelling that afflicted organized religion, Abraham Lincoln did believe in a Supreme Being, and he often said so. In his famous farewell address to the citizens of Springfield, before leaving Springfield for Washington and his inauguration, president-elect Lincoln told his audience, "I go to assume a task more difficult than that which devolved upon George Washington. Unless the great God who assisted him shall be with me and aid me, I must fail." He went on to say, "Let us all pray that the God of our fathers may not forsake us now."[3]

Throughout his life, Lincoln also read the Bible many times over. He often used biblical quotes in his political speeches, and he referred to the Bible as the Great Book: "In regard to the Great Book, I have but to say. It is the best gift God has given to man."[4] Although not deeply religious, Lincoln revered the Bible. He certainly had more regard for the Great Book than for any organized church or religion. Reading the Bible also had one great advantage over attending church, at least from Lincoln's point of view: he could read it at home without getting tangled up with the religious doctrines and controversies of the various denominations, which he thought to be so irritating.

But on this particular Sunday, President Lincoln decided to overlook his distaste for organized religion and go to church. He may just have wanted to get away from the White House and its pressures for a while. Hearing a good sermon and meeting people who were not members of his cabinet might help take his mind off the secession crisis and allow him to relax for an hour or two. The state of affairs in South Carolina was very much in his mind.

The secession crisis was on everybody's mind that Sunday. This item appeared in the March 10 edition of the *New York Times:* "There is but little doubt that the Government will order the evacuation of Fort Sumpter."[5]

# SECRET NEGOTIATIONS

**M**onday morning brought President Lincoln back to his office, where he spent much of the day tending to routine chores. He sent a note to Attorney General Edward Bates, which was actually a letter of introduction to the Honorable I. N. Morris. The president wanted Attorney General Bates to talk with Mr. Morris "in relation to the Russell fraud," which was a financial scandal involving the doings of a New York City firm. "I think it may subserve the public interest," he advised the attorney general.[1]

The president also sent a memo to Secretary of State William H. Seward, in which he recommended four candidates for diplomatic posts: "Dayton to England; Fremont to France; Clay to Spain; Corwin to Mexico." He ended his communiqué by adding, "This is suggestion merely, and not a dictation." Secretary Seward responded to the memo later the same day. He approved Cassius M. Clay as minister to Spain and Thomas Corwin to Mexico. But he preferred Charles Francis Adams for England over Lincoln's candidate, because Adams was "far above all others adapted to British Court &, society and infinitely more watchful capable."[2]

As far as the minister to France was concerned, Seward considered the president's suggestion totally unacceptable. Even though John C. Fremont was well known—he was a US senator from California and had been a candidate for president in 1856—Secretary Seward heard talk that Fremont was also "to be engaged in raising money there for his estates," which would cause "serious complications." But even more serious and complicated than his financial dealings was Fremont's personal background: "he is by birth and education a South Carolinian," Seward wrote. Actually, John C. Fremont was born in Savannah, Georgia, in January 1813, although he did attend the College of Charleston in Charleston, South Carolina, graduating in 1836. To Secretary Seward's way of thinking, appointing anyone with Fremont's Southern background as the US envoy to France would be inviting disaster. Seward was certain that Fremont would do his best to create bad feelings between the United States and France in the name of the Confederacy. There was no way to escape the problem of secession, not even within the rarefied circles of the diplomatic corps.[3]

President Lincoln also received a reply from General Winfield Scott on March 11, a message concerning the situation at Fort Sumter. The general's comments repeated exactly what he said at Friday's cabinet meeting. General Scott estimated that Major Anderson "has hard bread, flour & rice for about 26 days, & salt meat . . . for about 48 . . . . how long he could hold out . . . cannot be answered with absolute accuracy." In answer to whether Fort Sumter could be resupplied or reinforced, General Scott said straightforwardly, "No: Not within many months." And as far as what would be needed to supply and reinforce Sumter, the general was just as blunt: "a fleet of war vessels & transports, 5,000 additional regular troops & 20,000 volunteers. . . . would require new acts of Congress & from six to eight months."[4]

General Scott's reply to President Lincoln's inquiries neatly supported Secretary Seward's position regarding Fort Sumter—namely, that it must be abandoned. He was totally convinced that his way was the best way, if not the only way, to avert civil war and preserve the union. During the last weeks of the James Buchanan administration, Seward even went so far as to meet with Southern emissaries on the subject of the controversial fortress in Charleston Harbor. He "came to an understanding" with "certain of the leading Secessionists" that Fort Sumter would not be attacked by rebel forces "provided that the garrison should not be reinforced" by federal troops. And on March 5, the day after Abraham Lincoln's inauguration, "commissioners from the Rebel Government arrived in Washington and put themselves in communication with the

Secretary of State."[5] The three commissioners were Andre B. Roman of Louisiana, John Forsyth of Alabama, and Martin J. Crawford of Georgia. Secretary Seward assured the Southern emissaries that Fort Sumter would definitely be given up.

Seward's message was passed along to Jefferson Davis, who was living at the Confederate White House in Montgomery, Alabama. President Davis was relieved to hear what Secretary Seward had to say; he was under the impression that Seward was speaking on behalf of President Lincoln. The only trouble was that Seward was acting on his own; Lincoln knew nothing about his own secretary of state's activities with the Confederate representatives. As Gideon Welles phrased it, "the negotiations or understandings between him and the parties were not immediately detailed to the Cabinet." Secretary Seward intended to "effect a reconciliation" between North and South by himself, and inform President Lincoln after he had completed his negotiations.[6] The president's already unsettled state of mind was not being soothed by the behavior of his cabinet.

# THE PRESSURES OF OFFICE

One of the first items of business for President Lincoln on this Tuesday morning was a "private interview" with Joseph Holt, the former secretary of war. The meeting was to take place in the White House at eleven o'clock. The president did not mention the subject that he wanted to address during the interview, but it can be safely assumed that the conversation focused on Fort Sumter. President Lincoln's thoughts seldom strayed from the growing threat in South Carolina.[1]

The situation at Fort Sumter was turning President Lincoln into a nervous wreck, which is clearly evident in a note he sent to his friend and political colleague Jacob Collamer. He sent an agitated, almost hysterical, note of apology to Collamer for an offense that turned out to be imaginary. "My dear sir: God help me," the president wrote. "It is said that I have offended you. Please tell me how."[2]

When Jacob Collamer read the note, he was totally bewildered. He had no idea what President Lincoln was talking about and had no idea what prompted him to send such a baffling communiqué. "I am entirely insensible that you have, in any way, offended me," he said in response. "I cherish no sentiment towards you but that of kindness & confidence." President Lincoln sent an immediate reply: "My dear Sir I am much relieved to learn that I have been misinformed as to your having been offended."[3] Had President Lincoln really been informed of some offense that he might have inflicted upon Jacob Collamer, or were his nerves playing tricks on him? This small incident gives some insight into the president's mental condition in the days following his inauguration: frightened, confused, and, most of all, terrified that a bad decision on his part regarding Fort Sumter would start a civil war.

Another incident took place on March 12 that would further unnerve President Lincoln. Two of the Confederate emissaries who had arrived in Washington, John Forsyth of Alabama and Martin J. Crawford of Georgia, sent an official letter to Secretary of State Seward. The letter stated that "The Confederate States constitute an independent nation, de facto and de jure, and possess a government perfect in all its parts, and endowed with all the means of self-support." As representatives of the Confederacy, John Forsyth and Martin J. Crawford requested an appointment to meet with President Lincoln so that they might present their credentials and also to discuss "the objects of the mission with which they are charged."[4] The emissaries had been sent by the Confederate government in Montgomery, Alabama, "to open diplomatic relations with the Government of the United States."[5] Specifically, they had instructions to negotiate the transfer of Fort Sumter and Fort Pickens from the United States to the Confederacy.[6]

Secretary Seward had kept in touch with Messers. Roman, Forsyth, and Crawford by letter, but he had not had an actual conversation with them. The three emissaries—they actually preferred to be referred to as "ambassadors" because, as far as they were concerned, the United States was a foreign country—were anxious to have a meeting with both Seward and President Lincoln to discuss Fort Sumter and Fort Pickens. Secretary Seward informed the Confederate delegates that he would ask President Lincoln to agree to an in-person meeting with them; he also stated that all troops would be withdrawn from Fort Sumter.

Secretary Seward was doing his best to disrupt the secessionists, and used every means and method he could think of to frustrate their goals. He even went so far as to suggest that President Lincoln appoint George W. Summers, one of the leaders of Virginia's Unionist movement, as a Supreme Court justice. In Secretary Seward's opinion, appointing a leading Virginian as a justice to the US Supreme Court could only strengthen the Unionist cause. It would show the South that Lincoln and his administration had no animosity toward them. But President

Lincoln did not agree with Seward's opinion and, hence, did not appoint George W. Summers to the Supreme Court.

The Confederate representatives were encouraged by what Secretary Seward had to say in his letters, but they were also becoming impatient for a face-to-face meeting with Seward and, their ultimate goal, with President Lincoln. They agreed to wait a while longer, until March 28, but only on condition that Fort Sumter would not be reinforced. The secretary of state did his best to reassure the three men that the fort would be evacuated. He also informed a reporter writing for the *National Intelligencer*, probably the most widely read and influential newspaper in Washington, that all troops would be withdrawn from Sumter. When he spoke to the *Intelligencer*'s correspondent, Seward asked him to relay the news of the Sumter withdrawal to George W. Summers, an influential former judge and congressman from Virginia. Secretary Seward hoped that this news would help strengthen the position of the Unionists, and that the radical secessionists would begin to lose their influence, at least in the State of Virginia.

Secretary Seward's news regarding Fort Sumter was published in newspapers throughout the North and the South, and assured readers that Fort Sumter would definitely be evacuated. The *New York Herald* announced, "At ten o'clock tomorrow morning the Cabinet will meet to decide definitely the question of abandoning Fort Sumter." The article went on to say, "Advice received from various portions of the free States indicate that the Northern mind has already recognized the unavoidability of the abandonment and that no violent outbursts of opposition need be apprehended."[7] Newspapers in the Southern states said basically the same thing—there was no question in the minds of most editors that Fort Sumter was certain to be evacuated. And when George W. Summers was given Secretary Seward's message, he reacted as if the fort had already been turned over to the rebels: "The [report of the] removal from Sumter acted like a charm it gave us great strength," he said. "A reaction is now going on in the state. The outside pressure has greatly subsided."[8]

Many Northerners were glad to hear that Sumter would be evacuated and that war would be avoided. But probably just as many were angry that the fort would be given up without a fight. Much of their anger was directed at President Lincoln for allowing Fort Sumter to be abandoned, as well as for not having the Confederate commissioners arrested for treason. "Mr. Lincoln was bitterly blamed for this by over-zealous patriots," one historian wrote.[9] There were also several assassination threats. After dinner one night, the president and his entire family became sick; it was suspected that the fish they had eaten for dinner, a good-sized Maryland shad, had been deliberately poisoned.

To President Lincoln's family, along with members of the White House staff, it seemed that the president had aged several years during the week since his inauguration. The pressures of his office were visibly wearing him down. The negative reaction to the Confederate emissaries and their message regarding Fort Sumter, along with the assassination threats, depressed and frightened him. He was not sleeping well. His spirits may have been given a temporary boost by the visit of several army officers to the White House "at one p.m. to-day," as reported by a Washington newspaper. "They were of course in full dress, as is usual on such occasions."[10] But friends and family worried about him and wondered what would happen if the Sumter crisis did not end soon.

# MARCH 13, 1861, WEDNESDAY
## A NEW PLAN

President Lincoln had his usual desk full of work to deal with on this Wednesday. He sent a letter to Postmaster General Montgomery Blair, which was delivered by Mr. C. T. Hempston (or Hempstow—the spelling is not clear). In his letter, the president advised Postmaster Blair that the bearer of the note, "who is a Virginian," wanted to obtain "a small place in your Dept." for his son. "I think Virginia should be heard, in such cases." Lincoln hoped that showing preferential treatment to a Virginian in awarding a job, even a small one, might help improve relations between the State of Virginia and his administration. He was using every opportunity to make a favorable impression with Virginia Unionists. But despite the president's efforts and intentions, no appointment seems to have been made.[1]

Lincoln also sent memos concerning other appointments. He wrote to a Mark W. Delahay regarding some government positions in Kansas, including the post of surveyor general for the state. Mr. Delahay ended up receiving that particular job himself. The president also contacted a Mr. James Doolittle concerning the vacant position of agent for the Choctaw and Chickasaw Indians; he also sent a note to Secretary of State Seward about the appointing of the minister resident for Sweden and Norway. These were routine items, the sort of memos that the president wrote nearly every day.

But the president also sent another note to Secretary Seward; his second communiqué was anything but routine. In his second memo, the president informed Seward that he was not to have any face-to-face meetings with the three Confederate emissaries, despite any objections they might have—such a meeting would essentially serve as recognition of the Confederate States of America as a sovereign nation, independent of the United States. This was exactly what the president did not want to do; this would almost certainly lead to Britain and other nations recognizing the Confederacy as an independent country. Secretary Seward accordingly informed the commissioners that he would not be able to receive them. The reason he gave was because it "could not be admitted that the States referred to had, in law or fact, withdrawn from the Federal Union, or that they could do so in any other manner than with the consent and concert of the people of the United States, to be given through a National Convention, to be assembled in conformity with the provisions of the Constitution of the United States."[2]

Secretary Seward's refusal to meet with the Confederate representatives was not formally released until early April. But Confederate authorities acquired an unofficial version, at a much earlier date, most likely on March 13. Confederate president Jefferson Davis was not happy to hear that his commissioners would not be allowed to speak with the US secretary of state, and that they had been kept from this vital discussion by order of President Lincoln. He was hoping that negotiations between the emissaries and the US State Department would lead directly to the federal government turning Fort Sumter over to the Confederate government. President Davis described the fort as a standing threat to the chief harbor of South Carolina.

President Davis was both disappointed and upset. First, Secretary Seward had given his assurances that Sumter would be abandoned. A short time later, he was forbidden even to discuss the matter with Confederate officials. This did not improve the state of affairs in Charleston, at least not as President Davis saw it. He complained that, during the period of reiterated assurances to withdraw the garrison from Fort Sumter, Lincoln and his government were also devising plans for furnishing supplies and reinforcements for the garrison. The condition of affairs was deteriorating steadily, and as far as Jefferson Davis was concerned, it was all Abraham Lincoln's fault.

President Lincoln would not have been surprised by President Davis's unhappiness, but he would not have been overly upset by it, either. His main concern was still whether he should abandon Fort Sumter or strengthen its defense force. He had received some new information, a new idea, on how to resupply the fort—a new idea that gave him some encouragement that Fort Sumter might be resupplied and reinforced after all, despite what General Scott had said. Jefferson Davis's unhappiness was beside the point.

The new idea for resupplying Fort Sumter had been proposed by a former naval officer named Gustavus V. Fox, who had spent a considerable amount of time studying the geography of Charleston Harbor. After finishing his study, Fox came to the conclusion that it would be feasible to send supplies and reinforcements to Fort Sumter within a matter of days, not the many months that General Scott said would be necessary. His idea was fairly simple and straightforward: load the men and supplies aboard two borrowed New York City tugboats, which had shallow drafts and would be able to pass over the sand bar that blocked the harbor entrance. The tugs would be escorted by two warships, the *Pawnee* and the *Harriet Lane*, which would deal with any Confederate ships that might try to interfere with the operation. The landings would be carried out during the dead of night, when it would be difficult for Charleston's artillery batteries to see the approaching ships, let alone hit them with cannon fire. If all went according to plan, the landings would succeed despite any attempted opposition from the rebels, either at sea or from the harbor batteries, and Major Anderson would have everything he needed to retain Fort Sumter.

Gustavus Fox's strategy had originally been introduced earlier in the year, when James Buchanan was still president. But the plan was rejected at the time, because Buchanan's administration decided to take no action to relieve Fort Sumter. In mid-March, about a week after Lincoln's inauguration, Fox's idea came to the attention of Postmaster General Montgomery Blair. As soon as he read the plan, Postmaster Blair immediately telegraphed Fox to come to Washington and talk to President Lincoln.

When Fox arrived in Washington, Blair accompanied him to the White House to explain his idea.

President Lincoln was anxious to find a feasible way to get provisions and/or soldiers to Fort Sumter. The idea that Gustavus Fox was proposing sounded like just the plan he was looking for. From the way it was presented by Postmaster Blair and Gustavus Fox himself—including the fact that small tugboats would be almost impossible to hit by land-based artillery, especially at night—the strategy sounded as if it would be almost certain to succeed. Of course, there was also the question of what the secessionists would do if the plan *did* succeed. This was another major concern. The president decided to present the Fort Sumter question—if reprovisioning and reinforcing the fort was a good and feasible idea—to his cabinet on the following day. President Lincoln needed advice, advice that would help him to do something about Fort Sumter without starting a war. Hopefully, the cabinet members would offer counsel that would allow him to put an end to the problem in Charleston Harbor.

# ALMOST UNBEARABLE TENSION

**P**resident Lincoln spent most of the morning discussing Fort Sumter with his cabinet. According to the *New York Herald,* "the Cabinet met at ten A.M., and continued in session until one P.M."[1] Officers in the army and the navy also attended the meeting. The main topic of discussion was Gustavus Fox's idea for coming to the aid of Major Anderson and the Sumter garrison.

Although everyone who attended the meeting had a great deal to say, and was very generous—and sometimes over-generous—in giving their points of view, nothing that was said helped the president make up his mind over what to do about Fort Sumter. The cabinet members could not make up their minds, either. Neither could any of the army or navy officers, who tended to contradict each other. "The *army* officers and the *navy* officers differ widely about the degree of danger to rapidly moving vessels passing under the fire of land batteries," Attorney General Edward Bates wrote in his diary. "The *army* officers think destruction almost inevitable, where the *navy* officers think the danger but slight." He went on to say, "The naval men have convinced me fully that the thing can be done," but also were convinced that any landing at Sumter "would be almost certain to *begin the war*."[2]

A newspaper editor acquaintance gave President Lincoln a completely different tactic concerning the Sumter problem. In a letter dated March 12, 1861, J. Watson Webb of the *New York Courier and Inquirer* suggested an entirely unique approach, an approach that differed from the suggestions of both Lincoln's cabinet and the senior military officers—instead of attempting a secret landing in the middle of the night, Webb recommended that the president announce in advance his intentions to reinforce Fort Sumter. "Do this publicly and let the destination and purpose of the expedition be proclaimed," he wrote.[3] Lincoln should announce his plans to everyone in the country, including Jefferson Davis and South Carolina governor Francis Pickens, and let the Southerners react.

In his letter, Webb also suggested a different method of putting troops and supplies ashore on the island fortress. Instead of using tugboats and an escort of two warships, as Gustavus Fox had proposed, Webb advised sending a small flotilla of three warships for the expedition. According to Webb's plan, only two of the ships would actually carry troops and supplies. The third ship would sail a mile or so ahead of the others, acting as a decoy to draw enemy fire. "The fire having been thus opened by the Rebels upon Government vessels, nobody will censure Major Anderson or the Government, if he promptly, as he can, destroys *Moultrie* and the Battery on Morris Island."[4] The two ships carrying the men and provisions would be able to carry out their assignment at Fort Sumter, while the Charleston artillery batteries were preoccupied with the decoy ship.

J. Watson Webb had certainly given President Lincoln something to think about. Informing Jefferson Davis and Governor Pickens of his intentions regarding Fort Sumter was an idea worth considering—tell the Rebels what he had in mind and let them decide what to do about it. Another plan might be to send food and other necessities only, and announce that an expedition to supply a starving garrison would be dispatched. This would make the enterprise seem like a humanitarian effort. The president was still trying to make up his mind about how to deal with the situation in Charleston Harbor; Webb's letter gave him one or two more options.

A second cabinet meeting was held later in the day. It began at about 5:00 p.m., and was reported to have been quite a lively session. The main topic of discussion was the method for appointing officials in the western territories, and exactly who should decide which candidates for governor, marshal, judge, and secretaries of the various departments would be nominated. After the morning's tense discussion concerning

Fort Sumter, it must have come as a great relief for President Lincoln to talk about another subject.

The president had been under almost unbearable tension ever since he took office ten days earlier, and the strain certainly showed. "The President has been severely worked for the last few days, and to night looks severely jaded," a reporter from the *New York Herald* observed. The reporter went on to predict that, if the president did not curtail his activities and follow a less stressful schedule, "Mr. Lincoln will break down under the pressure made upon him, as General Taylor did before him."[5] President Zachary Taylor died on July 9, 1850, after only sixteen months in office. After his death, rumors began to circulate that President Taylor had been poisoned—assassinated by pro-slavery Southerners; he had planned to ban the expansion of slavery into the western territories.

# LINCOLN SENDS A MEMO

After tending to some routine appointments—naming Mark H. Dunnell as consul general for Canada and appointing Freeman H. Morse as consul to London—President Lincoln addressed the activity that concerned him most. He wrote a memo regarding the reinforcing of Fort Sumter to his cabinet. His secretary, John Nicolay, copied the memo for each member of the cabinet; each copy was signed by President Lincoln. The message was short and concise but let everyone know exactly what was on the president's mind: "Assuming it to be possible to now provision Fort-Sumpter, under all the circumstances, is it wise to attempt it? Please give me your opinion, in writing, on this question. Your Obt. Servt. A. LINCOLN."[1]

If President Lincoln was expecting a unified response from his cabinet, he was quickly disappointed. His seven advisors turned out to be as divided as ever.

Secretary Seward, as might be expected, advised him not to attempt reprovisioning, at least not yet. "If it were possible to peacefully provision Fort Sumter, of course I should answer, that it would be both unwise and inhuman not to attempt it. But the facts of the case are known to be, that the attempt must be made with the employment of military and marine force, which would provoke combat, and probably initiate a civil war. . . . I would not provoke war in any way now."[2]

Salmon Chase could not make up his mind whether he was in favor of taking any action. In one sentence, he said no, not if it meant going to war: "If the attempt will so inflame civil war as to involve an immediate necessity for the enlistment of armies . . . I cannot advise it." But on the other hand, he was all in favor of resupplying the fort if it did not result in

Salmon P. Chase, in a photo taken in 1870. He could not make up his mind whether he was in favor of taking any action to resupply Fort Sumter.

war: "But it seems to me highly improbable that the attempt . . . will produce such consequences. . . . I return, therefore, an affirmative answer."[3]

Secretary of War Simon Cameron said no, absolutely not: "it would be unwise now to make such an attempt. . . . I am greatly influenced by the opinions of the Army officers who have expressed themselves on the subject, and who seem to concur that it is, perhaps, now impossible to succor that fort, substantially, if at all. . . . All the officers within Fort Sumter, together with Generals Scott and Totten, express this opinion."[4]

Gideon Welles agreed with Secretary Seward and Simon Cameron and said no, arguing, "The question has two aspects, one military, the

Secretary of War Simon Cameron advised against resupplying Fort Sumter.

other political." As far as the military aspect was concerned, the "military gentlemen" were of the opinion that "it would be unwise" to support Fort Sumter "and I am not disposed to controvert their opinions." And in a political view, "I entertain doubts of the wisdom of the measure" and did not "think it wise."[5]

The secretary of the interior, Caleb Smith, said, "I have arrived at the conclusion that the probabilities are in favor of the success of the proposed enterprise, so far as to secure the landing of the vessels at the Fort, but . . . it would not be wise under all the circumstances." In other words, no.[6]

Montgomery Blair, the postmaster general, advised President Lincoln to do everything possible to retain the fort, and he blamed the "ambitious leaders of the late Democratic party," James Buchanan and his administration, for allowing the secession crisis to happen in the first place. "To the connivance of the late administration it is due alone that this Rebellion has been enabled to attain its present proportions," he said. He went on to advise that the evacuation of Fort Sumter "will convince the rebels that the administration lacks firmness." Montgomery Blair voted Yes on provisioning Fort Sumter.[7]

Attorney General Edward Bates advised against resupplying Fort Sumter. He admitted that the government "has the power and the means" to provision the fort, but went on to say that the "wisdom of the act must be tested by the value of the object to be gained and by the hazards to be encountered." The attorney general summed up his view in one sentence: "I am willing to evacuate Fort Sumter, rather than be an active party in the beginning of civil war."[8]

President Lincoln had the answers he had requested, but the answers were so split and indecisive—five against sending supplies, one in favor, and Salmon Chase undecided—that they could not possibly help him reach a decision regarding Fort Sumter. They also did not help settle his nerves or put his mind at ease. He was still as unsure of himself as ever.

The fact that the population of the North continued to be just as divided as his cabinet was another item that upset the president. A good many Northerners did not really care if the Southern states seceded or not, and agreed with Horace Greeley's opinion: "If the Cotton States shall become satisfied that they can do better out of the Union than in it, we insist on letting them go in peace," Greeley wrote. "The right to secede may be a revolutionary one, but it exists nevertheless. . . . And whenever a considerable section of our Union shall deliberately resolve to go out, we shall resist all coercive measures designed to keep it in. We hope never to live in a republic whereof one section is pinned to the residue by bayonets."[9]

Even members of President Lincoln's own political party did not stand behind him. A group of Republican congressmen were upset that Lincoln might not come to Major Anderson's rescue, but not for any patriotic reasons; they were afraid that abandoning the major would result in disaster for the Republican Party and for themselves. And Attorney General Bates was convinced that a sizeable percentage of Southerners were actually Unionists and anti-secessionists and were not in favor of leaving the Union at all. Bates wrote in his diary that these Unionists were anxious to rejoin the federal government, and that "in several of the misguided states of the South" the people "are really lovers of the Union" and are "anxious to be safely back under the protection of its flag." He went on to predict that "the nation will be restored to its integrity without the effusion of blood." Reinforcing Fort Sumter would only antagonize the loyal Unionists of the South, he insisted.[10]

President Lincoln realized that he still had a few weeks before Major Anderson ran out of food and supplies, which meant that he still had time to reach a decision. But it was becoming increasingly obvious that his cabinet was not going to help him make that decision. He was on his own, and he was all too aware that an incorrect or mistaken judgment could result in the end of his political career as well as in the end of the Union.

## MARCH 16 AND 17, 1861, SATURDAY AND SUNDAY

# A QUIET WEEKEND

**B**ecause no cabinet meetings were held over this particular weekend, President Lincoln had the time to tend to other business. One item on the president's agenda was to send a letter that formally recognized Luis Molina as envoy extraordinary and minister plenipotentiary of Nicaragua to the United States. It was a very friendly and diplomatic communiqué, welcoming "Mr. Molina" to Washington as well as acknowledging his rank and position. "Please communicate to his excellency the President of Nicaragua my high esteem and consideration, and my earnest wish for his health, happiness, and long life," the president wrote, which expressed the tone and sentiment of his entire letter.[1]

The president also sent two short requests to General Winfield Scott, both of which involved a Lieutenant John C. Howard. Lieutenant Howard had been court-martialed during President James Buchanan's administration, but President Buchanan disapproved of the sentence and Lieutenant Howard was released from arrest. A "retiring Union congressman from Texas" named Andrew J. Hamilton requested that President Lincoln restore Lieutenant Howard to his former post. President Lincoln agreed, writing to General Scott, "If Lieut. Genl. Scott perceives no impropriety in my granting Mr. Hamilton's request, made within, I should be gratified to do it."[2]

The second note to General Scott concerned a Major John C. Henshaw. "I have examined, to some extent, this case of Major Henshaw, and have been brought to deeply sympathize with him," the president wrote.

Major Henshaw had been court-martialed for refusing to allow troops under his command to apprehend runaway slaves. Because of this, US Army regulations prevented Major Henshaw from being restored to "line service"—any position that would put him in command of troops—but the major was asking to be assigned as paymaster at a military base. "He wishes to be appointed a Paymaster," the president continued, "and if, in the opinion of Gen. Scott, this can be done without impropriety, it would gratify me to do it." No record of General Scott's reply has been found, but Major Henshaw was appointed assistant adjutant general in August 1862 and eventually became judge advocate in 1864.[3]

President Lincoln had a high regard for soldiers and officers, and he always made it a point to intervene in their behalf whenever the opportunity presented itself. In the coming months and years, he would be depending on them more and more. His political career, including his hopes for being reelected in 1864, would rest entirely upon the success of Union troops in the field. Four years in the future, he would tell General U. S. Grant and his staff, "Your success is my success."[4] This was not just an empty compliment; Lincoln was fully aware that he was just stating the plain truth.

The most significant communiqué Lincoln wrote on March 16 was addressed simply "To the Senate," and was actually intended for the Committee on Foreign Relations. Its subject was a boundary dispute between the United States and Great Britain; the boundary in question was the line dividing Vancouver Island between the United States and Canada. The British government suggested that either Switzerland, Sweden, or the Netherlands be chosen to settle the dispute. President Lincoln asked, "Will the Senate approve a treaty referring to either of the Sovereign Powers above-named the dispute now existing between the Governments of the United States and Great Britain concerning the boundary line between Vancouver's Island and the American Continent?"[5]

This was a minor dispute, but it had the potential of growing into a major quarrel. Britain had already begun to take an interest in the American secession crisis, as well as in becoming involved in the disagreement between North and South. The last thing President Lincoln wanted was for any foreign country, including Britain, to intervene in what could very well deteriorate into a civil war. This was especially the case since Britain seemed to be favoring the South. "The South fight for independence," the British home secretary wrote, "but what do the North fight for, except to gratify passion or pride?"[6] The president wanted the Vancouver Island dispute ended before the British could use it as an excuse to involve themselves in the disagreement. The dispute was handed over to the Swiss government for arbitration, but nothing was resolved. Both countries maintained detachments on Vancouver Island until 1872, when the Royal Marines finally left the island. But Britain's interest in the conflict between North and South would continue to grow in the months to come.

Sunday was more or less a day of rest for President Lincoln. He went to church with General Winfield Scott that morning. According to one account, "The President and General Scott attended church in the forenoon, at the church of the Rev. Mr. Hynes."[7] But the president's visit to Reverend Hynes's church probably had more to do with a change of pace and a change of surroundings than with any desire to hear a good sermon. Just getting away from the White House, and all the pressures that went with it, must have been a great relief, even if it was just for an hour or so. President Lincoln knew that he would be needing all the relaxation he could get; he had the feeling that he would not be getting very much of it in the future.

# TARIFFS, APPOINTMENTS, AND A MEMO

After a fairly relaxed weekend, President Lincoln went back to his usual White House routine on Monday morning. This included a return to agonizing over Fort Sumter. He wrote a memo to himself listing the pros and cons of abandoning the fort, a sort of checklist to help him make up his mind. Lincoln called it "Some considerations in favor of withdrawing the Troops from Fort Sumpter, by President Lincoln."[1] The three-page document outlined the opinions given by Secretary Seward and the other members of his cabinet during their March 15 meeting.

Lincoln's memorandum is a fairly comprehensive listing of reasons for withdrawing the Sumter garrison, along with two objections for abandoning the fort. "The Fort cannot be permanently held without reinforcement" is the first reason given for withdrawing the garrison. Other explanations include the following: "[t]he Fort cannot now be reinforced without a large armament, involving of course a bloody conflict and great exasperation on both sides;" it is of no real military value and "is not necessary to protect the City of Charleston from foreign invasion;" "[t]he abandonment of the Post would remove a source of irritation of the Southern people and deprive the secession movement of one of its most powerful stimulants" and would also encourage Southern Unionists, "who while friendly to the Union are yet reluctant to see extreme measures pursued;" surrendering Fort Sumter would "confound and embarrass those enemies of the Union" who have insisted that the North was using "coercion" against the South by keeping a garrison at the fort.[2]

Two objections to surrendering the fort were also given. If Sumter were given up, Lincoln gave as his first objection, members of the

Republican Party would be demoralized by the "timidity" and "want of pluck" by the Lincoln administration and would desert the party. The second, and probably most important, objection was that the secessionists would view the abandonment of Fort Sumter as "a victory on their part."[3] According to this memorandum, there were a lot more reasons for giving up the fort than for reinforcing it. But this did not come as any surprise to President Lincoln; the members of his cabinet had said basically the same things at their meeting a few days earlier. Writing the memo did not help him come to a decision any more than his cabinet had done.

President Lincoln also had something else on his mind, something just as vital as Fort Sumter but in a different way. Treasury Secretary Salmon Chase urged "action in the revenue question at the earliest possible moment." Secretary Chase was referring to the collection of tariffs and customs from the seceded Southern states, including South Carolina. More specifically, he was talking about how to go about collecting these revenues. Because duties and tariffs were the main source of income for funding the federal government—between 90 percent and 95 percent of all funds came from collecting tariffs, since there was no income tax—the "revenue question" was a vital matter. "It will be the most delicate, complicated, and consequential topic yet submitted to the deliberation of the Cabinet."[4]

The president responded to Secretary Chase's revenue question with a question of his own—actually two questions. First, he wanted to know if "any goods, wares and merchandize" subject to the payment of duties were being "imported into the United States without such duties being paid"? In other words, were any imports being illegally smuggled into the country? President Lincoln also wanted to know if it would be possible for customs and tariffs to be collected by ships stationed off the coast of Southern ports—if "vessels off shore could be effectively used" to prevent smuggling as well as "to enforce the payment or securing of the duties." If so, the president went on, "what number, and description of vessels, in addition to those already in the Revenue service would be requisite?"[5] He wanted to make sure that the federal government would be collecting the revenue from any imported goods, and not the government of South Carolina or one of the other rebel states.

Secretary Chase did not really know the answer to President Lincoln's first question. He replied that he had no "official information" of any illegal smuggling operations, but he also admitted that there were no customs officials south of North Carolina, Tennessee, and Arkansas, and "consequently," he had "no reports" on any smuggling activities. Chase did say that offshore vessels would be able to "execute the revenue laws," but he added that all eleven vessels currently in service would have to be rearmed in case of attack by Southern warships. He also said that "naval protection" would be needed.[6]

Since the rearming and protecting of ships were both naval concerns, President Lincoln sent a short note to the secretary of the navy, Gideon Welles, to ask his opinion on the subject. "I shall be obliged if you will inform me what amount of Naval force you could at once place at the control of the Revenue service," he wrote. He also asked, "whether at some distance of time you could so place an additional force; and how much? and at what time?" If Secretary Welles was surprised by the president's request, he did not let it show. He replied that twelve naval vessels could be transferred to the revenue service immediately, and that four additional ships could also be withdrawn from "foreign service" within three months. Additionally, there were fifteen vessels "not in commission" that could probably be turned over to the revenue service as well.[7]

From the two replies he had received from Secretary Chase and Secretary Welles, President Lincoln was well satisfied that collecting revenues at sea was feasible, and also that any customs ships could be defended against any Southern raiders. But there was still one question that needed to be answered—was the collection of duties offshore legal and constitutional? To obtain advice on this particular item, the president wrote to his legal expert, Attorney General Edward Bates: "I shall be obliged if you will give me your opinion in writing whether under the Constitution and existing laws, the Executive has power to collect duties on ship-board, off-shore, in cases where their collection in the ordinary way is, by any cause, rendered impracticable." President Lincoln also asked if he had the power "to prevent the landing of dutiable goods, unless the duties were paid."[8]

No reply to this question was found in President Lincoln's papers. If Secretary Bates did send an answer, which is almost certain, he probably would have given his opinion that the president did not have the authority to do what he proposed without the consent of Congress. The Constitution gives Congress the power to lay and collect taxes, duties, imposts, and excises in Article I, Section 8. Congress gave the Executive Branch the power to negotiate tariff reductions in the Reciprocal Trade Agreement Act of 1934. President Franklin D. Roosevelt became the first president to have the authority to levy tariffs and negotiate bilateral trade agreements without the approval of Congress.[9] But the president had no such authority in 1861, which meant that he did not have the power to collect revenues offshore. This response would have come as yet another great disappointment to President Lincoln.

Another essential item on President Lincoln's agenda was to contact William H. Seward regarding the appointing of ministers to overseas posts. "I believe it is a necessity with us to make the appointments I mentioned last night—that is, Charles F. Adams to England, William L. Dayton to France, George P. Marsh to Sardinia, and Anson Burlingame to Austria." He stated that "Mr. Adams I take because you suggested him, coupled with his eminent fitness for the place." All of the appointments were made just as the president set them out in his letter except for Anson Burlingame, who was given an assignment in China.[10]

The most significant of these appointments was Charles Francis Adams as minister to Great Britain. In the coming months and years, Adams would use all of his diplomatic skills to keep Britain from intervening in the conflict on the side of the Confederacy. This would come as a great help, as well as no small relief, to President Lincoln. Adams's son, Henry Adams, observed that members of the British government were hoping that the seceded Southern states would become an independent country, which would greatly reduce the power and influence of the United States. As Henry Adams quoted British prime minister Lord Palmerston, Britain "desires the severance as a diminution of a dangerous power."[11] The president was determined that Palmerston would not have his desire granted, but his secretary of state lacked both the talent and the temperament— Seward held a deep prejudice against the British—to negotiate with the government in London. Charles Francis Adams was Lincoln's best hope of keeping the British out of the conflict between North and South.

# AN ORDER FOR CAPTAIN FOX

**P**resident Lincoln wrote a unique "To whom it may concern" memo as a favor to an acquaintance from his hometown. It was a short, one-sentence note: "I did see and talk with Master George Evans Patten, last May, at Springfield, Illinois. Respectfully A LINCOLN."[1] No one knows exactly who George Evans Patten might have been. He was probably a young friend of Lincoln's who wanted written proof that he had met and spoken with the then presidential hopeful in the spring of 1860, probably to satisfy some doubting friends.

It is not an important document, but it shows that the president was capable of taking time from his official responsibilities to write such a note for someone who could not possibly return the compliment or repay President Lincoln in any way. Doing such a small kindness for someone like Master George Evans Patten was simply part of Lincoln's character.

On the same day, the president consulted with Gustavus V. Fox regarding his most pressing anxiety and most frequently discussed subject: Fort Sumter and Major Anderson's situation. Following their discussion, the president ordered Captain Fox to travel to Fort Sumter and assess the state of affairs at the fort for himself. Fox wrote to his wife Virginia, "our Uncle Abe Lincoln has taken a high esteem for me and wishes me to take dispatches to Major Anderson at Fort Sumpter with regard to its final evacuation."[2]

Actually, the idea of visiting Fort Sumter was the idea of Captain Henry J. Hartstene of the Confederate navy. Captain Hartstene and Captain Fox had known each other for many years. They were both career naval officers, but in early 1861—after nearly thirty-three years in the US Navy—Hartstene was "in the rebel service at Charleston."[3] He was born in North Carolina and resigned his commission in the US Navy to join the Confederate navy. He had a good many Southern connections and was in a position to introduce Fox to Governor Francis Pickens of South Carolina. Later in the day, after leaving President Lincoln, Captain Fox received this order from General Winfield Scott: "I request that you will have the goodness to proceed to Charleston S.C. and obtain permission, if necessary, to visit Fort Sumter."[4] He left immediately and reached Charleston two days later, going by way of Richmond and Wilmington. President Lincoln would wait impatiently for his report.

# WHITE HOUSE ACTIVITIES

To President Lincoln's great relief, he received no official communiqués or messages regarding Fort Sumter on this Wednesday. There were other matters for him to deal with, routine items involving several political appointments and nominations that required the president's approval. But more urgent than any pending political activities was a medical issue involving his two boys, Tad and Willie—both were diagnosed with measles, which was a different sort of worry, and much closer to home than Fort Sumter.

Measles was still a fairly serious illness in 1861 and sometimes could be fatal. The Lincolns had already lost one son to sickness—Edward Baker Lincoln, who died of either diphtheria or tuberculosis in February 1850—and now both Tad and Willie had become ill at the same time. Both boys would get over the measles very quickly, but their parents had an anxious couple of days. President Lincoln already had enough on his mind; he did not need another source of anxiety.

The rest of the president's White House activities concerned more mundane matters, including the recommending of appointments for positions in the western territories. He made recommendations for the posts of governor, secretary, and surveyor general, along with other jobs, in the territories of Colorado, Nevada, and "Dacota" (Dakota). President Lincoln also instructed the secretary of the interior, Caleb B. Smith, to "make out and send blank appointments for all Indian places" in Wisconsin and Minnesota. All appointments were to be made "in favor of the persons unitedly recommended by the Minnesota Republican delegation in congress."[1] The president was fully aware that these appointments went along with being head of the Republican Party; he did not particularly like this part of his job but was resigned to dealing with it. Sometimes, filling these posts came with their share of difficulties. A note from one Robert Irwin asked President Lincoln to approve an attorney named George Denison for the post of naval officer of the Port of New York. Mr. Irwin inquired, with some annoyance, "for the last time . . . cannot you consistently give my Friend Denison the appointment he has solicited[?]"[2]

The president did not seem very sympathetic toward either George Denison or Robert Irwin. "I am scared about your friend Dennison," he responded, misspelling Denison's name. He went on to comment that competition for the post has been overwhelming, and that his appointing Denison "will appear too arbitrary on my part." With a note of sarcasm, President Lincoln added, "I have made no appointments at the city as yet; but it has pained me that among the scores of names urged, his has not occurred once." He signed the memo, "Your tired friend A. LINCOLN."[3] George Denison did not get the job, but A. Lincoln had his joke. During these times, the jokes were very few and far between.

# MARCH 21, 1861, THURSDAY
## CONFLICTING OPINIONS

The president spent at least part of his day working at his desk and arranging appointments. He sent a very short note to William H. Seward regarding one such position: "What says Gov. Seward to making the appointment mentioned within. LINCOLN."[1] The appointee mentioned in the memo was General Joseph G. Swift; the position was postmaster of Geneva, New York. As it turned out, General Swift did not receive the appointment. The job went to a William Johnson. President Lincoln also contacted Gideon Welles for some advice on naming a suitable candidate for the post of engineer in chief of the navy. "Will you please avail yourself of all the means in your power for determin[ing] and present me the name of [the] best man for the service[?]" No response from Gideon Welles has ever been discovered, but Benjamin F. Isherwood was appointed to the position.[2]

The president had other things to attend to besides political appointments. Most important among them was the state of affairs in Charleston, South Carolina. He still had not made up his mind about Fort Sumter and was looking for additional information to help him make a decision whether to reinforce or abandon. On this Thursday, two days after Gustavus V. Fox left for Fort Sumter, President Lincoln sent an old friend named Stephen A. Hurlbut on what amounted to a fact-finding assignment to Charleston. Stephen Hurlbut had lived in Illinois for a number of years, which is where he met Lincoln. He was born in South Carolina, however, and had the friends and connections needed to make contact with some of Charleston's more prominent citizens and find out their opinion regarding current events. Specifically, the president wanted Hurlbut to find out exactly what Charleston thought about secession,

Unionism, and Fort Sumter, along with other critical topics. William H. Seward held the opinion that a good many Southerners, if not the majority, opposed secession and wanted to remain loyal to the Union. Hurlbut's assignment was to find out if Secretary Seward's point of view was based upon solid fact or was just wishful thinking. Another of Lincoln's Illinois friends, Ward H. Lamon, went with him; it was hoped that Lamon's friendly and outgoing personality might help win a few friends for the Lincoln administration among the Charlestonians.

While Stephen Hurlbut and Ward Lamon were preparing to leave for Charleston, Gustavus Fox was just arriving. "We reached Fort Sumter after dark [March 21], and I remained about two hours," he would report. "Major Anderson seemed to think it was too late to relieve the fort by any other means than by landing an army on Morris Island." Morris Island was a section of land to the south of Fort Sumter. The major agreed with General Winfield Scott that approaching Fort Sumter from the sea would be impossible. But Captain Fox had formed another opinion—"as we looked out upon the water from the parapet" of the fort, it seemed to him that coming ashore at that point "seemed very feasible," especially at night. As Captain Fox and his escort stood talking among themselves, a small boat approached the parapet. Everyone could hear the sound of the oars as the boat approached the fort, which the sentry hailed, "but we could not see her through the darkness until she almost touched the landing."[3] If Fox could not see an approaching boat that was only a few feet away, how could the artillery crews in Charleston, a mile away, possibly detect any vessels approaching the fort? Captain Fox would report his thoughts on reinforcing Fort Sumter to President Lincoln. "It is very well understood that he had a plan for introducing reenforcements," a New York newspaper commented. Fox's plan "was regarded as measurably practicable," but "the probability if not certainty of collision" with the artillery batteries surrounding the fort was almost certain to take place. In other words, carrying out the plan would almost certainly lead to war.[4]

President Lincoln had his information, but he was no better off than he had been before. Captain Fox had obtained "accurate information in regard to the command of Major Anderson in Fort Sumter," as he had been ordered to do. He had spoken with Major Anderson as well as General Pierre G. T. Beauregard, the Confederate officer in charge of the batteries surrounding the fort. Captain Fox was of the opinion that an operation to reinforce Fort Sumter would succeed. Major Anderson was not nearly as enthusiastic about the situation as Captain Fox. "I have examined the point alluded to by Mr. Fox last night," he said. "A vessel lying there will be under the fire of thirteen guns from Fort Moultrie." He concluded by commenting, "The department can decide what the chances will be of a safe debarkation and unloading at that point under

General Pierre G. T. Beauregard, the Confederate officer in charge of the batteries surrounding Fort Sumter.

these circumstances."[5] Major Anderson thought that any attempt to resupply the fort would fail. Both officers agreed that any attempt to fortify Sumter would lead to war.

The president had two conflicting opinions, which did not help him in making a decision. Instead of helping put his mind at ease, Anderson and Fox had only made him even more anxious and apprehensive than before. As two of his biographers put it, "Lincoln did not deem it prudent to order the proposed expedition. Neither did his own sense of duty permit him entirely to abandon it."[6]

# A CABINET MEETING AND A RECEPTION

Presentident Lincoln spent a large part of his morning in a cabinet meeting. "The Cabinet came together at 10 o'clock this morning, and it is expected that their session of the day will last until nightfall," reported a Washington newspaper. "The Senate are anxious to get away, and are urging the President to send in all nominations with as little delay as possible." The senate was scheduled to adjourn for Easter recess and wanted to have all business concluded before the Easter holiday. The short article went on to report that a "large batch of nominations" went before the Senate, but "the only important one among them" was William Jane of Illinois, who was named as "Governor of the Dacotah Territory."[1]

But the day's main event had nothing to do with politics, at least not directly. The president and Mrs. Lincoln hosted their second White House reception since the inauguration. Their first gathering, on March 8, had been criticized for being "a motley crowd and a terrible squeeze."[2] But this "levee," although "not such a dense jam as that of two weeks ago, was very largely attended."[3] The main reason that this reception was not as crowded as the first levee was because guests from the Southern states declined to attend; they were clearly avoiding the Lincolns and the White House. This shortcoming did not seem to have any effect upon the hosts. In fact, the Lincolns might have enjoyed the party even more than their first simply because it was not such a "terrible squeeze." A reporter noted that "Mr. Lincoln was as cordial as usual, and seemed in fine spirits." Mrs. Lincoln arrived on the arm of Secretary of State Seward, at which time "the reception began again in earnest."[4]

For the next two hours, "the throng jammed through the doors as if they were about to overwhelm Mr. Lincoln." The gathering was entertained by the US Marine Corps band. One of the tunes that the band played was the "Grand Union Inaugural March," which was dedicated to Mrs. Lincoln. During the height of the festivities, a messenger arrived with a telegram for Secretary Seward. Everyone close to the secretary went silent and crowded around him, wondering what was wrong. But after the secretary opened and read the message and calmly declared that nothing startling had happened—he smiled and told the anxious crowd "Nobody's dead"—everyone breathed a sigh of relief. Nobody could relax these days, not even at a presidential levee.[5]

One of the guests informed the president that he was from Memphis, Tennessee, "which called forth some conversation," but President Lincoln was not at all flustered by the fact that one of the visitors was from the South. "Well, Tennessee's all right" he responded, in his best diplomatic tone of voice. This minor occurrence showed that the atmosphere inside the White House was just as tense as the rest of Washington; the mere presence of a visitor from Tennessee prompted uneasy comments from the other guests. Even though the president was enjoying himself, or at least doing his best to enjoy himself, there was no getting away from the impending crisis.[6]

# A MUCH-NEEDED REST

**P**resident Lincoln decided to take a much-needed rest during this Saturday and Sunday. The demands of office—including the endless political appointments, the constant disagreements among his cabinet members, and especially the escalating crisis at Fort Sumter—were putting the president under an ever-increasing mental strain. Friends and close advisors were becoming concerned with his health. He was working an average of twelve hours every day. His secretaries tried to persuade him to cut his hours to five or six per day, but to no avail—the president had too much on his desk, and on his mind, and simply could not accomplish everything he needed to accomplish in five or six hours. "The intense pressure does not seem to abate as yet," Lincoln's secretary John Nicolay commented, "but I think it cannot last."[1] Young Nicolay was wrong; the pressure and the constant work would go on. But President Lincoln did consent to take the weekend off, and announced that no business would be received and no business would be conducted during these two days. It would start all over again on Monday morning, however.

At the time of Abraham Lincoln's election, men who would become legends within the next four years were completely unknown to the public at large and were leading private lives.

Robert E. Lee was a colonel in the US Army, assigned to the Second US Cavalry. On Election Day 1860, Colonel Lee was stationed at Fort Ringgold, Texas, where he was preoccupied with the pursuit of a Mexican bandit named Juan Cortinas. Cortinas had been crossing into Texas and stealing horses and livestock from ranchers north of the Rio Grande, just as Pancho Villa would do in another era. He chased Cortinas for several hundred miles and, although he never did apprehend the bandit, managed to keep him away from the Rio Grande and the Texas border. In late February 1861, Colonel Lee was ordered to report to Washington, DC, and was in the capital on Inauguration Day. He was very much aware that seven Southern states had already seceded from the Union, and anxiously waited to see whether Virginia—which he described as "my native state"—would also secede.[2]

Ulysses S. Grant was an employee in his father's leather goods store in Galena, Illinois, waiting on customers and writing receipts. Toward the end of his life, he wrote that the winter of 1860–1861 was a time of excitement and anxiety. South Carolina and six other states had already seceded, and it looked as though other states "proposed to follow." It seemed to him that a civil war was unavoidable. As a graduate of West Point and a veteran of the Mexican War, Grant was certain that he would be recalled to the army when the fighting started. The hostile reaction of the South to the election of Abraham Lincoln only served to reinforce this feeling.[3]

James Longstreet would write that he "was stationed at Albuquerque, New Mexico, as paymaster in the United States Army, when the war-cloud appeared in the East." Like U. S. Grant, Major Longstreet was also a veteran of the Mexican War as well as a West Point graduate. Because of this, he realized that, if civil war came, he would almost certainly become involved in any fighting that might take place. Because he was a Southerner, born in South Carolina and spending most of his teen years in Georgia, he also knew that he would not be wearing the same uniform that he had worn in Mexico fifteen years earlier. "A number of officers of the post called to pressure me to remain in the Union forces," the major recalled. He responded by asking one of the officers what he would do if his state seceded and asked him to fight in its defense. "He confessed that he would obey the call," Major Longstreet said.[4]

In the early part of 1861, Actor John Wilkes Booth was performing on the stage in cities throughout the North and the South—Philadelphia, Richmond, Baltimore, and Albany, New York. He played the part of the villain Pescara in James Armstrong's play *The Apostate* in Albany on the same night that Abraham Lincoln was in Albany to have dinner with the governor of New York. Even though he was from Maryland, which had a sizeable pro-secessionist population, John Wilkes Booth had no interest in aligning himself with the Confederacy, at least not at that point in time. He promised his mother that he would not enlist in the Confederate army, and he kept his promise. Even though a number of his friends joined the Confederate forces, Booth did not. He did agree with many secessionists that slavery was more of a blessing than a curse, and he held the point of view that African slaves in the United States were better off than Africans anywhere else in the world. Even though he had rumors about assassination plots against Abraham Lincoln, Booth had no interest in getting involved in any of them. In short, he had no deep interest in politics. John Wilkes Booth was much too busy developing his already successful stage career to get involved with anything that might distract him from the profession of acting.[5]

In November 1860, William Tecumseh Sherman was superintendent of the Louisiana State Seminary of Learning and Military Academy in Pineville, Louisiana. He resigned his position in January 1861, when secessionists seized the federal arsenal at Baton Rouge and Louisiana seceded from the Union. In his letter of resignation, he stated, "on no earthly account will I do any act or think any thought hostile to or in defiance of the old Government of the United States."[6]

Toward the middle of March, he was introduced to President Lincoln by his brother, Senator John Sherman. Senator Sherman was in Washington to deliver some papers regarding some "minor appointments" in the state of Ohio, and he took his brother with him to the White House. He said, "Mr. President, this is my brother, Colonel Sherman, who is just up from Louisiana, he may give you some information you want." "Ah," the president reacted, "how are they getting along down there?" Sherman responded, "They think they are getting along swimmingly—they are preparing for war." "Oh, well," said he, "I guess we'll manage to keep house."[7]

Sherman was completely taken aback by the casualness of President Lincoln's reply. "I was silenced, said no more to him, and we soon left. I was sadly disappointed," he would write many years afterward. He told his brother "the country was sleeping on a volcano that might burst forth at any minute," and that the politicians "had got things in a hell of a fix." This included the president, who did not seem to be aware of what was happening and could only say that "we'll manage to keep house." Sherman was not impressed, either by President Lincoln or what he had to say.[8]

# WAITING FOR NEWS

**M**onday turned out to be another day of office routine, which meant another round of political appointments to handle. President Lincoln endorsed "Mr. Thomas Mustin, and Mr. Jones" to "retain their places." Thomas Mustin was a clerk in the Springfield, Illinois, auditor's office; Thomas Jones held a similar position in Springfield's census office. A Dr. Meredith Helm of Springfield had written to the president asking that the two men—one was Dr. Helm's brother-in-law; the other was his son-in-law—be permitted to retain their respective offices. Because of the president's endorsement, they were able to keep their jobs—in Lincoln's words, "for the present, at least."[1]

President Lincoln also received another request for his personal endorsement, a joint appeal from two Pennsylvania politicians: Senator Edgar Cowan and Congressman John Covode. The message was actually presented as a demand instead of a request: "We demand that the appointment named within be made at once." The request/demand concerned the appointment of Walter Burleigh of Pennsylvania to the staff of the Yankton Sioux Indian Agency. Once again, President Lincoln's approval served its intended purpose. Walter Burleigh received the appointment. His endorsement was short and to the point: "Let it be done. LINCOLN."[2]

The president's third appointment of the day was a straightforward favor; it had nothing to do with in-laws or demands from congressmen. He sent a message to William H. Seward stating that Senator Grimes wanted A. L. Wolff to be appointed as consul to Basel, Switzerland. Senator Grimes was a Republican from Iowa; August L. Wolff was a resident of Iowa and a friend of Senator Grimes. Senator Grimes's wishes also became President Lincoln's wishes, and August Wolff was soon on his way to Switzerland.[3]

The president had not yet heard anything from either Stephen Hurlbut or Ward Lamon about the situation in Charleston. Ward Lamon booked a room at the Charleston Hotel. Stephen Hurlbut was staying at his sister's house. Both men spoke with several South Carolina officials, including former South Carolina congressman and attorney general James L. Petigru. President Lincoln knew that Petigru was a staunch Unionist. He was well known, both in South Carolina and elsewhere, for his crack about the state after it seceded from the Union in December, 1860—"South Carolina is too small for a republic and too large for an insane asylum."[4] Petigru was completely pessimistic regarding any sort of peaceful solution to the secession crisis. He stated flatly that "the whole people were infuriated and crazed, and that no act of headlong violence by them would surprise him." The only way to avoid war would be to allow the states that had withdrawn from the Union to retain their independence—"peaceable secession or war was inevitable."[5]

Both Ward Lamon and Stephen Hurlbut stayed in Charleston for two days, talking to prominent individuals, collecting information, and forming opinions of what was likely to take place in the near future. Hurlbut was preparing a lengthy report on his findings, which he would submit to President Lincoln as soon as he and Lamon returned to Washington.

# MARCH 26, 1861, TUESDAY
## DENYING A REQUEST

This was another relatively quiet day for President Lincoln, although Fort Sumter was very much on his mind. He received a copy of a senate resolution requesting that he "communicate" Major Anderson's reports to the Senate regarding Fort Sumter. Apparently, the senators wanted a more detailed account of the defense of the fort, or at least a more detailed account than they had received from other sources. But the president turned down the senate's request. In a reply addressed "To the Senate of the United States," he said that, "[o]n examining the correspondence thus called for," he had "come to the conclusion that at the present moment the publication of it would be inexpedient." In his opinion, releasing Major Anderson's war office dispatches was not a good idea.[1]

The president did not give any reason for rejecting the request. Maybe it was just a diplomatic way of telling the senators to mind their own business—he wanted to make it clear that as president and commander in chief, the defense of Fort Sumter was *his* concern, not the senate's. Or he might have been afraid that the major's dispatches would fall into the hands of the press, who would distort the reports to suit their own purposes. Reporters had a way of writing their own version of official communiqués and reports. For instance, that morning's edition of the *New York Times* ran these headlines: "IMPORTANT INTELLIGENCE: LATEST REPORTS FROM FORT SUMPTER. Visit of the Special Government Messenger. The Fort Probably to Be Evacuated To-morrow."[2] And the *New York Herald* had been just as inaccurate on Sunday, March 24, with their own slip-up: "The Order Issued for the

Evacuation of Fort Sumter."[3] President Lincoln was all too aware that dramatic headlines did not necessarily have to be based upon fact.

The president's nerves were already getting the better of him. This request from the senate did not help calm him or put him in a better frame of mind. He already had enough to worry about concerning Charleston and Fort Sumter without the senate adding its own share of anxieties. The senate would not get its dispatches.

# MARCH 27, 1861, WEDNESDAY

# AN UPSETTING REPORT

nlike the previous two days, this Wednesday turned out to be anything but routine. But President Lincoln still had the usual chores to deal with—sending a diplomatic letter in response to an Italian envoy's speech and writing a couple of notes endorsing political appointees. The diplomatic letter was addressed to Joseph Bertinatti of Sardinia, representative of the Kingdom of Italy, who had just been promoted from consul to minister and recently made a short speech on the occasion of his promotion. The president offered Minister Bertinatti his very best wishes; the letter ended with: "Chevalier Bertinatti, your personal promotion is a subject of satisfaction to the Government of the United States." It was a very formal and polite little memorandum, the sort that government officials send all the time.[1]

President Lincoln also sent a letter to Attorney General Edward Bates endorsing George Howe as Attorney General of Vermont and C. C. P. Baldwin as marshal for Vermont. Both men received their respective appointments. Another note, from the "Hon. Mr. Blair of Pa." and dated March 27, called for Thomas P. Campbell Esq. to be appointed consul to Glasgow or "some other eligible appointment" in Pennsylvania. This request was made purely on political grounds: "Mr. Blair says his District does a large share of the voting, and never receives any thing." The note goes on to point out, "Therefore he is very anxious in this matter." But Mr. Campbell did not receive the appointment; it went to a James S. Prettyman of Delaware.[2]

The most significant item that President Lincoln had to contend with on this day had nothing to do with political appointments or partisan politics. Stephen Hurlbut and Ward Lamon had returned from their fact-finding assignment in Charleston, and Hurlbut submitted a report on what they had seen and heard while they were gathering their information; he addressed his report simply, "To His Excy Abraham Lincoln, President, U.S."[3] His account was highly detailed—it went on for eighteen handwritten pages—and summarized the meetings and conversations in which he and Lamon had taken part during their two days in the South. Hurlbut did not even make an attempt to be diplomatic or restrained in his description of Southern opinion concerning secession and other sensitive topics; he was deliberately straightforward, to the point of being blunt.

Stephen Hurlbut began by mentioning many of the people he had seen—"many of my old acquaintances and friends," including James Petigru—and concluded from his and Ward Lamon's conversations with these people that secession was inevitable and that the South was fully prepared to go to war. "From these sources I have no hesitation in reporting as unquestionable—that Separate Nationality is a fixed fact—that there is an unanimity of sentiment which is to my mind astonishing—that there is no attachment to the Union—that almost every one of those very men who in 1832 held military commissions under secret orders from Genl Jackson and were in fact ready to draw the sword in civil war for the Nation, are now as ready to take arms if necessary for the Southern Confederacy."[4]

This was exactly what President Lincoln needed to know—accurate information on the Southern outlook regarding independence from a trustworthy source. But this was not what he was expecting to hear. Secretary of State William H. Seward seemed so sure that the South was largely against secession and was devoted to the Union, but Hurlbut's statement divulged that this was absolutely not true and that Seward could not have been more wrong. Lincoln even believed this line of thinking himself at one time. Back in mid-August, before the election, he wrote, "The people of the South have too much good sense, and good temper, to attempt the ruin of the government."[5] Now his own line of thinking had been proven wrong as well. The president read Hurlbut's report and was completely stunned.

After making his declaration on "Separate Nationality," Hurlbut still had a lot more to say. He also stressed that the leaders of the Southern Confederacy were determined to gain their independence—peaceably if possible but by force of arms if necessary—and warned "there exists a large minority indefatigably active and reckless who desire to precipitate collision, inaugurate war & unite the Southern Confederacy by that means." Another item that must have come as a shock to President Lincoln was this statement: "The Seceding States are 'de facto' a Nation, they exercise to day every prerogative of sovereignty and within their limits are readily and cheerfully obeyed." Also: "they have an army—they are endeavoring to construct a Navy—they have Revenue Laws & will enforce them." As far as Fort Sumter was concerned, handing it over to the rebels would not prevent a war. "If Sumpter is abandoned it is to a certain extent a concession of jurisdiction which cannot fail to have its effects at home and abroad. . . . Undoubtedly this will be followed by a demand for Pickens and the Keys of the Gulf."[6]

In Stephen Hurlbut's opinion, there was nothing that the president could do to coax the seceded states back into the Union. "I solemnly believe that the Seven States are irrevocably gone—except perhaps Texas and Louisiana as to which I have no information. They have not gone out on the Negro question—their leaders in frank conversation do not say so. They have set up housekeeping for themselves and the only possible cure is to let them bear the burdens of housekeeping." Having said this, Hurlbut went on to reinforce his statement: "Nor do I believe that any policy which may be adopted by this Government will prevent the possibility of armed collision." In other words, civil war was unavoidable—there was no way to escape it. Any steps taken by the government to appease the seceded states would only serve to postpone the inevitable. He ended his report with this warning: "I cannot close without repeating to the President, that this is a time to expect and be prepared for the worst." If the president intended to yield to the rebels, "any yielding that the times

**101**

Stephen Hurlbut returned from his fact-finding assignment in Charleston with a startling report for President Lincoln—the South was fully prepared to go to war to create an independent nation.

may enforce has infinitely more value when it comes from a Government strong in fact and conscious of its strength—giving not from any suspicion of fear—but with the sense of power. And if no yielding takes place so much the more necessity for the most ample preparation."[7]

Ward Lamon presented his own share of bad news, which was not included in the Hurlbut account. He met with South Carolina governor Francis Pickens to discuss Fort Sumter during his two days in Charleston. Governor Pickens was adamant in his views regarding secession and the reinforcement of Sumter, and let Lamon know his opinions in no uncertain terms. "Nothing," he said, "can prevent war except the acquiescence of the President of the United States in secession, and his unalterable resolve not to attempt any reinforcement of the Southern forts." The governor went on to give this blunt warning: "Let your President attempt to reinforce Sumter, and the tocsin of war will be sounded from every hill-top and valley in the South."[8] The way Governor Pickens phrased it, South Carolina not only was fully prepared to go to war but also was actually looking forward to it.

Stephen Hurlbut's eighteen pages of observations and opinions did not contain a single word of encouragement. President Lincoln was both upset and depressed as he made his way through the report. According to Hurlbut's testimony, there was no way to avoid civil war. If he surrendered Fort Sumter, this would make him look weak and spineless and, at best, would only serve to postpone the coming war. If he decided to hold the fort, this would precipitate an armed conflict. The president's advisors were still divided over which course of action to take, which meant that the final decision would be up to him. And he would be damned whatever decision he made.

Sometime after breakfast, President Lincoln was introduced to London *Times* correspondent William H. Russell by Secretary of State William Seward. Russell was a well-known reporter, mainly because of his dramatic accounts of the Crimean War of 1853–1856. He had only recently arrived in the United States but, because of his reputation, was able to meet with Secretary Seward very shortly after his arrival. Seward arranged for the influential reporter to meet the president at the White House. While he was waiting to see President Lincoln, Russell accidentally ran into Joseph Bertinatti, the new Italian minister. Chevalier Bertinatti was wearing his full regalia; Russell thought he looked faintly ridiculous—he was decked out "in cocked hat, white gloves, diplomatic suit of blue and silver lace, sword, sash, and ribbon of the cross of Savoy," Russell recalled. He went on to note, "I thought there was a quiet smile on Mr. Seward's face as he saw his brilliant companion, who contrasted so strongly with the more than republican simplicity of his own attire."[9]

Russell, Secretary Seward, and the chevalier were escorted into "a handsome spacious room, richly and rather gorgeously furnished," where they waited for the president. President Lincoln entered the room within a very short time. Russell was anything but bowled over. He described Lincoln as having a "shambling, loose, irregular, almost unsteady gait, a tall, lank, lean man, considerably over six feet in height, with stooping shoulders, long pendulous arms, terminating in hands of extraordinary dimensions, which, however, were far exceeded in proportion by his feet."[10]

As Russell continued to give the president a good looking-over, his opinion of Lincoln's manner of dress and general appearance did not improve. "He was dressed in an ill-fitting, wrinkled suit of black, which put one in mind of an undertaker's uniform at a funeral; round his neck a rope of black silk was knotted in a large bulb, with flying ends projecting beyond the collar of his coat." Russell went on to comment, "A person who met Mr. Lincoln in the street would not take him to be what according to the usages of European society is called a 'gentleman;' and, indeed, since I came to the United States, I have heard more disparaging allusions made by Americans to him on that account than I could have expected among simple republicans, where all should be equals." But even though Abraham Lincoln might have been a sartorial horror, Russell admitted that, "at the same time, it would not be possible for the most indifferent observer to pass him in the street without notice." Because of his height, President Lincoln still managed to present an impressive appearance despite himself.[11]

The president advanced through the room, smiling "good-humoredly," until he met Secretary Seward and Chevalier Bertinatti. Seward formally introduced the chevalier to President Lincoln, who bowed stiffly from the waist; Chevalier Bertinatti responded with a bow of his own, and proceeded to read a long letter "accrediting him as minister resident." After the chevalier finished, "the President gave another bow still more violent," and proceeded to take a letter out of his pocket and read it in response to the chevalier's. After reading his letter, the president proceeded to shake hands with the minister. The awkward little ceremony was finally over, and the chevalier turned and walked out of the room.[12]

Secretary Seward then introduced Russell to the president, presenting the reporter as "Mr. Russell, of the London *Times*." President Lincoln extended his hand "in a very friendly manner" and said, "Mr. Russell, I am very glad to make your acquaintance, and to see you in this country. The London *Times* is one of the greatest powers in the world, in fact, I don't know anything which has much more power, except perhaps the Mississippi. I am glad to know you as its minister." Russell seemed to be very impressed by this greeting—he was probably expecting something awkward and a bit coarse, in keeping with the president's rough overall appearance. Conversation between the two continued "for some minutes" which, according to Russell, was genial and pleasant and "enlivened by two or three peculiar little sallies." In his diary, he mentioned that "I left agreeably impressed with his shrewdness, humor, and natural sagacity."[13]

President Lincoln could see that he had made a favorable impression with the British journalist. It was nice to know that he had a new ally, if not exactly a new friend. His conversation with Russell was probably one of the high points of his day. He was still shaken by Stephen Hurlbut's report, and was all too aware that if civil war came he would be needing all the allies he could get, on both sides of the Atlantic Ocean.

MARCH 28, 1861, THURSDAY

# A MEMO FROM GENERAL SCOTT

**P**resident Lincoln was notified that the Senate would be adjourn-
ing for their Easter recess, a routine message that did not come
as any surprise. He also received another communiqué, a memo from
his general in chief, Winfield Scott, which came as a very unpleasant
and disturbing surprise. In his memo, General Scott gave the president
his point of view concerning Fort Sumter and Fort Pickens—he told
Lincoln that *both* forts should be surrendered to the rebels. According
to the general, evacuating both Sumter and Pickens would placate the
slave states that had not seceded, including Virginia, and would convince
them to remain in the Union. Just abandoning Fort Sumter would not be
enough; Fort Pickens would also have to be given up.

The president was completely taken aback by what General Scott
had to say. The general wrote that he was doubtful "whether the volun-
tary evacuation of Fort Sumter alone would have a decisive effect upon
the States now wavering between adherence to the Union and secession."
But, on the other hand, he said, "Our Southern friends, however, are
clear that the evacuation of both the forts would instantly soothe and
give confidence to the eight remaining slave-holding States, and render
their cordial adherence to this Union perpetual."[1] President Lincoln's
most valued military advisor was recommending that he should give in
to the rebels and their demands.

Lincoln still had not been able to reach a decision regarding Fort
Sumter—whether to evacuate or reinforce—which was making him
increasingly anxious and depressed. General Scott's recommendations
made him feel even worse. Winfield Scott was probably the most
respected military advisor in the country; he was the hero of the War of

1812 and the Mexican War, and he was also the highest-ranking officer in the US Army. The president was hoping that General Scott would supply him with some reliable guidance and advice on how to retain Fort Sumter without going to war. Instead, he was advised to surrender Sumter *and* Pickens in order to appease Virginia and the other slave states that had not left the Union. It was not what he was expecting.

That night, the president and Mrs. Lincoln hosted their first formal dinner party at the White House, which is usually described as a "state dinner." President Lincoln tried his best to play the role of gracious host, smiling and shaking hands with all the guests, but he could not get General Scott's memo out of his mind. Despite the president's mental state, the dinner was declared a success. "The Cabinet Dinner given by the President on Thursday last is spoken of an all sides as a most agreeable affair," wrote the *Evening Star.* "Twenty-eight persons were present, including the members of the President's family, Cabinet officers and families."[2] Winfield Scott was supposed to have attended the dinner, but it was announced that he was "indisposed" and would not be present.

William H. Russell of London's *Times* was also there, and it did not seem to him that the president was in any sort of melancholy mood. In fact, he thought Lincoln was in top form as a wit and raconteur. Where some diplomats or professional statesmen might make a polite speech to make a point, Russell pointed out that "Mr. Lincoln raises a laugh by some bold west-country anecdote, and moves off in the cloud of merriment produced by his joke."[3] After everyone was seated for dinner, the dining room buzzed with "a Babel of small talk round the table . . . except when there was an attentive silence caused by one of the President's stories."[4] Russell enjoyed hearing the president's amusing stories as much as Lincoln enjoyed telling them. He thoroughly enjoyed the evening and appreciated the president's company. After the party was over, he told a New York reporter, "I think a great deal of Mr. Lincoln, and that I am equally pleased with my dinner."[5] President Lincoln was doing a very effective job of covering up his worries.

Russell was introduced to Mary Lincoln shortly after he arrived at the White House. His description of the president's wife was straightforward, and not very flattering. "She is of the middle age and height, of a plumpness degenerating to the embonpoint natural to her years; her features are plain, her nose and mouth of an ordinary type, and her manners and appearance homely." In other words, he thought that she was a fat little middle-aged housewife. "She handled a fan with much energy, displaying a round, well-proportioned arm, and was adorned with some simple jewelry." Russell also thought that she was very self-conscious of her position as First Lady, "that her position requires her to be something more than plain Mrs. Lincoln, the wife of the Illinois lawyer."[6] His observations were probably not meant to be nasty, but they were certainly not very complimentary.

Just as the dinner guests were leaving the White House, President Lincoln asked the members of his cabinet to join him in an adjacent room. He wanted to talk to them about General Scott's memorandum. When the door was closed and the president was able to talk freely, "he informed them, with evident emotion, that General Scott had that day advised the evacuation of Fort Pickens as well as Fort Sumter."[7] As he spoke, the president was clearly agitated and upset; his facial expression and his voice conveyed the strain he was feeling at that particular moment. Everyone in the room was as surprised by Lincoln's demeanor as by the contents of General Scott's message—he had seemed so relaxed and cheerful a few minutes before, and now he was visibly distraught.

General Scott's recommendations were met by a "long pause of blank amazement" by the cabinet members; they sat and stared at the president in silence for a few moments, not knowing what to say or how to react. Finally, Postmaster General Montgomery Blair broke the silence with a "strong denunciation, not only of this advice, but of Scott's general course regarding Sumter." In Blair's opinion, General Scott was "playing politician" instead of performing his duties as an officer and as the president's chief military advisor. He was also behaving as a Virginian instead of an American. In his denunciation of General Scott, everyone realized that Blair was also criticizing William H. Seward for his often-stated views that Fort Sumter should be given up.[8]

The group agreed with the attorney general and unanimously condemned General Scott's recommendations, although there was no formal vote on the subject. The president thanked everyone for coming to his impromptu meeting as well as for their opinions. Before the meeting broke up, President Lincoln requested the cabinet members to attend a formal council the next day. With that, the group dispersed, and the president went up to bed.

But he could not go to sleep; he was much too keyed up and worried. He realized that he could not depend upon generals or cabinet members to make the decision whether to surrender the forts, a decision that might very well result in war. He was president; he would have to decide the issue himself. One of Lincoln's many biographies put it this way: "It was apparent that the time had come when he must meet the nation's crisis."[9] As he worried his way through the long night, unable to close his eyes, President Lincoln thought about his options and almost certainly made up his mind about what he was going to do regarding the Sumter and Pickens predicament. But he would ask his cabinet for their opinion tomorrow afternoon, just to sound them out before he made his own opinion known to his advisors.

# THE PRESIDENT ORDERS AN EXPEDITION

After spending a sleepless night thinking about Stephen Hurlbut, Winfield Scott, Fort Sumter, and Fort Pickens, President Lincoln said that he was "in the dumps" when morning finally arrived.[1] Besides being anxious and distressed, he was also a nervous wreck. It seemed to him that no matter what he did, and what course of action he decided to pursue, the end result would be civil war. President Lincoln had done his best to avoid war. But it now seemed inevitable that, despite all his efforts to appease South Carolina and the other Southern states, an armed conflict was inescapable. It was not a good morning for the president.

Besides the impending crises in Florida and South Carolina, President Lincoln also had two routine political appointments to deal with. He sent a note to Hiram Barney, described as "a prominent New York City attorney," to arrange a meeting at the White House. Additionally, he recommended eleven candidates for various positions in California. Not surprisingly, all eleven received the jobs for which they had applied. Even with the possibility of war becoming increasingly likely, the wheels of the political machine still kept turning.[2]

The prearranged cabinet meeting began around noon, with every cabinet member in attendance except for Simon Cameron, the secretary of war. The conference started out as a general conversation about what should be done about the forts. It was an informal discussion, not meant to resolve anything. Attorney General Edward Bates listened to what everyone was saying for some time, and he made a suggestion to the president: instead of carrying on with what was basically an aimless chat session, each cabinet member should give his opinion, in writing, of General Scott's recommendation to give up both Sumter and Pickens. "I proposed that the President should state his questions, and require our opinions *seriatim*," with each member reading his own opinion. President Lincoln liked the attorney general's idea, and he instructed each individual to commit his point of view to paper and read it out loud.[3]

The attorney general spoke first—"I immediately wrote and read the following memorandum," he recalled. He was in favor of reinforcing Fort Pickens but was vague concerning Fort Sumter: "As to Fort Sumter, I think the time is when it ought to be either evacuated or relieved."[4] This was not any kind of answer—it was what everybody had been saying for the past several weeks, and was not the reaction President Lincoln either wanted or needed. Secretary of State Seward next read his reply—he advocated holding Fort Pickens and, just as he had been saying since early March, advised ordering Major Anderson to withdraw from Fort Sumter. Secretary of the Navy Gideon Welles supported reinforcing Fort Pickens and resupplying Fort Sumter. Interior Secretary Caleb Smith also recommended defending Fort Pickens, but he thought it best to surrender Fort Sumter. Postmaster General Montgomery Blair strongly advised the president to hold both Fort Sumter and Fort Pickens.

President Lincoln listened attentively to each opinion. He was not surprised to hear that Secretary Seward still did not want to reinforce Fort Sumter; Seward was not the type to change his mind, especially on such a vital issue. And Attorney General Bates's vague, sitting-on-the-fence response probably amused the president more than irritated him. He was glad to have the opinions of his cabinet, but he had already decided what he was going to do. Since it was fairly clear that there was no real possibility of avoiding war, President Lincoln ordered that a combined army and navy force be sent to reinforce Fort Sumter. As far as he was concerned, this would only be carrying out his presidential duties—in his inaugural address, he promised to hold, occupy, and possess all federal installations. If the rebel states were determined to start a war, Fort Sumter was as good a place as any.

Shortly after Secretary Seward and all the other cabinet members left the White House that afternoon, President Lincoln sent identical orders to Gideon Welles and Simon Cameron: they were to prepare an "expedition" to relieve Fort Sumter—"Sir: I desire that an expedition, to move by sea, be got ready to sail as early as the 6th. of April next, the whole according to memorandum attached; and that you co-operate with the Secretary of War [the Navy] for that object. Your Obedient Servant. A. LINCOLN."[5] The brackets indicate whether the addressee was Cameron (War Department) or Welles (Navy Department).

The president also issued specific orders to Secretary Welles and Secretary Cameron: "Navy Dept. Stmrs *Pocahontas* at Norfolk, *Pawnee* at Washington, and Revenue Cutter *Harriet Lane* at N. York to be ready [under sailing orders] for sea with one months stores" and "War Dept. Two hundred men at N. York ready to leave garrison—one years stores to be put in a portable form."[6]

Issuing these orders must have greatly relieved President Lincoln. His nerves were still in an uproar, but at least he could be satisfied that he had taken a direct action regarding the Sumter crisis. The next move would be up to the rebel forces in Charleston—whether or not they would begin hostilities by opening fire on the expedition or on the fort itself. One writer put it this way: on March 29, 1861, "Lincoln began to act as commander in chief."[7]

# POLITICAL APPOINTMENTS

Aﬅer the critical cabinet meeting of the day before, and the momentous decision that came as a result of it, Saturday turned out to be calm and routine. This was fortunate for President Lincoln—he needed a day to catch his breath and concentrate on routine matters. The tensions of the past weeks were taking their toll on his health. He woke up with a debilitating headache and, to his wife's alarm, keeled over from stress and fatigue. In an attempt to do *something* to relieve the pressures of his office, President Lincoln decided to reduce the time he spent talking to the public. Instead of spending up to twelve hours every day with visitors and office seekers, he would decrease his visiting period to five hours per day, from 10:00 a.m. to 3:00 p.m. The president still wanted to talk to members of the public, but he also had to look after his own well-being, both physical and emotional. Five hours per day should be enough time to see visitors, he decided.

Despite the problems he faced dealing with secession and the Sumter crisis, President Lincoln also had his share of political correspondence to deal with every day. A "particular friend" of his, Jesse K. Dubois, asked the president to use his influence to secure a job for his son-in-law, a John P. Luse. The post was superintendent of Indian affairs for Minnesota. But, for political reasons, Lincoln was not able to comply with Dubois's request. "I was nearly as sorry as you can be at not being able to give Mr. Luce the appointment you desired for him," he wrote to Jesse Dubois.[1]

President Lincoln also had other letters to write concerning political appointments. He sent a note to Interior Secretary Caleb B. Smith, in which he requested that the son of a high-ranking naval officer be retained as an agent for the Ponca Indian tribe in the Dakota Territory. The president also recommended the brother-in-law of an acquaintance, who was "an out and out Republican," for a consulship in Panama, and endorsed "about fifty five Californians" for federal posts in that state.[2]

The most difficult, and potentially controversial, appointment involved naming one of his wife's relatives, Elizabeth Todd Grimsley, as an official in the Springfield, Illinois, post office. He had already appointed several friends to important government positions, including territorial governor. If he acquired a prominent post for "Cousin Lizzie," Mary Lincoln's cousin, it might give the impression that he was giving out good jobs just to his friends, associates, and relatives. "The question of giving her the Springfield Post-office troubles me," he said.[3] But the incumbent official remained in office until August, when he was replaced by someone who was not a Lincoln appointee. The issue of nepotism disappeared before it could become a problem.

While the president was tending to politics and political job hunters, Mary Lincoln was having her own problems. In her role as First Lady and now as "First Hostess," she announced that she would be giving an "at home" at the White House every Saturday afternoon between two and four o'clock. To inaugurate this new social event, Mrs. Lincoln gave a reception at three o'clock on this day. Reporter William H. Russell of London's *Times* attended the reception, and he did not seem to be very impressed. He was not in his hotel room when the invitation arrived and, subsequently, did not arrive at the White House until late in the afternoon. By the time he finally was able to present himself at the White House, the party was nearly over. "It was rather late before I could get to the White House," he recalled, "and there were only two or three ladies in the drawing-room when I arrived."[4] He was told that attendance at Mrs. Lincoln's gathering was "very scanty." A good many Washington ladies did not have a very high opinion of the First Lady or of the guests who accepted Mrs. Lincoln's invitation. "They miss their Southern friends, and constantly draw comparisons between them and the vulgar Yankee women and men who are now in power."[5] President Lincoln was not in attendance, which was just as well; he would not have been very happy about the way his wife was treated by the Washington socialites, who seemed to be mainly pro-Southern in sympathy.

# MARCH 31, 1861, EASTER SUNDAY
## A VITAL DECISION

**P**resident Lincoln did not go to church on this Easter Sunday, or at least there is no record of it. If he and Mrs. Lincoln had attended Easter services, this would have been mentioned prominently in the Washington press. But no mention appeared in any newspapers about the president and his wife having gone to any of the Washington churches. The president was preoccupied with other matters.

He was certainly in a prickly and cantankerous mood; his anxiety and his jangled nerves were still very much in evidence. When some politicians came to the White House to complain about the way he and his allies had been handling the distribution of government jobs, President Lincoln was not in the frame of mind to listen to them or to their grievances. He bellowed at the astonished representatives, ripped up the listing of complaints they had brought for him to read, threw it into the fireplace, and gave them a good ticking off. After finishing his tirade, the president escorted his visitors to the door and threw them out with a few more well-chosen words. He did not win any friends, but getting rid of the intruders must have been highly satisfying as well as extremely therapeutic.

A few hours later, he received Captain Montgomery Meigs and Lieutenant Colonel Erasmus D. Keyes to discuss a plan to relieve Fort Pickens, off the Florida coast. By this time, the president was in a much better mental state. The two officers had already worked out a proposal to reinforce Fort Pickens, as they had been ordered by Secretary of State Seward, and had gone to the White House at around three o'clock in the afternoon. Both the president and Secretary Seward were present when they arrived. President Lincoln listened to what Captain Meigs and Colonel Keyes had to say, but he was still in a highly nervous state. "Mr. Lincoln was sitting behind the table near the end; his right leg, from the knee to foot, which was not small, rested on the table, his left leg on a chair, and his hands were clasped over his head," Colonel Keyes recalled. But the president could not sit still; he uneasily kept on moving his arms and legs throughout the meeting. "These positions were changed frequently during the conference, and I never saw a man who could scatter his limbs more than he."[1]

Captain Meigs read the report that Colonel Keyes and himself had written, which mainly concerned itself with the engineering features of the operation. President Lincoln asked the captain if he thought that Fort Pickens could be reinforced successfully. Captain Meigs told him that if the attempt was made, "a fleet steamer under a young and enterprising officer should be dispatched immediately." The "enterprising officer" would have to act quickly—"run the batteries, enter the harbor, and prevent any expedition of Bragg's crossing the harbor in boats to assault Fort Pickens."[2]

When Captain Meigs finished reading his report, President Lincoln instructed Meigs and Colonel Keyes to visit General Winfield Scott at his home and inform him that their plan had his approval. General Scott was to put their proposal into operation unless he had "strong reasons to the contrary." As Captain Meigs recalled, "We went to the house of General Scott, showed him our papers, which he approved saying there was nothing in them not necessary and little to be added as necessary. Mr. Seward came in and the matter was talked over and resolved upon."[3]

The president had now ordered the relief of both Fort Pickens and Fort Sumter. He realized that the next step was to wait and see exactly how the South would react to his decision. Waiting would not improve either his nerves or his disposition.

# APRIL 1, 1861, MONDAY
# "*I* MUST DO IT"

Presdent Lincoln signed more correspondence than usual on this Monday. A large number of these notes and letters concerned the customary political appointments—federal appointments, State of California appointments, and requests from friends for appointments, along with requests from political acquaintances. But the most pressing communiqués had nothing to do with politics.

The president's main activity concerned issuing a series of orders relating to the relief of the two controversial Southern ports, mainly Fort Pickens. Specifically, his directives involved the heavily armed sidewheel steam frigate USS *Powhatan* and in making it ready for sea as soon as possible. The warship was slated to escort the relief convoy that would be sent to Fort Pickens. He sent two notes to the director of the Navy Yard in Brooklyn, New York, Andrew H. Foote, to "fit out the *Powhatan* without delay." In his directive, President Lincoln added that the *Powhatan* "is bound on secret service, and you will under no circumstances communicate to the Navy Department the fact that she is fitting out."[1] He did not want any senior naval officials, including Secretary of the Navy Gideon Welles, to know anything about the *Powhatan* leaving Brooklyn or, especially, its destination. William H. Seward had warned that naval officers sympathetic to the South—and there were very many of these—would report news of the *Powhatan* to Confederate agents. This deliberate failure to communicate with the Navy Department would lead to a great deal of confusion regarding efforts to reinforce both Fort Sumter and Fort Pickens.

President Lincoln also sent an order to the *Powhatan*'s captain, Samuel Mercer, relieving him of command. Captain Mercer was informed that he would be replaced "for a special purpose" by another officer, "an officer who is duly informed and instructed in relation to the wishes of the Government."[2] This "duly informed and instructed" officer was Lieutenant David D. Porter, who also received orders from the president. These orders came in the form of two letters. The first letter directed Lieutenant Porter to "take command of the steamer *Powhatan*, or any other United States steamer ready for sea which he may deem most fit for the service to which he has been assigned by confidential instructions of this date." In other words, the president wanted Lieutenant Porter to take an armed vessel, the *Powhatan* or any other warship that had been fitted out and was ready for action, out to sea as quickly as possible. The letter was signed "Abraham Lincoln," but also contained the note, "Recommended: WM. H. SEWARD."[3]

The second letter directed Lieutenant Porter to "proceed to New York" and "assume command of any naval steamer available." It went on to say: "Proceed to Pensacola Harbor, and at any cost or risk prevent any expedition from the mainland reaching Fort Pickens." The president made no mention of Fort Sumter, possibly on Secretary Seward's advice. This dispatch was also signed by President Lincoln and accompanied by the note, "Recommended: WM. H. SEWARD."[4]

Two separate reinforcing expeditions had been scheduled: a naval expedition to Fort Sumter commanded by Gustavus Fox, and an army mission to support Fort Pickens headed by Montgomery Meigs. Secretary of State Seward—who wanted to give up Fort Sumter and was not enthusiastic about defending it—favored the Fort Pickens operation and wanted the *Powhatan* for the Pickens force. Gideon Welles wanted the heavily armed warship to sail to Charleston as Captain Fox's flagship. Because the two flotillas were assembled separately, and in secret, blunders and mishaps were bound to happen. And they did happen. President Lincoln would unintentionally sign an order assigning the *Powhatan* to both the Sumter force *and* the Pickens force. The *Powhatan* would wind up sailing off to Pensacola, and Captain Fox would lose his flagship. Gideon Welles would blame Secretary Seward for the mix-up;

the president did not want to precipitate a feud between two of his cabinet members, and would assume full responsibility for the incident. But even though he would blame himself for not paying attention when he signed the orders, the incident did nothing to endear Secretary Seward to President Lincoln.

By this time, the president had resigned himself to the thought that war was almost a foregone conclusion, and busied himself in making preparations for it. He issued an order addressed to "All officers of the Army and Navy," which directed them to give all possible support to Colonel Harvey Brown, "supplying him with men and material and cooperating with him as he may desire."[5] Colonel Brown commanded the expedition to reinforce Fort Pickens. Another executive order, marked "Confidential," was sent to Gideon Welles at the Navy Department. President Lincoln advised Secretary Welles that Captain Silas H. Stringham would be proceeding to Pensacola "with all possible dispatch." When he arrived at Pensacola, Captain Stringham would assume command "of that portion of the home squadron stationed off Pensacola."[6]

General Winfield Scott also received a communiqué from President Lincoln, which was more in the way of a request than a direct order. President Lincoln asked the old general, "Would it impose too much labor on General Scott to make short, comprehensive daily reports to me of what occurs in his Department. . . . If not I will thank him to do so."[7] General Scott would usually comply with the president's request; he sent reports to the White House on most days, although he would sometimes forget.

During the course of the day, President Lincoln also received a strange sort of memo from Secretary of State Seward; the memo was dated April 1. Actually, it was not so much a memorandum as a listing of grievances against the president and his activities since taking office. The note, which Secretary Seward called, "Some thoughts for the President's consideration," was in the handwriting of his son Frederick.[8] The secretary's own handwriting was so illegible that it frequently could not be deciphered by anyone.

In his very first sentence, Secretary Seward laid his opinions right on the line: "We are at the end of a month's administration and yet without a policy either domestic or foreign"—according to Seward, President Lincoln had not made any decisions at all regarding plans or procedures since he had been in office. This lack of executive leadership had occurred, Secretary Seward continued, because of Lincoln's "need to meet applications for patronage"—the president was spending too much time handing out jobs to his friends and political allies, which "prevented attention to other and more grave matters." He goes on to warn that "further delay to adopt and prosecute our policies for both domestic and foreign affairs would not only bring scandal on the Administration, but danger upon the country."[9]

One piece of advice Seward offered the president was to change his focus from slavery to a policy of maintaining the Union—"Change the question before the Public from one upon Slavery, or about Slavery for a question upon Union or Disunion." He insisted that the public saw the occupation or evacuation of Fort Sumter as part of the slavery issue; as such, Fort Sumter should be surrendered—keeping it had nothing to do with preserving the Union. But all of the Gulf of Mexico forts should be reinforced and defended, and warships should be recalled "from foreign stations" and deployed for a blockade.[10]

Secretary Seward also had a few definite ideas on the subject of foreign policy. His major concern was the possible intervention of European countries in any future war between North and South. "I would seek explanations from Great Britain and Russia, and send agents into Canada, Mexico and Central America, to rouse a vigorous continental spirit of independence on this continent against European intervention." He also wanted the president to demand "explanations" from Spain and France, but he did not specify exactly what sort of explanation he was looking for. If a "satisfactory explanation" was not received, Secretary Seward recommended convening Congress and declaring war against both France and Spain—he did not mention going to war against Britain or any other country.[11]

"But whatever policy we adopt, there must be an energetic prosecution of it," Secretary Seward concluded. And as far as carrying out those policies, both foreign and domestic, "Either the President must do it himself," or he must "[d]evolve it on some member of his Cabinet"—meaning himself. Secretary Seward did not exactly come right out and declare that he was much more qualified to carry out the duties of chief executive than President Lincoln, but he certainly implied it very emphatically.[12]

President Lincoln read Secretary Seward's memo on the same day that it was written. As might be expected, the president was not exactly overjoyed to read what Seward had to say. He already had enough problems with Jefferson Davis, General Winfield Scott, and the governors of all the seceded Southern states, especially Governor Francis Pickens of South Carolina. He certainly did not need his own secretary of state telling him how to do his job, and suggesting that he could do it much better. Actually, there were a good many people, both North and South, who were in full agreement with Seward. One of them was Confederate president Jefferson Davis. President Davis called Seward "the 'power behind the throne,' greater than the throne itself."[13]

The president immediately sat down and wrote a reply to Secretary Seward's memo. Already under so much pressure that he was becoming physically unwell, his reaction reflects his agitated mental state—he was extremely angry and upset, and was letting it show. President Lincoln first took issue with Secretary Seward's claim that his administration had no policy, either foreign or domestic. He reminded his secretary of state that at his inauguration he firmly stated, "The power confided to me will be used to hold, occupy and possess the property and places belonging to the government," and went on to say that "[t]his had your distinct approval at the time." In the same paragraph, Lincoln went on to scold Seward again, telling him "that comprises the exact domestic policy you now urge," except for the abandoning of Fort Sumter.[14]

As far as Fort Sumter was concerned, President Lincoln had this to say: "I do not perceive how the reinforcement of Fort Sumpter would be done on a slavery, or party issue, while that of Fort Pickens would be on a more national, and patriotic one." In other words, reinforcing Fort Sumter was a bad idea because Seward was against it, but bolstering the defenses of Fort Pickens was a good, patriotic idea because Seward favored it. Although he did not exactly call Secretary Seward a hypocrite, he came very close.[15]

Secretary Seward's remarks on foreign policy did not receive much comment from President Lincoln, although he did allude to the recent (March 16) Spanish annexation of Santo Domingo. He tartly informed Seward that American diplomats and ministers had been given full instructions and information regarding the situation in that country, adding that everything had been carried out "all in perfect harmony, without even a suggestion that we had no foreign policy."[16] The president was letting Seward know that he could be very cynical and sarcastic, and sometimes just plain nasty, when he felt the need.

President Lincoln saved his most direct, and personal, comments for last. Secretary Seward stated that whatever policy was adopted must be prosecuted energetically, and that either the president himself or a member of his cabinet must direct it and must not allow any debate relating to it—"Once adopted, debates on it must end, and all agree and abide."[17] The president's reaction to this was direct and straightforward, almost belligerent: "I remark that if this must be done, *I* must do it," he fairly shouted at the top of his voice. He went on to say that when a "general line of policy" is adopted, this policy would not be changed "without good reason" and would also no longer be the subject of "unnecessary debate." But as president, he added with some sarcasm, he was "entitled to have the advice of all the cabinet." Having said everything he had set out to say, the president ended his little tirade by signing his letter, "Your Obt. Servt. A. LINCOLN."[18]

President Lincoln had certainly given his secretary of state a piece of his mind. But there is no evidence that he actually sent his letter to Secretary Seward. After blowing off steam, Lincoln most likely put the note in his files and allowed himself to cool off. According to one source, "Lincoln may have thought better of rebuking his secretary in writing and handled the matter orally."[19] When he had calmed down, the president would have met with Secretary Seward privately and discussed the contents of his memo in a cool and restrained manner, although there is no record of when this meeting actually took place. President Lincoln knew that he would be needing the counsel and advice of his secretary of state in the coming months and years, and he did not want to alienate him. At their meeting, the president basically would have said the same things he put in his letter, but in a more diplomatic manner.

But whether the president actually sent his letter is beside the point. The language and tone of voice he used in his response shows exactly how much he had changed and grown since his inauguration on March 4. After four weeks in office, Lincoln was no longer the newly sworn-in candidate depending heavily upon his cabinet for guidance. He had learned that he could not depend upon his advisors to make his decisions for him. If he had ever been intimidated or awe struck by William Seward's two terms as governor of New York or twelve years as a US senator, he certainly was not any longer. President Lincoln respected Secretary Seward's opinion, and would frequently come to reply upon it during the next four years. But all final decisions would be made by the president himself, as he made clear in his letter to Seward—"*I must do it.*" Lincoln would continue to grow throughout his presidency, both as chief executive and as the commander of all Union forces.

The president's "oral handling" of the dispute with Secretary Seward had its desired effect—Seward stopped scolding the president for his lack of leadership. But even though President Lincoln had a major disagreement, he did not allow this to stand in the way of his relationship with Seward. He did not hold a grudge. As one of his biographers put it, "now that Seward had given up trying to run the administration, Lincoln liked him as a man and thoroughly enjoyed his company."[20] President and Mary Lincoln often visited Seward and his wife at their home. The Lincolns and the Sewards sometimes went on Sunday outings together. Lincoln and Seward both had a well-developed sense of humor, and often told jokes that left each other in hysterics. They became such good friends that other members of the president's cabinet complained that Lincoln confided in his secretary of state far too often and paid too much attention to his advice. Actually, Seward's personality and sense of humor helped President Lincoln deal with his own anxieties—at least until the next day's assortment of worries presented themselves. And each day would bring its share of worries.

APRIL 2, 1861, TUESDAY

# AN UNPLANNED VISIT

Thomas Tuesday turned out to be a fairly relaxed and routine day, with the usual appointments taking up the morning hours. President Lincoln nominated his friend Ward H. Lamon for the post of marshal of the District of Columbia; he also appointed Simeon Smith of Minnesota as commissioner of pensions. One of the president's happiest chores was writing a "Thank You" note to Mrs. Mary Hancock Colyer of Bleeker Street, New York City. Mrs. Colyer was a niece of John Hancock, the president of the Continental Congress and premier signer of the Declaration of Independence. On March 22, 1861, she wrote to the president, "I take pleasure in presenting . . . a share ticket issued by the province of Massachusetts Bay, 1765, for the rebuilding of Faneuil Hall, signed by John Hancock, and endorsed on the back by Abraham Lincoln . . . one of your ancestors."[1] In a letter dated April 2, President Lincoln replied, "Permit me to express my cordial thanks for the interesting relic you were so kind as to send me, as well as for the flattering sentiment with which it was accompanied."[2] He was clearly delighted to have received Mrs. Colyer's gift—her "favour," as he called it—and was more than pleased to send his personal thanks.

The issue of reinforcing federal installations also had to be addressed. By this point in time, Fort Sumter and Fort Pickens had become a major part of the president's routine. He wrote a short note to Secretary of State Seward in which he directed that $10,000 be paid to Captain Montgomery Meigs "from the secret service fund."[3] Captain Meigs accompanied a Colonel Harvey Brown on the expedition to reinforce Fort Pickens. President Lincoln also wrote a memo to the secretary of the navy, Gideon Welles, informing Welles that Mr. Gwinn

H. Heap will john Captain David D. Porter if so ordered. Heap did leave his job at the Navy Department temporarily, and was attached to USS *Powhatan* as acting paymaster.[4]

During the afternoon, the president and his family left the confines of the White House to visit Washington Navy Yard. The visit was unplanned; its purpose was to give President Lincoln a chance to unwind for a few hours. The officers and men stationed at the navy yard were taken completely by surprise when Lincoln and his family turned up, but they did their best to make the Lincolns feel at home. "The party were saluted by 21 guns," and were personally escorted through the facility by the base commander, Captain Franklin Buchanan.[5]

The Lincolns spent about two hours at the yard, examining and inspecting the base's "machinery and work," according to one account. At the end of their visit, the president said that he was "highly pleased" with everything he had seen.[6] The stopover probably upset the staff at the facility as much as it had given Lincoln some much-needed relaxation—presidential visits were not designed to soothe the nerves of base commanders—and they were probably very glad to see him depart. But this would not be the last time President Lincoln would hear from Franklin Buchanan. In less than three weeks, Buchanan would resign his commission in the US Navy and would be given a captain's commission in the Confederate navy. He would command the ironclad CSS *Virginia* (*Merrimack*) in the battle with USS *Monitor* at Hampton Roads, Virginia, in March 1862.

# APRIL 3, 1861, WEDNESDAY
## INCREASING WAR NERVES

**P**resident Lincoln's ravaged nerves were making themselves known again, this time as the result of a political appointment. William Kellogg of Illinois had come to the White House to speak with the president during the morning; the subject of the conversation was obtaining a post for a Major John C. Henshaw. The meeting had apparently not been either successful or very pleasant. "I regret to again trouble you, and hope never again to feel the humiliation I did in our interview of this morning," William Kellogg scolded in a note he sent to Lincoln, "or again to solicit patronage."[1]

The president was obviously shaken by both the interview and the note. "Mr. Kellogg does me great injustice to write in this strain," he protested. Lincoln went on to say that Kellogg "has had more favors than any other Illinois member." He ended his short memo by saying exactly what was on his mind, a genuine *cri de coeur*: "Is it really in his heart to add to my perplexities now?"[2] He already had enough on his mind and certainly did not need any more problems from some political opportunist from Illinois.

One of the issues on the president's mind, and adding to his perplexities, was an order he signed for Lieutenant Colonel Erasmus D. Keyes. This order was actually an authorization to begin preparations for the reinforcing of Fort Pickens: "You will proceed forthwith to the city of New York to carry out the instructions which you have received here."[3] The instructions were to land troops at the fort with support from an escorting warship, which was to be on hand to prevent a Confederate counterattack—"get a good-sized steamer and six or seven companies of soldiers, and to carry the latter, with a number of large guns and a quantity of munitions of war, to Fort Pickens, land them on the outside of the fort under the guns of a ship of war, and the fort would soon be made impregnable."[4] Colonel Keyes had actually written the order himself and had originally taken it to General Winfield Scott for his signature. But when General Scott read the document, he handed it back to Colonel Keyes and said, "You had better get the President to sign that order." The colonel did what General Scott suggested. He went directly to the White House, "and Mr. Lincoln signed it without a moment's hesitation."[5] Along with Captain David D. Porter and Captain Montgomery Meigs, Colonel Keyes left Washington for New York that night. During their time in New York, the three officers "busied themselves with assembling men, horses, and guns and in chartering steamers to carry them to Florida."[6]

President Lincoln also sent a directive, marked "Confidential," to Secretary of the Navy Gideon Welles. The president instructed Secretary Welles to "cause three complete sets of signal books telegraphic & common to be delivered to the bearer."[7] The "bearer" has never been identified. The signal books may have been intended for delivery to Major Anderson at Fort Sumter; if so, he never received them. The lost books certainly contributed to the failure of the naval task force to reinforce Sumter—the army personnel inside the fort could not decipher the signals of the navy's warships just outside the harbor.

The April 3, 1861, edition of the *New York Times* featured an editorial with the following headline: "Wanted: A Policy." The article essentially made the same points that Secretary of State William Seward made in his note of two days earlier, "Some thoughts for the President's consideration"—namely, that the Lincoln administration had not formed any policy at all, either foreign or domestic. The author of the article was identified only as "[t]he Washington correspondent of one of our morning contemporaries." His main point was made about a quarter of the way through the essay: "The fact is, our Government has done absolute nothing, towards carrying the country through the tremendous crisis which is so rapidly and so steadily settling down upon us. It allows everything to drift,—to float along without guidance or impulse of any kind." The article ended with this pronouncement: "In a great crisis like this, there is no policy so fatal as that of having no policy at all."[8]

President Lincoln may or may not have read the article, but it would not have fazed him if he did happen to see it. He had already gone over the issue of official policy with Secretary Seward, and had nothing more to say about the subject. Also, the president had too much on his mind to be worried about the opinion of some anonymous newspaper correspondent.

War was becoming more of a possibility with each passing day, and the preparations for war were taking up an increasing amount of the president's time.

# APRIL 4, 1861, THURSDAY
## A DISAPPOINTING MEETING

At the end of March, Major Robert Anderson sent a letter to Colonel Lorenzo Thomas, General Winfield Scott's chief of staff, advising that he was planning to evacuate the laborers working at Fort Sumter. His supplies were running low, he explained—he was down to his last barrel of flour—and he could not afford to feed the extra hands. "If the Governor permits me to send off the laborers we will have rations enough to last us about a week."[1] But the "Governor," actually the secretary of war for South Carolina, would not give his permission for the workers to be sent ashore.

The news of Major Anderson's predicament came as a very unpleasant surprise for President Lincoln. Secretary of War Simon Cameron sent Anderson a note to say that the president "had supposed you could hold out till the 15th. inst. without any great inconvenience," and that Lincoln "had prepared an expedition to relieve you before that period." Secretary Cameron went to instruct Major Anderson, "You will therefore hold out if possible till the arrival of the expedition." But he ended his communiqué by advising the major, "if at all, in your judgment, to save yourself and command, a capitulation becomes a necessity, you are authorized to make it."[2]

During the early afternoon hours of this Thursday, President Lincoln had a meeting with John B. Baldwin, a Unionist member of the Virginia Convention. The Virginia Convention had convened on February 11 to consider whether Virginia should secede from the Union; John Baldwin was a delegate to the convention. He had only just arrived in Washington that morning; he was escorted to the White House by Secretary of State Seward around noon. Both Secretary Seward and President Lincoln

**131**

hoped that a meeting with a leading member of the convention might lead to better relations between Richmond and Washington, and might even result in Virginia deciding to remain in the Union—John Baldwin had a great deal of influence among the convention members. Actually, Secretary Seward had more optimism concerning the possible results of the talk than President Lincoln. Although the president himself had authorized the meeting with Baldwin, he had more than his share of doubts about having a conversation with a member of the Virginia Convention, even if he happened to be a Unionist.

The president was not in a very positive frame of mind when he went into the meeting. The first thing he said was, "Mr. Baldwin, I am afraid you have come too late."

John Baldwin was taken aback by this remark. "Too late for what?" he replied.

President Lincoln had a quick response to this. "Why do you not all adjourn the Virginia Convention?" Baldwin was surprised by this, as well. "Adjourn it!—how? do you mean *sine die*?" He was asking if the president meant that the convention should be adjourned with no plans to reconvene at any future date.

"Yes," he said, "*sine die*; why do you not adjourn it; it is a standing menace to me, which embarrasses me very much."

The interview was not going in the way that John Baldwin expected. Instead of at least making an attempt to be diplomatic, President Lincoln was angry and belligerent. Baldwin had no way of knowing that President Lincoln's nerves were on edge, and that he was taking all of his anxieties out on him. He tried to explain that he left Virginia for Washington "by the shortest and most expeditious mode of travel known," that he could not have arrived any sooner, and had come to discuss the Virginia Convention in a reasonable manner. But the president did not seem interested in what he had to say. With a hint of irritation in his voice, Baldwin went on to say that the convention was in the hands of Unionists, who had a three-to-one majority over the secessionists. If the convention were adjourned, the secessionists would probably form a new and radical convention of their own. And if that happened, there would be no question that Virginia would leave the Union within a matter of days.

President Lincoln asked Baldwin straightforwardly, "What is your plan?" meaning what was his plan to avert a civil war. Baldwin's reply was just as direct: he wanted Lincoln "to withdraw the forces from Sumter and Pickens, declaring that it was done for the sake of peace, in the effort to settle this thing." Lincoln was not satisfied with this solution. For one thing, he said, the US Treasury would lose $50 or $60 million in revenue per year if he should give up Fort Sumter, along with access to the port of Charleston—"What would I do about the collection of duties?" Baldwin pointed out that it would cost a lot more than that to pay for a civil war—$60 million per year would be "a drop in the bucket compared with the cost of such a war as we are threatened with." He also warned that "if you intend to do anything to settle this matter you must do it promptly. I think another fortnight will be too late. You have the power now to settle it."[3]

The conversation did not produce any favorable results for either side. John Baldwin did not agree to an adjournment of the Virginia Convention; President Lincoln would not abandon Fort Sumter or Fort Pickens. Toward the end of the meeting, which lasted about an hour, Baldwin told the president, "I tell you, before God and man, that if there is a gun fired at Sumter this thing is gone. And I wish to say to you, Mr. President, with all the solemnity that 1 can possibly summon, that if you intend to do anything to settle this matter you must do it promptly." He also said that if Fort Sumter was fired upon, Virginia would secede from the Union within forty-eight hours—"Virginia herself, strong as the Union majority in the Convention is now, will be out in forty-eight hours." When he returned to Richmond, Baldwin reported that he had reached no sort of agreement with President Lincoln: "No pledge; no undertaking; no offer; no promise of any sort."[4]

President Lincoln had already decided to reinforce Fort Sumter. Secretary of War Simon Cameron had informed Major Robert Anderson that an expedition would be sent to relieve him before April 15, although the local authorities refused to permit the messenger to deliver the letter to Major Anderson. On this same Thursday, President Lincoln gave the order to send Captain Gustavus Fox's task force to Fort Sumter. He summoned Captain Fox to the White House and said that he had decided "to let the expedition go."[5] General Winfield Scott summarized the president's directive in a letter to an aide-de-camp, explaining that Captain Fox had been given command of an expedition to reinforce Fort Sumter. The aide-de-camp, Lieutenant Colonel H. L. Scott, was to embark with Captain Fox and "cause a detachment of recruits, say about two hundred, to be immediately organized at Fort Columbus [New York] with a competent number of officers, army ammunition and subsistence." General Scott went on to direct the colonel, "Some fuel must be shipped. All artillery implements, fuses, cordage, slow match, mechanical levers and guns, etc., etc. should also be put on board."[6] The force would not leave New York for a few days, but the president wanted to be prepared for whatever might take place in Charleston Harbor.

## APRIL 5, 1861, FRIDAY
# THE PRESIDENT SIGNS TWO SETS OF ORDERS

The president spent at least part of this Friday obtaining, or at least trying to obtain, political appointments for his friends and relatives. An "old acquaintance" of thirty years, Ethelbert P. Oliphant, asked for "a judgeship in the swamp land division of the General Land Office" in Nebraska. But in his letter, Mr. Oliphant also added, "I think I am deserving of something better." Apparently, President Lincoln agreed with him; he appointed Oliphant to the post of associate justice of the Washington Territory.[1]

President Lincoln also sent a note to Ira P. Rankin, the collector of customs in San Francisco, asking Rankin to award the position of custom house drayman to Lockwood M. Todd. Lockwood M. Todd just happened to be the cousin of Mary Todd Lincoln, the president's wife. But Rankin replied by informing Lincoln that "a formal protest" had been lodged against Mr. Todd's appointment; the protest had been signed by "a large number of the Republicans of Solano County." The reason behind this protest was that Todd was considered "a most bitter and violent opponent of the Republican party" and, as such, was not considered worthy of the president's backing. Todd did not receive the drayman job, or at least there is no record of the appointment. Instead, he was named commissary of subsistence, with the rank of captain.[2] But the protesting Republicans actually did Todd a favor. A captain with the US Army's supply department was several steps above drayman; "Custom house drayman" was a sort of glorified deliveryman, which means that Lincoln actually did manage to help his wife's cousin get a decent job despite the political opposition.

The president had other chores to tend to. He received his first pay voucher, his first salary as president, in the amount of $2,083.33. The largest bank, and probably the best-known bank, in Washington at the time was Riggs and Company at Ninth and F Streets. President Lincoln opened an account at Riggs and promptly deposited his first month's salary in the new account. But he noticed a mistake in the request to pay him his salary. The document stipulated that he should be paid on the first of every month. Lincoln realized that his first full day as president was March 5, not March 1. He did not want credit for days he did not work, and would not sign the request until he crossed out the word *first* and replaced it with *fifth*—"On to-day, and on the first fifth of each month, please to send me a Warrant for the amount of my salary as President of the United States."[3] The edited note was passed along to Salmon Chase, the secretary of the treasury, who duly paid the president on the fifth of every month. Lincoln was not always honest, and could sometimes be out-and-out arbitrary, but on this day he was the "Honest Abe" of legend.

An article appeared in Washington's *Evening Star* mentioning that "President Lincoln sat for his portrait at Brady's galleries" on the previous day. The short notice went on to report that "Brady will soon publish a large picture of the President and Cabinet, which will be the finest work of the kind ever issued." This was the first of many photos that the Brady gallery would take of President Lincoln; the event served as a nice change of pace for the president—it took his mind off his troubles as president for a short while, at least. A visitor to the White House on this Friday observed that the president was looking troubled and ill at ease, considering the strain Lincoln had been enduring for the past month.[4]

The president would have been even more upset if he had known about a blunder involving the reinforcement of Fort Sumter, especially since he was responsible for the blunder. Two sets of orders had been issued to the captain of the USS *Powhatan*. One copy sent the *Powhatan* to Fort Sumter; the second assigned it to support the Fort Pickens expedition at Pensacola, Florida. President Lincoln accidentally signed both documents—he had not read them and had signed them in haste. The

*Powhatan* had originally been assigned to the Fort Sumter task force by Gideon Welles, secretary of the navy, who issued instructions that sent the warship to Charleston. But William Seward favored a plan to reinforce Fort Pickens instead; he presented President Lincoln with orders that would send the *Powhatan* to Florida. When the two sets of orders were placed on the president's desk, Lincoln signed both documents without looking at them—he did not realize that he was sending the *Powhatan* to Fort Sumter and Fort Pickens at the same time. Among other problems, the tensions of the past month were also affecting the president's ability to concentrate.

The Sumter expedition consisted of *"Pocahontas* at Norfolk, *Pawnee* at Washington, *Harriet Lane* at New York, to be under sailing orders for sea, with stores, etc., for one month. . . . Supplies for twelve months for one hundred men to be in portable shape ready for instant shipping." The *Powhatan* would be the flagship, and it would carry an additional three hundred sailors. The ships would leave their ports and rendezvous at Charleston Harbor.[5] Secretary of the Navy Gideon Welles instructed Samuel Mercer, captain of the *Powhatan*, "You will leave New York with the *Powhatan* in time to be off Charleston bar, ten miles distant from and due east of the light house, on the morning of the 11th instant, there to await the arrival of the transport or transports with troops and stores."[6] Captain Mercer prepared his ship to go to sea on the following day.

But before Captain Mercer could leave port, Lieutenant David D. Porter boarded the *Powhatan* with a completely different set of orders, which were also signed by President Lincoln: "Lieutenant D. D. Porter will take command of the steamer *Powhatan*. . . . All officers are commanded to afford him all such facilities as he may deem necessary for getting to sea as soon as possible."[7] Because the president's authority was higher than Secretary Welles, Captain Mercer yielded the ship to Lieutenant Porter. By 2:45 p.m., USS *Powhatan* left Brooklyn Navy Yard for Fort Pickens with Lieutenant Porter in command. The Fort Sumter expedition had lost its flagship and its most heavily armed warship. And President Lincoln was not even aware of the mix-up, a mix-up that was of his own doing.

APRIL 6, 1861, SATURDAY

# "THE REBELLION WAS RAPIDLY CULMINATING"

**E**ven though President Lincoln had already made up his mind to reinforce Fort Sumter, Secretary of State Seward nevertheless advised him to notify South Carolina officials that a relief expedition would be on its way. Seward was still hoping to defuse the situation in Charleston, and he thought that an advance notice from Lincoln might provide a step in that direction. The president complied with Secretary Seward's request; he agreed to inform South Carolina governor Francis Pickens that he was sending a convoy that would carry supplies and provisions only. But he was under no illusion that informing Governor Pickens would change the governor's point of view, or would have any effect on the situation. President Lincoln knew that the gunners in Charleston Harbor would open fire on any Union ship that approached Fort Sumter. Only the week before, on March 27, Stephen Hurlbut warned, "I have no doubt that a ship known to contain only provisions for Sumpter would be stopped & refused admittance."[1] The president had no reason to disbelieve Hurlbut's warning.

On April 3, the latest incident involving Charleston's artillerymen had taken place. The schooner *Rachel H. Shannon*, on its way from Boston to Savannah with a cargo of ice, encountered dense fog off Charleston and made a detour into the harbor. A battery on Morris Island, inside the harbor, fired a shot at the schooner, a signal for the ship to heave to. The captain was very much astonished by this and "ran up the Stars and Stripes to show that he was all right." According to General Abner Doubleday, who was stationed at Fort Sumter, "This was regarded as a direct defiance and a heavy cannonade was at once opened on the vessel." The schooner's captain was "[v]ery much puzzled to account for this hostility, he lowered his flag, and the firing ceased." A boat was sent from Charleston to investigate the schooner, and its crew was satisfied that the boat and its crew had no hostility in mind when entering the harbor. Artillerymen at Fort Sumter stood by their guns but were not ordered to open fire.[2] A Georgia newspaper carried the story of the schooner, "The Vessel Fired Into at Charleston," and reported that several shots "were fired into his rigging, one of which passed through his main-sail and another through his top-sail."[3]

President Lincoln probably heard about this incident, although General Doubleday reported that "this affair attracted very little attention or comment at the North."[4] It certainly would not have come as any surprise to him. But despite what happened to the *Rachel H. Shannon*, and despite Stephen Hurlbut's warning, the president still intended to send South Carolina advance notice of the relief expedition. He hoped that this might reduce the tension surrounding Fort Sumter. Any attempt at reconciliation would be well worth the effort, even if the effort did not succeed. To make contact with South Carolina authorities, the president decided to send a messenger, a clerk from the Department of State named Robert S. Chew, to Charleston with a letter. Robert Chew was an aide to Secretary Seward but, even more important to the president, also had vital connections with the Virginia Unionists; this connection might prove useful in making contact with Governor Pickens. His orders were to proceed directly to Charleston and, if Fort Sumter was still in Union hands and not under attack, to arrange an interview with Governor Pickens and to read this message to the governor:

I am directed by the President of the United States to notify you to expect an attempt will be made to supply Fort-Sumpter with provisions only; and that, if such attempt be not resisted, no effort to throw in men, arms, or ammunition, will be made, without further notice, or in case of an attack upon the Fort.[5]

After reading the president's message, Chew was to leave a copy of it with Governor Pickens and retain the original. But if Fort Sumter had already surrendered when he arrived in Charleston, he was to return to Washington at once without speaking to the governor. Chew left for Charleston at 6:00 p.m., along with army captain Theodore Talbot. Captain Talbot had been stationed at Fort Sumter when he was still a lieutenant. He would be carrying a letter to Major Anderson at Fort Sumter, informing the major that a convoy was on its way.

Even though President Lincoln had almost no faith at all in the success of Robert Chew's mission to Charleston, he realized that the assignment was a strategic masterstroke. As one historian put it, "In effect Lincoln flipped a coin with Confederate president Jefferson Davis, saying: 'Heads I win; tails you lose.'"[6] If the Confederates allowed the supply convoy to land its cargo of provisions, this would avert a confrontation, at least temporarily, and would make President Lincoln look the part of peacemaker—doing his best to prevent civil war from breaking out despite Southern threats and bluster. But if the Charleston gunners opened fire on the convoy, Jefferson Davis and the Confederates would be blamed for starting the hostilities. Lincoln would emerge as the winner no matter what President Davis decided to do. Honest Abe could be devious and conniving when it suited his purpose.

In mid-afternoon, Gideon Welles arrived at the White House along with a naval aide and some disturbing news. The aide had just come up from Pensacola with a letter from Captain Henry A. Adams, US Navy, commander of the task force standing off Fort Pickens. In his letter, Captain Adams informed Secretary Welles that, despite orders that had been issued by General Winfield Scott to land troops at Fort Pickens, he would not allow any such landing to take place. Secretary Welles would later write, "Captain Adams, the senior naval officer, would not recognize the orders of General Scott."[7] In his letter, Captain Adams justified this refusal by explaining that he already had orders, issued by the Navy Department, which prohibited him from instigating any sort of belligerent action at Pensacola. This included reinforcing Fort Pickens. It seemed to him that allowing a landing force to be put ashore would be a violation of his orders from the Navy

Department. In other words, the navy had no obligation to take orders from the army, even if those orders were issued by the army's senior general. Secretary Welles realized this was a matter for the president to deal with and, accompanied by the naval aide, went directly to the White House with Captain Adams's letter.

Gideon Welles's message was exactly what President Lincoln did not want to hear, especially with the situation at Fort Sumter coming to a boil. He already had enough trouble with Secretary of State Seward; he did not need any problems with the navy. Secretary Welles suggests that new orders immediately be sent to Captain Adams by special messenger, orders directing Adams to give his full cooperation in putting troops ashore at Fort Pickens. "Prompt action was all-important," Welles said, "for the rebellion was rapidly culminating."[8] President Lincoln agreed, and new instructions were written out for the captain. But even after the orders were written, the president's worries were still not over. It took a couple of hours before a trustworthy officer could be found to deliver the orders—meaning an officer who was not sympathetic with the South or, as Secretary Welles put it, "whose fidelity and energy were unquestioned."[9]

An officer who met Secretary Welles's qualifications was found that afternoon: Lieutenant John L. Worden from New York. Secretary Welles read Captain Adams's orders to the lieutenant and also gave him a copy of the document. He advised Worden to commit the contents of the paper to memory so that he would be able to destroy it if it became necessary—Lieutenant Worden would be traveling by train through Richmond to Florida and ran the risk of being captured. When the lieutenant left Washington for Pensacola on the following morning, President Lincoln had one less thing to worry about, at least for the time being.[10]

President Lincoln still had not had any word regarding the *Powhatan* fiasco. At the very end of the day, he was finally informed.

Captain Montgomery Meigs learned about the two sets of orders for USS *Powhatan* earlier in the day, and he telegraphed Secretary of State Seward concerning the state of affairs. Sometime near 11:00 p.m., Secretary Seward and his son Fred walked over to Willard's Hotel to show

Captain Meigs's telegram to Gideon Welles—he knew he would have to give some sort of explanation sooner or later. Secretary Welles read the telegram but did not understand a word of it—the *Powhatan* was supposed to be on its way to South Carolina, not Florida. When he finally understood the situation "after a few minutes of conversation," which included "some excitement on my part"—Gideon Welles must have been absolutely livid that his orders had been countermanded—Welles and the two Sewards decided that they had better go and see President Lincoln at the White House. Secretary Seward also sent for Captain Silas H. Stringham, who had been given command of the flotilla assigned to defend Fort Pickens. Captain Stringham was also staying at Willard's; Welles thought Captain Stringham's testimony might be needed during their White House visit.[11]

Even though it was almost midnight, President Lincoln was still at work in his office when the four men arrived. This was Gideon Welles's second visit since mid-afternoon, which must have taken the president by surprise. He took one look at the expression on Secretary Welles's face and playfully asked, "What have I done wrong?"[12] Secretary Welles explained what had happened regarding the *Powhatan*'s botched orders; Captain Stringham confirmed what Welles told him. After absorbing everything that had been said, the president turned to Secretary Seward and declared that the *Powhatan* must be returned to Captain Mercer, and that "on no account must the Sumter expedition fail or be interfered with."[13] Fort Pickens could wait, but no time was to be lost with regard to Fort Sumter.

The president was fully aware that Secretary Seward favored a plan to give priority to reinforcing Fort Pickens; Welles would later write that Seward "had his heart set on" the Pickens expedition; he also accused Seward of interfering with managing the Navy Department.[14] Simon Cameron seconded Welles's grievance; he complained that Seward was trying to run the War Department. But President Lincoln took full responsibility for the *Powhatan* incident. He insisted that if he had paid more attention to what he was doing, and if he had not signed both orders because of his own negligence, the *Powhatan* never would have been sent off to Florida. As Gideon Welles put it, "He took upon himself the whole blame, said it was carelessness, heedlessness on his part, he ought to have been more careful and attentive."[15] This is absolutely true—the president was completely at fault for the disaster. Secretary Welles seemed somewhat surprised that President Lincoln did not at least shift some of the blame to Seward for his "interference," as he called it. "President Lincoln never shunned any responsibility," and he often took the responsibility for mistakes that his cabinet committed—at least in Welles's opinion.[16] But Lincoln was not the type to blame someone else for his own shortcomings, as Secretary Welles would often discover for himself during the next four years.

# A BLEAK DAY

The foul weather—rain with sporadic downpours throughout the day—did not help steady President Lincoln's nerves on this otherwise quiet Sunday. But the weather was the least of the president's concerns. All the Sunday newspapers were filled with stories about Charleston and Fort Sumter, which increased the president's melancholy; his mind was already preoccupied with thoughts of Sumter, along with Fort Pickens. A nice, sunny day might have helped lift his spirits a little bit.

During the early evening hours, at about seven o'clock, former congressman John Minor Botts of Virginia came to the White House to confer with President Lincoln. Congressman Botts recalled, "we had a great deal of conversation upon the general affairs of the country, and especially in reference to the condition of things in Virginia." Their main topic of conversation was the president's meeting with John Baldwin three days earlier, especially their discussion of the Fort Sumter situation—the fort was running out of provisions. The president went on to explain to Congressman Botts that he had sent a messenger to Governor Pickens of South Carolina regarding the emergency at Sumter with this proposal: if the governor will allow Major Anderson to obtain his provisions at the Charleston market, no effort will be made to provision the fort; but President Lincoln insisted "he will not permit these people to starve, and that I shall send provisions down—that I shall send a vessel loaded with bread." The president continued to say that "I shall at the same time send a fleet along with her, with instructions not to enter the harbor of Charleston unless that vessel is fired into; and if she is, then the fleet is to enter the harbor and protect her."[1]

During the course of the conversation, Congressman Botts also claimed that Lincoln made this proposal to John Baldwin: he would evacuate Fort Sumter if the Virginia Convention agreed to adjourn. According to Botts, the president said to Baldwin: "[I]f you will go back to Richmond and get that Union majority to adjourn and go home without passing the ordinance of secession, so anxious am I for the preservation of the peace of this country, and to save Virginia and the other border States from going out, that I will take the responsibility of evacuating Fort Sumter."[2] But John Baldwin did not mention any such proposal in his own version of his conversation with the president. In fact, he said just the opposite—no pledge or proposal of any sort was made by President Lincoln. No one has ever been able to say for certain which version—Botts's or Baldwin's—is accurate. As one source understates the matter, "The differences between the Baldwin and Botts accounts have perplexed historians."[3]

According to John Botts, Baldwin rejected the president's proposal out of hand. Botts recalled that he was "very much incensed" by Baldwin's reaction and immediately asked, "Mr. Lincoln, will you authorize me to make that proposition to the Union men of the Convention? . . . I will take the steamboat tomorrow morning and have a meeting of the Union men tomorrow night." He was quite certain that the convention members would accept the proposal "willingly and cheerfully," since adopting President Lincoln's plan would be the only way to save the country from civil war. But the president said, "it is too late, the fleet has sailed, and I have no means of communicating with it." John Botts had another suggestion: "will you authorize me to mention this circumstance for your own benefit?" He would be willing to tell the Virginia Convention that he did offer to evacuate Fort Sumter. Botts felt certain that Southern "demagogues" would blame President Lincoln for starting the war, and that informing the convention of his offer would refute this. But the president was not interested. His reaction to this idea was, "Well, not just now, Botts; after awhile you may." Botts thought that this lack of interest was caused by his anxiety over "ruinous and destructive war which he foresaw."[4]

Whether this conversation took place or not, John Botts's story does show President Lincoln's very troubled state of mind during the early days of April. In another account, Botts gives another insight into Lincoln's mental state. He quotes the president as saying, "What do I want with war? . . . I am no war man; I want peace more than any man in this country, and will make greater sacrifices to preserve it than any other man in the nation."[5] But war was coming, he could see that, no matter what he said or did. The Southern states were determined to have their independence, and there was nothing he could do to stop them apart from going to war.

# GROWING TENSIONS

I n a letter dated "Charleston, S.C. April 8th 1861," Robert S. Chew informed President Lincoln that he had met with South Carolina governor Francis W. Pickens on Saturday, April 6. In accordance with his instructions, he read Lincoln's "provisions only" letter to the governor during the meeting and had also given the governor a copy of the letter. After accepting the letter, Governor Pickens said that he would submit it to General Pierre G. T. Beauregard, who had been given command of all forces in Charleston by Confederate president Jefferson Davis. According to Robert Chew's communiqué to President Lincoln, "Genl. Beauregard was accordingly sent for, and the Governor read the paper to him." Governor Pickens made a remark about giving a reply to Chew regarding President Lincoln's message, but Chew responded, "I informed him that I was not authorised to receive any communication from him in reply."[1] Captain Talbot asked General Beauregard for permission to communicate with Major Anderson at Fort Sumter. The general refused.

Later in the day, General Beauregard wrote this message to the Confederate secretary of war, Leroy P. Parker, in Montgomery, Alabama: "An authorized messenger from President Lincoln just informed Governor Pickens and myself that provisions will be sent to Fort Sumter peaceably, or otherwise by force."[2] General Beauregard meant his communiqué to be confrontational—in his letter to Governor Pickens, President Lincoln made no mention of using force. What he said was that no effort to land soldiers or weapons would be made without further notice.

It was just as well that Robert Chew had not been allowed to bring a message from Governor Pickens back to Washington. President Lincoln could guess what Pickens had to say in reply to his letter; he already had enough bad news to deal with and did not need any more. He realized that his letter to the governor would trigger a reaction against Fort Sumter; General Beauregard's message to Secretary of War Parker only served to worsen the already belligerent situation in Charleston. The Confederates had two choices: either back down and allow the US convoy to land its supplies, or take aggressive action against Sumter. President Lincoln knew they would not back down.

President Lincoln was not the only one in Washington who could see the outbreak of war coming closer with each passing day. General Winfield Scott advised the president that more troops were needed as soon as possible to deal with the impending crisis, specifically the transfer of militia units from states throughout the North to the regular army. He also sent a message to Secretary of War Simon Cameron suggesting that ten companies of state militia be requisitioned. The small (sixteen-thousand-man) regular army would not be nearly large enough to deal with the coming emergency.

The president agreed with his senior general and began taking steps toward expanding the army. He sent for the governor of Pennsylvania, Andrew Curtin, to discuss the possibility of increasing the Pennsylvania state militia. Pennsylvania bordered on Maryland and was uncomfortably close to Virginia. Both were slave-holding states that might very well secede from the Union and join the Confederacy. Governor Curtin did not need very much persuasion from President Lincoln to prepare the state militia against a possible Southern invasion. He returned home to Harrisburg and petitioned the Pennsylvania legislature to raise the funds for additional state troops.

This was just what the president wanted to hear—more soldiers were being recruited for the hostilities that were almost certain to come, and would be coming very quickly. He sent an encouraging note to Governor Curtin, "I think the necessity of being *ready* increases. Look to it. Yours truly A. LINCOLN."[3]

One of the president's more routine tasks on this Monday was to appoint two candidates to the newly created Yankton Land District in

South Dakota. In fact, his first directive was to create the district itself, according to "the boundaries described" in a letter from the new district's commissioner. Next, he named a Virginian, Jesse Wherry, to be the receiver of public monies, and selected Henry A. Kennerly of Missouri as the Land Office register. Lincoln was doing his best to keep both Missouri and Virginia from leaving the Union, and he hoped these two nominations might sweeten the opinion of the two states toward him and his government. The coming conflict was never far from President Lincoln's mind, not even when making political appointments.[4]

APRIL 9, 1861, TUESDAY

# DECEPTIVE CALM

**T**he atmosphere inside the White House was calm and free of controversy on this Tuesday, at least on the surface. President Lincoln tended to three routine appointments while he was waiting for news regarding the reprovisioning of Fort Sumter. All three appointments were ordinary and typical: approving Joseph H. Barrett for the post of commissioner of pensions in Cincinnati, Ohio; authorizing an old friend, James Short, to be supervisor of the Round Valley, California, Indian reservation; and naming Christian Metz as collector in Buffalo, New York. Although he gave the impression of being calm, the president was just as nervous and anxious as he had been since inauguration day.

Several hundred miles to the north of Washington, DC, Gustavus V. Fox departed New York Harbor for Charleston. He wrote to Postmaster General Montgomery Blair, "At 8 A.M. of the 9th inst. we discharged the pilot" and headed out to sea.[1] Fox was aboard the steamer SS *Baltic*, a luxury liner that had been leased by the US government from the North American Steamship Company. In the spring of 1861, the US Navy was critically short of warships. During the coming months, the Navy Department would find itself fighting along an extended front with fewer than a dozen modern, steam-powered ships available for service against the Confederacy. The bulk of the navy's warships had been assigned to overseas duties, including special duties in Japanese waters. To make up for this shortage, at least in part, civilian ships were chartered from civilian shipping firms—SS *Baltic* was leased at a rate of $1,500 per day. During the 1850s, SS *Baltic* had been the fastest liner to cross the Atlantic but, in recent times, had been operating out of New York and assigned to domestic service. The *Baltic*'s sister ship,

SS *Atlantic*, was also chartered by the government, and at the same daily rate. Gideon Welles would be needing all the help he could get, and he was glad to have the two passenger ships.

Gustavus Fox was also glad to have the *Baltic* as part of his provisioning convoy. The revenue cutter *Harriet Lane*, along with two tugboats, also joined Fox's group. "One of my tugs went to sea Sunday night, another one followed the *Baltic*," he later wrote.[2] The sloop of war *Pawnee* sailed from Norfolk, Virginia, also on April 9. Fox thought that he would have the steam frigate *Powhatan* as well. He had no way of knowing that his flagship was now on its way to Pensacola.

Confederate authorities were being kept well informed of the navy's movements by the Northern press. This item appeared in the Washington *Evening Star*'s April 9 edition: "The steamer *Baltic* still lies at pier forty-two, at the foot of Canal Street, and is being loaded with freight as expeditiously as possible." The account goes on to report, "Orders were issued this morning that she should make ready for sea by three o'clock this afternoon." Another article appeared in the same edition: "This morning the revenue cutter flag on the *Harriet Lane* was hauled down, and the Stars and Stripes run up at her peak. . . . The cutter is heavily armed, and her crew increased to eighty men."[3]

If President Lincoln happened to read these two articles, he would have been even more worried and upset than before. He was well aware that newspapers from the North were being carried into the Southern states by those who sympathized with the secessionists, as well as by ordinary travelers. The information in these two reports meant that the War Department in Montgomery, Alabama, knew as much about the *Baltic* and the *Harriet Lane* as he knew himself. The president did not need another cause for worry.

# WAITING FOR NEWS

Almost all of President Lincoln's day was occupied by the crisis in Charleston, South Carolina, and the increasing prospect of war. He received a request from Pennsylvania governor Andrew Curtin involving the state militia. Governor Curtin's main concern was preparing the troops for combat, which he was certain they would be facing in the not-too-distant future, and asked to be sent a drill officer to help organize the men and oversee their training. The president was more than willing to oblige. He sent Secretary of War Simon Cameron this slightly whimsical message: "Dear Sir: Gov. Curtin telegraphs us to send him a drill-officer. Better send one at once."[1]

Newspapers were filled with rumors that were accepted as truth by their readers, which only helped intensify the crisis. The *New York Herald* featured these headlines on its front page:

OPENING OF CIVIL WAR
Immense Excitement in Charleston[2]

The front page story goes on to give detailed particulars of Charleston and its defenses, along with a map of the harbor and its fortifications and a listing of Confederate troops billeted in the vicinity of Charleston. Everything on the page gives the indication that war had already broken out. This sort of sensational journalism not only alarmed the paper's readers in New York but also was read and believed by government officials, North and South. The three Southern commissioners who had been sent to Washington in February, Martin J. Crawford, A. B. Roman, and John Forsyth, sent this dispatch to General Beauregard in Charleston: "Washington, April 10, 1861. General G. T. Beauregard: The 'Tribune' of to-day declares the main object of the expedition to be the relief of Sumter, and that a force will be landed which will overcome all opposition. Roman, Crawford, and Forsyth."[3]

The three commissioners went back to their home states after sending their message. But their "a force will be landed" statement was not based on anything resembling solid information. All they had to go on was "public rumor and the newspapers," which were never very reliable sources even under the best and unemotional of circumstances.[4] Roman, Crawford, and Forsyth were not the only ones who were in the dark. No one knew exactly what was happening in Charleston except what the papers were saying, and these reports were largely inaccurate.

President Lincoln was not exactly certain, either. He was waiting for word from Gustavus Fox regarding the Fort Sumter expedition—on whether the convoy had delivered its supplies to Sumter, or even if it had arrived in Charleston at all. He also did not know how much popular support he would receive when the war actually began—at this stage, with the Fox expedition on its way to Charleston, the president was certain that civil war was only a matter of days away. There were still quite a few people, both in and out of political office, who held the opinion that the seceded states should be allowed to go in peace. President Lincoln was certain that most Republicans would support him and the war; whether the Democrats would follow suit was open to question. It would certainly have put his mind at ease if he could have counted on the support from Congress and the public at large. But everything connected with Charleston, and Fort Sumter remained uncertain and undecided.

## APRIL 11, 1861, THURSDAY
# AN UNACCEPTABLE DEMAND

The president spent a good deal of his morning making political endorsements for candidates in several states. He asked Montgomery Blair to intercede on behalf of a John S. Scott for the position of postmaster general in Covington, Kentucky, adding "I know nothing as to the propriety of this; but write to keep a promise."[1] Salmon Chase received a similar note from the White House, a request to find a job for a loyal supporter "who co-operated with us in 1858 & 1860. . . . Can any thing be found for him—permanent, or temporary? Please try."[2] President Lincoln also recommended three other political appointees, including a candidate for deputy surveyor of Philadelphia. He also designated the *National Republican* as the official Washington newspaper "for the publication of notices and advertisements from the Executive departments."[3] Even with war posing an immediate threat, President Lincoln still had his hands full with the business of everyday politics. He was not allowed to forget that he was not only president and commander in chief but also head of the Republican Party.

President Lincoln also had several activities directly connected with preparing for the impending war. He had a conversation with Carl Schurz, a German immigrant who backed Lincoln in the 1861 presidential campaign and was in favor of reinforcing Fort Sumter. He also favored strengthening the US Army in preparation for the coming war—like the president, Schurz was convinced that civil war was unavoidable. During their meeting, Schurz and President Lincoln talked about the formation of four regiments, including a cavalry regiment. In a letter to the president, dated April 11, Schurz advised Lincoln "to furnish good arms to the four regiments without delay, and also uniforms to those who are not already uniformed."[4] Carl Schurz was not given command of any of the regiments he mentioned. He was appointed minister to Spain in July and managed to persuade the Spanish government not to support the Confederacy. When he returned from Spain at the end of 1861, Schurz received a commission as a general in the Union army.

The president also spent a good part of his day with the governor of Maryland, Thomas H. Hicks. Governor Hicks told President Lincoln that he did not agree with the government's current policy toward the seceded states. It seemed to him that Lincoln was pursuing a "coercive" program regarding South Carolina and the other slave states, and he was not at all happy with "the course the Administration was taking." This was actually an understatement. The governor was more than unhappy with President Lincoln; he was furious. But the president offered this statement in the way of explanation of his policies. "There is a steady, deliberate, and cool intention to show the world one of two things—either that we have a government worth preserving, or that it is so imbecile that a few slaveholders on this continent can set themselves up as superior to it and more powerful." When the governor heard President Lincoln's explanation, "he modified his opinion to a very great extent." This came as wonderful news for the president, the best news he could have hoped for—he desperately needed the support of Maryland and of its governor. Washington, DC, was completely within the borders of Maryland, which was a slave state that had voted overwhelmingly against Lincoln in the 1860 election. If Maryland joined the Confederacy, this would have isolated the capital and would have almost guaranteed its capture by Southern troops. Lincoln's meeting with Governor Hicks, which was described as lasting for "several hours," was probably his most productive discussion of his entire presidency.[5]

The situation in Charleston had reached the crisis point. General Beauregard sent Major Anderson a letter in which he demanded the evacuation of Fort Sumter in the name of the Confederate government. He wrote, "the Confederate States can no longer delay assuming actual possession of a fortification commanding the entrance of one of their harbors, and necessary to its defense and security." The general went on to say that "[a]ll proper facilities" would be put at Major Anderson's disposal for the removal of his command and all weapons and private property "to any post in the United States which you may elect." But before surrendering the fort, Major Anderson was given permission to salute the Stars and Stripes before lowering them for the last time.[6]

In his letter to Major Anderson, General Beauregard neatly gave the Confederacy's official position regarding Fort Sumter. President Jefferson Davis wrote, "the ground on which Fort Sumter was built was ceded by South Carolina to the United States in trust for the defense of her own soil and her own chief harbor."[7] President Davis also blamed President Lincoln for the fact that the men stationed inside the fort were on the verge of starvation. "Lincoln will know that, if the brave men of the garrison were hungry, they had only him and his trusted advisors to thank for it." The soldiers "had been kept for months in a place where they ought not to have been."[8] In other words, Fort Sumter was never a US government installation to begin with. And its garrison was not really made up of soldiers at all; they were just trespassers. General Beauregard's demand amounted to an eviction notice: get out before I throw you out!

After finishing his letter, the general gave it to his aides for delivery to Major Anderson. The two aides—Colonel James Chesnut Jr. and Captain Stephen D. Lee—were rowed out to Fort Sumter by two crewmen. Colonel Chesnut and Captain Lee presented themselves to Major Anderson and handed him Beauregard's letter as soon as they landed at the fort. Major Anderson read what General Beauregard had to say and called a meeting with his officers to discuss the letter's contents. At the end of two hours, the major returned with a reply, which was written in typical mid-nineteenth-century fustian: "General: I have the honor to acknowledge the receipt of your communication demanding the evacuation of this fort; and to say in reply thereto that it is a demand with which I regret that my sense of honor and of my obligations to my Government prevents my compliance."[9] Major Anderson would not surrender. He also matter-of-factly informed Colonel Chesnut and Captain Lee that the Sumter garrison would be starved out in a few days, anyway, even if the Charleston artillery did not batter the fort to pieces in the meantime.

The two aides were rowed back to Charleston, where they delivered Major Anderson's letter to General Beauregard. They also relayed the major's verbal message about the garrison being on the verge of starvation. After reading the letter and listening to what Chesnut and Lee told him about the food situation at the fort, General Beauregard sent the two aides back to Sumter with another letter for Major Anderson. In this new communiqué, Beauregard once again asked the major to evacuate the fort, especially in view of the fact "that you would in a few days be starved out if our guns did not batter you to pieces—or words to that effect"—this was a new tactic to induce Major Anderson to surrender. If the major would state the time at which he would evacuate Fort Sumter, "we will abstain from opening fire upon you."[10]

By this time it was very late. Colonel Chesnut and Captain Lee made their third trip to visit Major Anderson, taking General Beauregard's latest surrender request out to Fort Sumter. The major read the letter and, in a response dated April 12, 1861, at 2:30 a.m., said that he was prepared to evacuate Fort Sumter by noon on April 15, "should I not receive, prior to that time, controlling instructions from my Government, or additional supplies."[11]

This was not even close to being acceptable; Major Anderson's reply was rejected out of hand. At 3:20 a.m., five minutes after the major wrote his communiqué, he was handed this response: "Sir: By authority of Brigadier-General Beauregard, commanding the provisional forces of the Confederate States, we have the honor to notify you that he will open the fire of his batteries on Fort Sumter in one hour from this time."[12] The note was signed by Colonel Chesnut and Captain Lee. After reading the note, Major Anderson told the two aides that he hoped to see them in heaven if he did not meet them again on earth.

Gustavus Fox's task force would not be able to offer any help to Major Anderson. A powerful storm, usually described as a "gale," slowed the rescue fleet and scattered its ships. Fox's expedition had been a fiasco from the very beginning. First, the *Powhatan* had been diverted to Pensacola by mistake. Then the remainder of the fleet had been waylaid by bad weather. For the past two days, Fox noted that the convoy "had constant steady bad weather and heavy sea."[13] A newspaper account gave a more detailed summary: "The non-arrival of the squadron off Charleston is doubtless due to the heavy gale that has prevailed along the Southern coast for the past two or three days." The report goes on to elaborate, "The storm was so severe that a large number of vessels, including several steamers, were obliged to take refuge in Hampton Roads."[14] During the next twenty-four hours, Fox's luck would not get any better.

President Lincoln had no way of knowing about the notes that had passed between General Beauregard and Major Anderson, but he would not have been surprised by them or by their contents. It had become increasingly evident, more evident with each passing day, that the South was prepared to go to war over Fort Sumter. The president was all too aware that war was very close at hand. But when he went to bed on Thursday night, he had no idea that the war would already have started by the time he woke up on Friday morning.

# THE CRISIS REACHES A CLIMAX— A LAST PEACEFUL DAY AT THE WHITE HOUSE

**"A**ccording to the notice given by General Beauregard, fire was opened upon Fort Sumter, from the various batteries which had been erected around the harbor, at half-past four o'clock on the morning of Friday, the 12th of April, 1861."[1] Jefferson Davis wrote this terse, matter-of-fact description of the opening salvoes against Fort Sumter many years after the event. Mary Boykin Chesnut, the wife of Colonel James Chesnut, General Beauregard's aide, wrote from a far more personal point of view. Mary Chesnut was living in Charleston at the time, and was kept from sleeping by the incessant cannon fire. At four-thirty on that Friday morning, she wrote in her diary that she was shocked by "the heavy booming of a cannon. . . . The shells were bursting . . . I knew my husband was rowing about in a boat somewhere in that dark bay, and that the shells were roofing it over, bursting toward the fort."[2] By this time, Gustavus Fox had finally arrived at Charleston. "At 3 A.M. of the 12th reached the rendezvous 10 miles east of Charleston light—found only the H. Lane [the revenue cutter *Harriet Lane*]," he noted in his diary. Three hours later, the sloop *Pawnee* was sighted. Captain Fox boarded the sloop and told its captain that he intended "going in to offer to land provisions" and "asked him to stand in with me." The *Pawnee*'s captain explained that he had been ordered to remain ten miles east of the light and await the *Powhatan*. "I took the H. Lane as an escort, and as we drew in saw that the forts had all opened fire upon Sumpter and that Major Anderson was replying gallantly."[3]

When President Lincoln woke up several hours later, he had no idea that Fort Sumter had been attacked. He carried on with his usual office business from the White House. Political appointments were his main activities. Two senators from Pennsylvania were appointed to positions in their state by presidential authority. A senator from Ohio received an appointment for the post of marshal of that state, and a nomination for collector of the Port of Philadelphia was made. The morning was calm and routine.

At around noon, the cabinet held its usual weekly meeting. Secretary of State William Seward proposed sending Massachusetts congressman George Ashmun on a secret diplomatic mission to Canada. Congressman Ashmun's assignment was "to keep political feelings right" between the United States and Canada—in other words, to give the Canadian government the North's view of the crisis at Fort Sumter. Secretary Seward's proposal was approved, and Congressman Ashmun was sent to Canada at a fee of $10 per day, plus expenses.[4] Next on the agenda, Secretary of War Simon Cameron read a letter from Texas governor Sam Houston to the commanding officer of US Army troops in Texas. In his letter, Governor Houston declined the offer of using federal troops against any secessionists in the state. President Lincoln also had a topic to discuss, advising the cabinet that he had a conversation with the mayor of Washington, DC, regarding the resumption of work on the Treasury Building. The main portion of the building had been completed in the early 1840s, but work on the west wing had been suspended. The president favored resuming work on the west wing "to keep the people of Washington in good humor." The cabinet members agreed with him, and construction resumed.[5]

The two messengers who had gone to Charleston on April 8 with President Lincoln's "provisions only" letter, Robert S. Chew and Captain Theodore Talbot, had just arrived from Charleston in time for the cabinet meeting. Both gave their versions of what had happened on April 8—meeting with Governor Pickens, and being refused permission to communicate with Major Anderson by General Beauregard. Captain

Talbot even brought back the letter to Major Anderson that President Lincoln had given him; it was still in its envelope, unopened.

Throughout the meeting, President Lincoln gave the impression of being calm and businesslike. He did not seem to be nervous or anxious at all, not even when Chew and Talbot gave their accounts of what had happened at Charleston. Even though much of the news he heard was anything but encouraging, the president was not discouraged, or at least did not seem to be.

By mid-afternoon, word of the Fort Sumter attack was beginning to spread—by telegraph, by word of mouth, and by rumor. British reporter William H. Russell first heard the news of Fort Sumter in Baltimore at about 8:00 p.m. The proprietor of the Eutaw House Hotel, where Russell was staying, took him aside and said, "The President of the Telegraph Company tells me he has received a message from his clerk at Charleston that the batteries have opened fire on Sumter because the Government has sent down a fleet to force in supplies."[6]

Word of the attack reached New York in time for newspaper editors to publish special evening editions about Fort Sumter. Newsboys were out on the street shouting, "Extra! Extra! Read all about the bombardment of Fort Sumter!" People who were just getting out of work scanned the headlines and read the reports as they headed for home. Some were angered by what they read, some were frightened, and others found the stories hard to believe. "I can hardly hope," one man said, "that the rebels have been so foolish and thoughtless as to take the initiative in civil war and bring the matter to a crisis. If so, they have put themselves on a horribly false situation."[7]

The war that Abraham Lincoln hoped to avoid, and eventually was forced to accept as inevitable, had finally started. A British biographer commented, "In effect, the Civil War began on Lincoln's very first day in office."[8] Now that the crisis had at long last come to a head and the shooting had begun, President Lincoln must have been relieved. The waiting was over, along with all the tension that went with it. There would be no more worries about reinforcing Fort Sumter, or over offending Governor Pickens. His main worry would now be how to go about restoring the Union—fighting the war and winning the war. He did not know it at the time, but this would turn out to be a lot more difficult than he thought. Fighting the war and winning the war would produce an entirely different assortment of problems for him to worry about, the problems of a wartime president.

# VISITORS

Saturday morning's newspaper headlines were full of nothing but Fort Sumter and Charleston. Most of the headings, along with the accompanying stories, were surprisingly low keyed. "Commencement of Hostilities—Bombardment of Fort Sumter" one front page matter-of-factly stated.[1] Others were just as unemotional: "THE WAR COMMENCED: The First Gun Fired by Fort Moultrie against Fort Sumter."[2] "THE WAR BEGUN: Very Exciting News from Charleston."[3] But this reticence did not last very long. Within the coming days and weeks, news reports—throughout the North and the South—would go berserk with their flag waving and name calling. Throughout the North, crowds held raucous gatherings and assemblies to support the Union and damn all secessionists. Even residents of New York City, who had frequently been emotional in their support of the South, held patriotic rallies in support of the Union after Fort Sumter.

The bombardment of Fort Sumter united the North in a frenzy of patriotism. Winston Churchill would write that Fort Sumter "roused and united the people of the North. All the free states stood together."[4] The attack has been compared with Pearl Harbor. If nothing else, it abruptly ended all the arguments and debates regarding the pros and cons of secession—there would be no more editorial opinions supporting a Southern Confederacy. An editorial in the *New York World* neatly summed up the prevailing point of view north of the Mason-Dixon Line: "We have, at last, thank God—and most reverently do we say it— we have, at last, a united North."[5]

Young men from every Northern state rushed to join their local regiments. A nineteen-year-old from Providence, Rhode Island, wrote in his diary: "Military spirit runs high and I, in common with the other young men, feel that it is my duty to serve in the field."[6] A New Jersey private remarked that the state government "cooperated heartily and cordially with the President and Secretary of War in all their efforts to suppress the rebellion in its infancy."[7] The flag had been insulted and disgraced, and the North reacted with an outpouring of fury.

But Fort Sumter unified the South as well. Now that the war had begun, Southerners rallied to defend what they now thought of as their own country, a land different and apart from the Northern states. They now had a nation worth fighting for. A twentieth-century British writer pointed out that "Southerners had a homeland in a sense that the North did not . . . with a literature, an idiom, a diet, mores" separate from the North.[8] Jefferson Davis insisted that "the southern States had rightfully the power to withdraw from a Union into which they had, as sovereign communities, voluntarily entered."[9] In other words, Southerners were of the opinion that they had every right to fight for independence. A Tennessee newspaper ran this headline: "INDEPENDENCE, NOW AND FOREVER!"[10]

On the first full day of civil war, President Lincoln held a meeting with three members of the Virginia Convention at the White House. The delegates were political leaders of long standing: William B. Preston, a member of the Confederate Congress; Alexander H. H. Stuart, elected to the Virginia senate; and George W. Randolph, who would become the Confederate secretary of war in 1862. The convention sent the president a letter of inquiry, usually referred to as a "resolution," on April 8. The purpose of this resolution was to ask President Lincoln to advise the convention of "the policy which the Federal Executive intends to pursue in regard to the Confederate States."[11]

President Lincoln had already written his reply to the resolution and proceeded to read the text to the three delegates. It was a strange sort of document, not exactly belligerent but not a peace offering, either. The first part of his response was an apology for not making his policy clear or "what course I intend to pursue." The policy he intended to follow had already been set down in his inaugural address, President Lincoln explained. He then proceeded to read the relevant passage from his address: "The power confided to me will be used to hold, occupy, and possess, the property, and places belonging to the Government, and to collect the duties, and imposts; but, beyond what is necessary for these objects, there will be no invasion—no using of force against, or among the people anywhere." He went on to elaborate that by "property and places belonging to the government" he was referring to "the military posts, and property, which were in the possession of the Government" when he took office. After reading this section, the president read a passage that he had inserted that morning, a section mentioning Fort Sumter: "But if, as now appears to be true, in pursuit of a purpose to drive the United States authority from these places, an unprovoked assault has been made upon Fort-Sumpter, I shall hold myself at liberty to re-possess, if I can, like places which had been seized before the Government was devolved upon me."[12]

The next item President Lincoln read to his three visitors was his intention to "repel force by force." He also said that "I shall perhaps, cause the United [States] mails to be withdrawn from all the States which claim to have seceded," but only if reports that Fort Sumter had been attacked turned out to be true. As of that morning, according to the *Baltimore Sun*, no government official had received any official word regarding Sumter; only newspaper reports and rumors had reached Washington up to that time.[13] Another point Lincoln wanted to make was that the military posts within the states "which claim to have seceded" still belonged to the US government "as much as they did before the supposed secession." President Lincoln wanted the Virginia delegates to know that he considered the secession of the seven Southern states to be altogether illegal.[14]

After explaining that he would repel force by force and that he held himself at liberty to repossess military installations that had been seized by states that claim to have seceded, President Lincoln went on to repeat his earlier remark: "I shall not attempt to collect the duties, and imposts, by any armed invasion of any part of the country," although he might "land a force, deemed necessary, to relieve a fort upon a border of the country."[15] On the one hand, he was prepared to "hold, occupy, and possess" any government installation, but he went on to declare that he would not attempt any sort of invasion or use of force in any part of the country, including any of the so-called seceded states. The president realized that he had a war on his hands, but from what he had to say to the Virginia delegates, it seemed that he was intending to have a "soft war," a limited war: no invasion of any sort of any of the seceded states, except possibly an attempt to recapture a fort or an installation "upon a border of the country." The three delegates listened to the president's answer, and went back to Richmond to report what they had been told regarding Lincoln's policy regarding the Confederate States. A Washington newspaper reported, "The *on dit* [rumor or gossip] here is that they are much pleased with the President's reception of them," but also somewhat ominously stated that "though as yet it is hardly possible that much of a definite character could have transpired in the matter between themselves and the Government."[16]

At about the same time that President Lincoln was speaking with the Virginia delegates, Gustavus Fox was outside Charleston Harbor aboard the warship *Pawnee*. Captain Fox could see that Fort Sumter was on fire and was being pounded by artillery fire from the batteries in the harbor. "As we drew near I saw, with horror, black volumes of smoke issuing from Sumpter," he later would write. "The barbarians, to their everlasting disgrace be it said, redoubled their fire, and through the flames and smoke the noble band of true men continued their response."[17] Major Anderson surrendered the fort later that day, at 2:00 p.m. The *Baltimore Sun* reported in a dispatch dated Charleston, April 14: "The negotiations between Major Anderson and General Beauregard were completed last night, and Major Anderson, with his command, will evacuate Sumter this morning, and will embark on board one of the war vessels off our bar."[18] Anderson and his men, except for one soldier who was killed by an exploding cannon during a salute to the Stars and Stripes, embarked for New York. The "battle" had been a one-sided affair; there was no doubt as to how it would end.

Along with Secretary of War Simon Cameron and writer James R. Gilmore, President Lincoln met with the former senator from Mississippi, Robert J. Walker, to hear Walker's views of the South. As the president put it when he was introduced to Walker, "this is the gentleman who knows all about the South, and can tell us how high that raccoon is going to spring." Senator Walker certainly did know a great deal "about the South;" although he was born in Pennsylvania, he served ten years as US senator for Mississippi. Despite this, he supported the Union; his son Duncan would become a brigadier general in the federal army. But James Gilmore did almost all of the talking, giving his own observations of the South and its inhabitants. Among the things he said to the president: Southerners "were of the same race as ourselves, but unmixed with our degraded foreign element, and with our every trait intensified in consequence of having a servile race to support them in idleness," and also that "the good [were] very good, the bad not fit to feed the pigs."[19]

During the two-hour meeting, President Lincoln was also advised "that the slave-owners, who were the inciters of the present trouble, were a very small minority of the Southern people, numbering, all told, only about 200,000." Small slaveholders were mostly planters; many were of the opinion that they could raise their crops more cheaply by hired than by slave labor. And non-slaveholders were generally satisfied "to let things go on as they were;" they did not care very much which party was in power, the Republicans or the Democrats. But this attitude changed when Lincoln was nominated for the presidency. Southerners were told that he was an abolitionist, and worse, "that he had negro blood in his veins," and that "both from blood and principle he was bound to go to the length of freeing the slave, and placing him on a political equality with the white." This would lead not only to political equality but also to "negro domination, and the domination of the lowest type of negro, which no Southern, or even Northern, white man would submit to."[20]

President Lincoln was surprised to hear this. But he was also informed that "[t]he slave-owners control the South, control it because of their wealth, and their wealth is in their slaves. A man in the South is not worth so many dollars, but so many negroes. They have gone into the rebellion to protect that kind of property, and you can't put it down until you deprive them of it."[21]

"But you are aware that I have no constitutional right to abolish slavery," the president responded.

"Except as a war measure," Gilmore said. "But seven States have already declared themselves independent, and begun a war in Charleston harbor."

"Yes," President Lincoln agreed, "such doings look like war; but whether we have had cannon-balls enough to justify extreme measures is the question. We won't discuss that." This coincided with what he had told the three Virginia delegates earlier that day—he was hoping for a limited war.[22]

Gilmore was not yet finished; he still had a few more things to say. He advised the president to warn the seceded states that if they did not rejoin the Union within a specified time—"say ninety days"—he would free all the slaves within those states. President Lincoln was not impressed by Gilmore's recommendation. His first response was, "do you suppose the North would sustain me in any such measure?" and quickly added that abolitionists had been "working for thirty years to bring the North to that way of thinking" with nothing to show for it. He also said, "you must bear in mind that I have no right to emancipate the slaves, except for the preservation of the Union."[23] Freeing the slaves was not even close to being a top priority for Lincoln. He dismissed Gilmore's suggestion—"shoved slavery under the rug"—because he was concerned about Northern unity. He won last November's election with less than 50 percent of the vote, and he feared that many of those who voted for him, along with most of those who voted against him, "would have refused to countenance an antislavery war." As such, he thought it best "to keep a low profile on the slavery issue."[24] According to his point of view, keeping the North united and containing the war were more important than freeing the slaves.

Gilmore also addressed his concern over Secretary of State William Seward; he was especially worried about what he perceived as the hatred of the South toward Secretary Seward. "They regard him as their arch enemy; and from his prominence and ability they will believe that he is really the soul and brains of your administration," he informed Lincoln. The president had heard that one before. "Then they consider Seward as the King-devil?" he said with a smile.[25]

But Gilmore did not see the humor of the situation. He insisted "both politicians and people regard him as the incarnation of all evil." He went on to advise, "If the leaders had not thought him a coward, I question if they would have fired upon Fort Sumter." They would not have done so if Senator Walker was a member of the president's cabinet, Gilmore insisted. This caused Senator Walker to chime in. "Come, come, Mr. Gilmore," he said, "omit any reference to me."[26]

President Lincoln was just as amused as before by Gilmore's remarks about Secretary Seward. "Well, well," he said, still smiling, "I guess the Southern people would hang Seward if they should catch him. But now tell me how you would go to work to put down this rebellion?"[27]

Gilmore's advice was to follow the plan the British intended to use against the American colonists during the War of Independence. "The plan was to divide the Southern colonies by a line running westward from Charleston, also to separate New England from the middle colonies by the Hudson River, and to crush each section separately." The president seemed impressed by this idea—"divide and conquer." In his memoirs, Gilmore noted that General William T. Sherman would use this plan during his march to the sea in 1864.[28]

With this piece of advice, the meeting ended and the guests left the White House. President Lincoln did not learn very much as a result of the meeting, but he did seem very relaxed, sometimes even whimsical, during the two-hour session. He had not been either relaxed or very whimsical in the weeks since he had taken office, and the meeting seemed to have soothed his nerves, if it accomplished nothing else. Listening to the opinion of someone else on the subjects of the rebellion and freeing the slaves might even have helped him make up his mind on these two taxing and distressing items.

# MORE VISITORS

President Lincoln attended services at New York Avenue Presbyterian Church on this Sunday morning. He attended this church regularly, even though neither he nor his wife ever became members of the congregation. The sermon was delivered by Reverend Phineas D. Gurley, DD. Reverend Gurley still favored peace, and told the congregation, "God has afforded another opportunity for pause, for appeal to Him for assistance before letting loose upon the land the direst scourge which He permits to visit a people—a civil war." But after making these opening remarks, he prayed that all future decisions of President Lincoln's administration—meaning all of his decisions as a war president—"might be sanctified and blessed." The reverend did not mention Fort Sumter, but everyone present, including the president, knew what he meant—he was acknowledging the fact that war had already started. Lincoln appreciated these sentiments. Shortly after arriving in Washington, he had expressed his desire to attend a church in Washington whose pastor was "aloof from politics." In Reverend Gurley, he found the pastor he was looking for. The pastor "created a place where Lincoln could go to hear a good sermon and avoid the clamor of politics." There were not very many places in Washington where anyone could escape the stress and strain of partisan politics, but the president managed to find a place where he could put his mind at rest for at least an hour or so.[1]

Shortly after returning from church, President Lincoln held a cabinet meeting at the White House. The president and the members of his cabinet, along with "sundry military officers," met to give "final shape" to a proclamation that he had written himself. The proclamation called into service seventy-five thousand militia for three months. The document was dated April 15, but it was drafted and signed on Sunday the 14th. After the president signed the proclamation, it was sent to the State Department to be filed and distributed for publication in the next morning's newspapers.[2]

A piece of legislation passed by Congress in 1795, which is usually referred to as the Militia Act, gave the president the authority to take command of state militia units and transfer them to the federal forces in an emergency—in other words, the militia would then become units of the US Army. President Lincoln made use of his legal training in drafting the proclamation; he closely followed the language of the 1795 Militia Act when writing the call for militia. He began by stating that the laws of the United States "for some time past" have been opposed and obstructed by the States of South Carolina, Georgia, Alabama, Florida, Mississippi, Louisiana, and Texas, "by combinations too powerful to be suppressed by the ordinary course of judicial proceedings, or by the powers vested in the Marshals by law." Because of these combinations, he "thought it fit to call forth" the militia of several states of the Union "to the aggregate number of seventy-five thousand" to "cause the laws to be duly executed" in the seven states mentioned in the proclamation. President Lincoln also summoned Congress to convene on July 4 in a special session, a meeting to consider his proclamation and to appropriate funds for the actions he called for.[3]

"Hopeful, moderate, steadfast," was one description of President Lincoln during the meeting. He was optimistic about the proclamation, that the ninety-day militia would "ultimately translate itself into armed might," but he was not excessively optimistic. When one of the president's advisors made some negative remarks about the South and its ability to hold its own against the men and resources of the North, Lincoln had a ready response for this attitude. "We must not forget," he said, "that the people of the seceded States, like those of the loyal ones, are American citizens, with essentially the same characteristics and powers." He went on to say, in a very quiet and matter-of-fact tone of voice, "We must make up our minds that man for man the soldier from the

South will be a match for the soldier from the North and vice versa." The president was still hoping for a short and limited war but was preparing himself mentally for something a lot longer and bloodier.[4]

In accordance with the terms of surrender, Major Robert Anderson and his command formally evacuated Fort Sumter on Sunday afternoon. "With banners flying, and with drums beating 'Yankee Doodle,' we marched on board the transport that was to take us to the steamship *Baltic*, which drew too much water to pass the bar and was anchored outside." An officer on Major Anderson's staff, Captain Abner Doubleday, gave his recollections of the evacuation. "We were soon on our way to New York."[5] Major Anderson also gave his own concise account of the withdrawal, via telegram to Secretary of War Cameron. He ended his telegram by reporting that " [we] marched out of the fort Sunday afternoon the fourteenth inst. With colors flying and drums beating. Bringing away company and private property and saluting my flag with fifty guns."[6]

When his cabinet meeting ended, President Lincoln's day was far from over. Visitors continued to turn up at the White House throughout the rest of the afternoon and into the night, mostly to pledge their help and backing or to give advice. "The President's room was filled all day as by a general reception,"[7] one biographer wrote. One of the callers was Stephen A. Douglas, Lincoln's opponent since the 1850s as well as in the recent presidential election, who came to offer his support. He told the president that, although he was "unalterably opposed" to the administration "on all its political issues," he was "prepared to sustain the president" in all of his efforts to preserve the Union, to maintain the government, and to defend the capital. Throughout their two-hour conversation, Douglas "spoke of the present and future without any reference to the past."[8] Among the topics they discussed was the president's proclamation. Douglas agreed that state militias should be called up, but he thought that two hundred thousand men should be nationalized instead of seventy-five thousand. President Lincoln was very grateful to have the support of his old adversary. "Now Lincoln could be thankful that across the years of political strife between him and Douglas" the two of them had never deeply offended each other and that "their personal elations had never reached a breaking point."[9]

Douglas was as good as his word. Shortly after his White House visit, he told a sizeable Chicago gathering that there could be no neutrals in the war, only patriots or traitors. "He knew he had trumpets left, and he blew them to mass his cohorts behind Lincoln's maintenance of the Union."[10] This backing was much appreciated by President Lincoln. He was well aware that he would be needing all the help he could get in days to come.

APRIL 15, 1861, MONDAY

# A DEPRESSING MEETING

President Lincoln released his militia proclamation on this Monday morning. The actual text of the document was sent to the press via telegraph, which would allow it to be published in newspapers that day. A passionate outburst of patriotism was the overall reaction to the proclamation throughout the North. In the South, the overwhelming attitude was of hatred for the North and for Abraham Lincoln.

Some newspaper accounts did not indulge in any editorial opinions at all, and simply printed the proclamation as it was issued. Washington's *Evening Star* was one such newspaper. The editor ran the declaration on page 2, under the simple heading, "The President's Proclamation."[1] The *New York Herald's* headline also tried its best to be unbiased toward the South: "A WAR PROCLAMATION: Seventy-Five Thousand Men Ordered Out."[2] The *Philadelphia Inquirer*, on the other hand, was thoroughly prejudiced and made no attempt to hide it. "VOLUNTEERS! VOLUNTEERS!! VOLUNTEERS!!!" began one article. "Young men desirous of rallying round the Standard of the Union, and willing to maintain its time-honored folds unsullied over the ramparts of Fort Sumter, will enroll themselves immediately in the new volunteer Light Artillery Regiment, now rapidly filling up."[3]

And the volunteers came—in Philadelphia, in New York, in Chicago, and in every city and town throughout the North. Governors of every Northern state contacted the War Department to ask how many men they should send in response to the president's proclamation. The governor of Ohio, William Denison, telegraphed President Lincoln, "What portion of the 75,000 militia . . . do you give to Ohio? Great rejoicing here over your proclamation." The president replied, "Thirteen

Regiments."[4] Throughout the day and for many days to come, President Lincoln received many similar messages. Because of Fort Sumter and the president's call for volunteers, the population north of the Mason-Dixon Line was almost rabid with patriotism. Veterans of the War of 1812 and the Mexican War made passionate speeches to civic groups on the subject of loyalty to the Union. In New York City, 250,000 people waved flags and sang "Yankee Doodle" at a pro-Union rally. So many volunteers answered the president's call that some states were overwhelmed by the number that showed up at recruiting stations. The governor of Iowa telegraphed Washington that he raised ten regiments—he had been asked to recruit only one. He had the men, the governor said. What he needed now was for the government to send enough weapons to arm and equip them.

As might have been expected, President Lincoln's proclamation produced just the opposite effect throughout the South. Newspaper editorials railed against Lincoln and his attempt to "coerce" the seceded states into rejoining the Union. Northerners who lived in the Southern states were accused of being spies, and were strongly advised to go back where they came from before they were hanged. As far as the South was concerned, Abe Lincoln could go straight to hell and take his seventy-five thousand volunteers with him.

The governors of the upper South—including Kentucky, Tennessee, and Missouri—were as vehemently against the president's proclamation as the Northern governors were in favor of it. They flatly refused to send any men at all in response to Lincoln's order. The governor of Kentucky telegraphed that his state "will furnish no troops for the wicked purpose of subduing her sister Southern States." Tennessee's governor sent a similarly scathing telegram: his state "will not furnish a single man for the purpose of coercion, but fifty thousand if necessary for the defense of our rights and those of our brethren."[5] In Missouri, the governor sent his defiant message directly to the president: "Your requisition is illegal, unconstitutional, revolutionary, inhuman. . . . Not one man will the State of Missouri furnish to carry on any such unholy crusade."[6] The governors of North Carolina and Delaware also refused to obey President Lincoln's proclamation. Maryland remained "ominously silent."[7]

Not very many people throughout the South were silent. Fanatical anti-Lincoln and pro-Southern rights demonstrations had been in progress since the attack on Fort Sumter on April 12. When word of Lincoln's proclamation reached Richmond and other Southern cities on April 15, the excitement became even more strident. The reaction was the same as in the North, except in reverse—instead of rallying to support the Union, Southerners took to the streets and carried on in support of "Jeff Davis and the Southern Confederacy." In the seceded states, President Lincoln's call for troops increased animosity toward the North as much as it increased hostility toward the South in places like Ohio and New York.

The president and his cabinet went into session at ten o'clock; the meeting lasted nearly all day long. During the course of the session, Secretary of War Simon Cameron agreed not to make any sort of decision without first consulting with General Winfield Scott—rumors had been circulating that Cameron and General Scott did not get along, and that they refused to work together. Secretary Cameron's remark was copied by most of the major newspapers; the *New York Times* reported that "all statements of a difference existing between them" were "without foundation."[8]

The major topic of discussion was the defense of Washington, DC. The Confederate secretary of war, LeRoy Pope Walker, made a well-publicized boast that Confederate troops would capture Washington before the first of May. Two prominent Pennsylvania republicans, Governor Andrew Gregg Curtin and Alexander K. McClure, asked General Scott if this was a possibility. The general admitted that the capital would not be easy to defend, and that General Beauregard had a large army under his command, but he insisted that Washington was not in any real danger and could not be taken. While this conversation was going on, President Lincoln sat and quietly listened. He did not agree with General Scott's opinion, and remarked that if he were General Beauregard he would take Washington.[9]

President Lincoln knew that the capital was in danger. If General Beauregard moved his army across the Potomac over the Long Bridge, there would not be very much that Lincoln could do to stop him. The city was defended mainly by volunteers—well-meaning but undertrained amateurs in uniform. General Beauregard could brush these amateurs aside and do anything he wanted, including capture the president and his entire cabinet. The president was both frightened and depressed by this awareness. If rebel forces captured Washington—which seemed more than possible at the time—the civil war would be over before it started.

Abraham Lincoln was melancholy and depressed by nature. Knowing that the US government could be overthrown by a determined force of secessionist soldiers, even a small force, made him feel even more dismal than usual. "For Lincoln, the plain physical realities of war rang in his ears and marched in front of his eyes and registered painfully in his melancholy mind," a biographer commented.[10] He desperately needed some good news, or at least some small piece of encouragement. Instead, he heard nothing but things that made him feel unhappy and dejected.

# APRIL 16, 1861, TUESDAY

# AN UNEVENTFUL DAY

ollowing a long and not very encouraging day on Monday, President Lincoln was relieved that Tuesday turned out to be relatively calm and uneventful. The newspapers were filled with talk about the war and what had happened in Charleston during the past week, but there was nothing that was particularly alarming. One headline stated, "THE NORTH AROUSED FOR WAR."[1] The president already knew this; he did not need a newspaper headline to remind him.

The only correspondence President Lincoln sent was a note to Secretary of War Simon Cameron. He asked the secretary to appoint Benjamin Hardin Helm to the post of paymaster for the Union army. Benjamin Helm was married to Emilie Todd, the half sister of Mary Todd Lincoln, which made him the president's brother-in-law. He did not accept the position. Instead, he accepted a commission in the Confederate army—he was born in Kentucky—and was promoted to the rank of brigadier general. General Helm died of wounds received at Chickamauga, September 21, 1863. The president also requested one Robert A. Kinzie to be appointed paymaster of Kansas. He had no other activities: no meetings, no conferences, no speeches. The calm and uneventful days would be few and far between from now on, as the president probably guessed, and he did his best to relax as much as possible—as much as possible for him, at least.

Ulysses S. Grant heard the news of Fort Sumter in Galena, Illinois, where he was still a clerk at his father's leather goods store. When "the call of the President for 75,000 men was heard throughout the Northern states," a meeting to organize a company of volunteers was held in the town's courthouse. Because Grant was a West Point graduate and had seen active service during the Mexican War, he was asked to preside over the meeting. As soon as the quota of men for the volunteer company was met, which did not take very long, he announced that he "would aid the company in every way that I could." Many years later, Grant announced, with some emphasis, "I never went into our leather store after that meeting, to put up a package or do other business." He left Galena behind and never looked back.[2]

James Longstreet was paymaster at Albuquerque, New Mexico, when the news of Fort Sumter ended all speculation concerning the "war-cloud" in the east, as he put it. He had already made up his mind that, when the war finally came, he would resign his US Army commission and join the still-organizing Confederate forces. Several of Longstreet's fellow officers tried to talk him out of leaving the Union army. One of the officers was a Captain Gibbs of the Mounted Rifles. During the course of a "long but pleasant conversation" with Captain Gibbs, Longstreet asked him what he would do if his state seceded from the Union and called upon him to defend its borders. Captain Gibbs admitted that he would "obey the call" and fight for his state.

Not every Southerner who felt duty bound to join the Confederate forces was an officer. Another member of the Mounted Rifles, a sergeant from Virginia, asked if he would be able to follow Longstreet's example—resign from the US Army and return to his native state. Longstreet explained that private soldiers and non-commissioned officers could not leave the army without the permission of the War Department, and that the sergeant would not be able to join the Confederate army until his enlistment expired. Officers could resign their commissions, but privates and non-coms did not have that option; they were bound by their oaths and by the terms of their enlistment. A good many soldiers would simply ignore their enlistment terms and would join the Confederate army despite their oaths.

Somewhere during the long journey from Albuquerque to Richmond, where he would report to General Beauregard at the War Department, someone asked Longstreet how long he thought the war would last. "At least three years," he responded. This came as a surprising answer—most people, on both sides, expected the war to be over by the end of the year, if not sooner. It turned out to be a lot longer and costlier than anyone, including James Longstreet, could ever have imagined.[3]

After resigning his position as superintendent of the Louisiana State Seminary of Learning and Military Academy in January, William Tecumseh Sherman became president of the Fifth Street Railroad in St. Louis. He later recalled that everyone talked of war. A house near the Sherman residence, on the northwest corner of Fifth and Pine, served as Confederate headquarters, where a Confederate flag was publicly displayed. There was also a "rebel" camp in the vicinity, along with several companies of US Army troops. Sherman tried his best to keep out of the dispute but, after Fort Sumter, knew that he would have to become involved—like his friend Ulysses S. Grant, he was a graduate of West Point. He was more than correct. At the end of May, he received a message from his brother Charles in Washington—he had been appointed a colonel of the Thirteenth Regular Infantry, and that he was wanted in Washington "immediately."

When he arrived in Washington, Sherman discovered that President Lincoln had called for seventy-five thousand state militia volunteers— "I . . . found that the Government was trying to rise to a level with the occasion." He was surprised by the news; somehow, he must have missed it during his move from Louisiana to St. Louis. He was even more surprised by the number of men that had been called up, and remarked that even this number "seemed to me utterly inadequate . . . still it was none of my business." He had come to Washington to join his regiment, not second-guess the president. "I took the oath of office, and was furnished with a list of officers, appointed to my regiment, which was still incomplete."[4]

Now that he had been officially commissioned as a colonel of the Thirteenth Infantry Regiment, Sherman sent his wife and family back to Lancaster, Ohio, his hometown. He also resigned his position as president of the Fifth Street Railroad, to take effect at the end of May, after only two months' service, and began his career as an army officer. The war was going to be a very long one, he said, longer than any of the politicians thought, and he would play a very crucial part in it.[5]

# INCREASING ANXIETIES

President Lincoln spent part of his morning tending to political appointments. He asked Secretary of State William H. Seward to send his brief on candidates for secretary of the Nebraska Territory, and sent a memo to Attorney General Edward Bates requesting the names of candidates for a judge as well as for the attorney general of that territory. He also commissioned one Albert T. Enos, who was a friend of a friend, as major in the Eighth Pennsylvania Regiment, and asked Gideon Welles to add his recommendation to an acquaintance seeking a position in the army, presumably as an officer. This was part of the president's usual morning routine; political appointees were always presenting themselves, looking for contacts and positions.[1]

But something completely out of the ordinary, an event that would change the entire course of the war, was taking place about a hundred miles south of the White House. In Richmond, the Virginia Convention voted to secede from the Union, by a vote of 88 to 55. During the course of that session, former governor Henry Wise announced that units of the Virginia militia were in the process of capturing the federal armory at Harpers Ferry at the very moment. Governor Wise knew all about that operation because he had planned it himself. Actually, Wise was being premature; the attack on Harpers Ferry did not take place until the next day, April 18, but the consequence was the same. Virginia had not only divorced itself from the Union and joined the Confederacy but also had declared war on the United States. The capture of the Harpers Ferry arsenal was a foregone conclusion—the Forty-Seventh US Army defenders were easily overwhelmed by several companies of Virginia militia. Before abandoning the fort, the army regulars set fire to the building and left it to the attackers. The fires were quickly extinguished. All of the machinery and equipment was saved, and every salvaged weapon—about sixteen thousand rifles—was sent off to Richmond, where they were distributed to units throughout the Confederacy.

The loss of Virginia both depressed and angered President Lincoln. Virginia was the most heavily populated of the Southern states, as well as one of the wealthiest. Now all of that wealth and all those resources would be turned against the United States. The Tredegar Iron Works in Richmond, which had manufactured cannon and heavy artillery for the US Army, would now be making weapons for the Confederacy. Also, the president feared that other states in the upper South, including the vital states of Kentucky and Maryland, would be encouraged to leave the Union by Virginia's example. "Yes, Lincoln was angry with the people of Virginia," one historian wrote. They had allowed their rebellion to take hold within sight of his office windows at the White House. The president could actually see Confederate flags waving just across the Potomac in Alexandria. "If he had to, he would use force against those people over there." It was becoming increasingly evident that he would have no other option except using force.[2]

President Lincoln's anger with "those people over there" increased exponentially when he read what Jefferson Davis had to say about him and his call for seventy-five thousand volunteers. President Davis made his statement, which amounted to his counterproclamation to Lincoln's decree, from the Confederate capital at Montgomery, Alabama. But this made no difference to Lincoln. In his counterproclamation, Davis accused Abraham Lincoln, by name, of planning to invade the Confederacy "with an armed force" with the purpose of subjugating the "free people" of the South "to the dominion of a foreign power." Because of Lincoln's planned invasion, it was the duty of the Confederacy to "defend the rights and liberties of the people by all the means which the laws of nations and the usages of civilized warfare place at its disposal."[3]

In his proclamation, President Davis went on to name exactly how he intended to wage war against Lincoln and his "wanton and wicked aggression"—he would ask the owners of civilian ships to apply for "letters of marque and reprisal," which was a license issued by the Confederate government for ships owned by private individuals to attack any merchant ship flying the Stars and Stripes.[4] The Confederacy could not afford its own navy, so President Davis asked private individuals to employ their ships to conduct open warfare against the US merchant fleet. These vessels, usually referred to as "privateers," would keep anything they managed to take from these captured merchant vessels. Privateers had a slightly different standing under international law than did pirates. Privateers performed the same function as U-boats in another war, except that U-boats were commissioned as warships by a belligerent nation.

If President Lincoln still harbored any notions of a limited war at this point in time, Jefferson Davis's proclamation calling for privateers put an abrupt end to them. He not only had an insurrection on his hands, but now had a naval war to deal with as well. During the next three months, Confederate privateers would capture two dozen merchant vessels. Owners of Northern shipping firms panicked. The president now looked for a way to counter Jefferson Davis's latest challenge.

Another problem, a lot more immediate, also worried the president. During the morning, he conferred with General Winfield Scott on the subject of the defense of Washington. The general reported that three or four regiments from Massachusetts were expected to arrive here "in two or three days." President Lincoln was hoping they would arrive a lot sooner than that. Washington had become an isolated city, and was threatened by attack from both Virginia and possibly from Maryland as well. Another regiment had been sent to Fort Monroe, about 180 miles south of Washington near Hampton Roads, Virginia. And a third was slated to defend Harpers Ferry. Harpers Ferry was captured before any reinforcements could arrive, but Fort Monroe remained in Union hands throughout the war. General Scott also had the idea of reinforcing Gosport Navy Yard, in Portsmouth, Virginia, recommending "two or three companies of regulars to assist in the defence of that establishment." But the shipyard was also captured, along with all of its weapons and facilities. The general sounded optimistic about surrounding the capital with federal troops, telling the president, "To night, all the important avenues leading into Washington, shall be well guarded." President Lincoln's fears were not lessened by what General Scott had to say. He wanted those Massachusetts regiments in Washington as quickly as humanly possible, before secessionist forces could seize the city along with its government buildings and facilities, including the White House.[5]

One thing, at least, went right for the president on this mostly dismal day—USS *Powhatan* finally arrived at Fort Pickens. Six hundred men, along with their equipment and horses, landed at the fort during the night and continued going ashore into the morning hours. President Lincoln wanted Fort Pickens to be held by Union forces at all hazards, as he announced; he finally had his wish granted. The harbor, one of the best and most strategic in the Gulf of Mexico, would remain in Union hands throughout the war.

# APRIL 18, 1861, THURSDAY
## A REGRETTED LOSS

Among the things on President Lincoln's mind on this Thursday morning was a misunderstanding with his secretary of state, William H. Seward. Secretary Seward apparently told someone that the president had some sort of disagreement with Thurlow Weed, an advisor and associate of Lincoln's, and that the two were no longer on friendly terms. He sent a short and to-the-point note to Seward to straighten him out on the matter. "You astonish me by saying Mr. Weed understands there is some alienation, or enmity of feeling, on my part towards him," President Lincoln wrote. "Nothing like it. I shall be glad to see him any time, & have wondered at not have [*sic*] seen [him] here already. Yours very truly." With all the other problems that occupied the president's thoughts, he did not need his secretary of state to spread gossip about him and his political allies. He sent off his sharp little note and got on with the rest of his day.[1]

And there were a great many things for him to deal with, none of which were as easily disposed of as his minor dispute with Secretary Seward. One of the most prominent items was the matter of Colonel Robert E. Lee, and what the colonel was going to do now that Virginia had seceded from the Union. President Lincoln sent Frank Blair Sr., the father of Postmaster General Montgomery Blair, to meet with Colonel Lee and ask him to become commander of all Union forces—to replace General Winfield Scott, who realized that he was too old and infirm to carry on as general in chief. The two met at the Blair residence in Washington on this Thursday, the day after the Virginia Convention voted to secede. After the war, Lee would recall that he had a conversation with "Mr. Francis Blair" regarding command of the US Army, "which was at his invitation, and, as I understand it, at the instruction of President Lincoln." After listening to what Blair had to say, Colonel Lee remarked, "I declined the offer he made me . . . stating, as candidly and courteously as I could, that, though opposed to secession and deprecating war, I could take no part in an invasion of the Southern States."[2]

Immediately after leaving the Blair residence, Colonel Lee went to see General Scott. "I went directly from the interview with Mr. Blair to the office of General Scott: told him of the proposition that had been made to me, and my decision."[3] During the course of the meeting, General Scott "used every argument he could bring to bear to induce him to remain with the Union." The general also implied that, when he retired, he "felt sure that Robert Lee would be offered his position," the position being general in command of all Union forces.[4] But Colonel Lee told General Scott the same thing he said to Francis Blair: he could not, and would not, take any action against the South, especially against Virginia. Two days later, on April 20, he submitted his formal resignation to General Scott: "Since my interview with you on the 18th instant I have felt that I ought not longer to retain my commission in the army. I therefore tender my resignation, which I request you will recommend for acceptance."[5]

Robert E. Lee considered himself to be a Virginian, not an American. "At base, Lee was more Southern than he was American," one biographer was moved to comment.[6] He was certainly a Virginian first and an American second. Virginia had been the home of the Lee family long before the United States ever came into existence. Colonel Lee's great-great-grandfather, Richard Lee, lived in Virginia as early as 1646. Even though he had spent his entire adult life in the US Army, Colonel Lee could not bring himself to fight against what he described as his "native state." He told General Scott, "Save. in the defence of my native State, I never desire again to draw my sword."[7]

General Scott was disappointed by Colonel Lee's decision. He had served with Lee in the Mexican War, when Lee was Captain Lee of the Engineers; Captain Lee was probably one of General Scott's most trusted officers. He knew that he lost his best commander; he referred to Robert E. Lee as "[t]he very best soldier" he "ever saw in the field."[8]

The news of Robert E. Lee's defection put President Lincoln in one of his deep depressions, which made him feel miserable, anxious, and apprehensive. He could not fathom how an officer with Colonel Lee's background, training, and experience—a West Point graduate, a veteran of the Mexican War with a brilliant war record, superintendent of West Point—could give up his career and join forces with turncoats and deserters. "In Lincoln's view," a biographer wrote, "Lee was a strange and inexplicable man."[9] As far as President Lincoln was concerned, Robert E. Lee was nothing but a traitor. It would take three years for him to find a replacement for this extraordinary officer, three years and several generals and numerous lost battles before he discovered Ulysses S. Grant.

Robert E. Lee was not the only officer who resigned his commission. About one-third of all the US Army's officers also transferred their allegiance to the Confederacy. Among them were Thomas J. "Stonewall" Jackson, Nathan Bedford Forrest, Albert Sidney Johnston, Jeb Stuart, Ambrose P. Hill, and John Bell Hood, all of whom would become prominent generals in the Confederate army and would wreak havoc on Union forces during the early part of the war. Their defection left the US Army in a shambles. Only Winfield Scott and one other general, seventy-seven-year-old John Wool, had ever commanded armies. But of all the officers who went South with their states, President Lincoln would regret the loss of Robert E. Lee most of all. A prominent Civil War historian was moved to remark that "perhaps the greatest asset that Virginia brought to the cause of Southern independence was Robert E. Lee."[10]

After having gone through another less-than-encouraging day, President Lincoln decided to go to bed early. But he had not been asleep very long when he was awakened by his private secretary, John Hay, who had some distressing news. Hay had been told that a young Virginian was in town boasting that he was going to carry out some sort of sinister and spectacular plot within the next forty-eight hours. This plot sounded suspiciously like an attempt to assassinate the president; with the cur-

When Virginia seceded from the Union, Robert E. Lee resigned his commission in the US Army. President Lincoln knew that he lost his best commander.

rent atmosphere in Washington, and given the attitude of secessionists toward the president, such a threat was more than feasible. But the president was not impressed by Hay's warning. It would take a lot more than a vague threat to make him get out of bed and interrupt a good night's sleep. After listening to what his secretary had to say, President Lincoln just "quietly grinned."[11]

# A CONTROVERSIAL PROCLAMATION

**P**resident Lincoln was becoming more anxious and depressed with each passing day. He was all too aware that Washington was in grave danger—the city was under siege. Frederick W. Seward, son of Secretary of State William Seward, wrote that the capital had been "suddenly transformed into an isolated city, in an enemies' country, threatened with attack from the hostile communities all around it."[1] The city was surrounded by secessionists; an attack was expected at any time. Telegraph lines had been torn down by Confederate sympathizers, which made the situation inside Washington even more tense—rumors were now the primary source for news and all information.

And the news was not good, at least not for the residents of Washington—the latest word was that armed secessionist mobs and members of the Virginia militia were on the march to capture the city and overthrow the government. The president heard these rumors, along with everyone else, and was even more worried. He realized that Washington was inadequately defended, to put it mildly—only six companies of regular soldiers, about six hundred men, and about twice than many undertrained volunteers were on hand to guard against an attack. Additionally, about five hundred members of the Pennsylvania militia had arrived the day before. But these men were even less prepared for a fight than the other volunteers—they arrived without any weapons or equipment. When these volunteers passed through Baltimore on their way to Washington, they were given some very hostile stares from that city's residents—Northerners, especially members of the volunteer militia, were anything but welcome.

President Lincoln recognized that he did not have nearly enough troops on hand to protect Washington from a determined mob of secessionists. Reinforcements were on their way from other Northern cities—one unit reported to be heading to Washington was the Sixth Massachusetts Regiment—but he had no idea when they might arrive. It was a helpless feeling. Actually, the Sixth Massachusetts had already arrived in Baltimore, on their way to Washington. No railway line ran directly through Baltimore, which meant that the troops had to leave the train at the city's eastern terminal and move through the city on foot to the Camden Station before they could board the Washington train. "At the Washington depot an immense crowd assembled," according to a newspaper account of what happened next. "The rioters attacked the soldiers, who fired on the mob. Several were wounded, and some fatally."[2]

The rioters threw bricks and paving stones at the troops; the soldiers of the Sixth Massachusetts responded by firing into the crowd. The Massachusetts men did manage to make their way across town to the Camden Station, but four men were dead by the time they reached their destination. Twelve civilians also died, and many more on both sides were wounded.

President Lincoln was officially informed of the melee later in the day, via a telegram that was signed by the governor of Maryland, Thomas Hicks, as well as by the mayor of Baltimore, George W. Brown. The telegram stated that "a collision between citizens of Baltimore and troops" had taken place.[3] Mayor Brown also sent a letter dated April 18, only the day before, to warn that the residents of Baltimore were "exasperated" by federal troops passing through their city. "It is my solemn duty to inform you," Mayor Brown wrote, "that it is not possible for more soldiers to pass through Baltimore unless they fight their way at every step." His warning turned out to be chillingly correct.[4]

With everything else that was worrying him, President Lincoln did not need a riot in Baltimore to increase his anxiety. He would have been even more angry and upset if he had known that the governor of

Virginia, John Letcher, had sent two thousand muskets to the Baltimore rioters, and that Jefferson Davis was encouraging Governor Letcher to keep on supplying them with weapons. "Sustain Baltimore if practicable," Davis wrote to the governor. "We will reinforce you."[5] Baltimore was only forty miles away from Washington. Jefferson Davis's next move might be to reinforce the Virginia militia and direct Governor Letcher to attack the capital. "From the mountain-tops and valleys to the shores of the sea, there is one wild shout of fierce resolve to capture Washington City at all and every human hazard," the *Richmond Examiner* barked.[6]

So many Confederate sympathizers lived in Maryland and in Washington itself that rumors began to spread of a plan to kidnap President Lincoln and his wife Mary. General Winfield Scott advised Mrs. Lincoln to leave Washington and return to Springfield, Illinois, with her sons Tad and Willie. But Mary Lincoln refused to go—she had no intention of leaving the White House for the provinciality of Springfield, and she also did not want to leave her husband. She enjoyed being First Lady. She also felt perfectly safe and well protected in the White House. General Scott and his suggestions were both quietly ignored.

Something else occupied the president's thoughts this Friday morning, an item that was not nearly as pressing or immediate as the capture of Washington but was just as vital in dealing with the war against the Confederacy. In response to Jefferson Davis calling for privateers to operate against Northern merchant shipping, President Lincoln announced that he was imposing a blockade of all the ports of seven seceded states. The offending states were listed in the proclamation's first sentence: "the States of South Carolina, Georgia, Alabama, Florida, Mississippi, Louisiana, and Texas." The declaration went on to state that any person who "shall molest" a vessel of the United States "under the pretended authority of the said States" would be "held amenable to the laws of the United States for the prevention and punishment of piracy."[7] In other words, any crew member of any privateer who acted under the authority of one of Jefferson Davis's letters of marque would be treated as a pirate and hanged.

Mary Lincoln refused to leave Washington despite rumors of a plot to kidnap her.

Despite President Davis's declared intention to attack US merchant vessels on the high seas, President Lincoln's blockade proclamation did not meet with unanimous support throughout the North. The main objection was that, by blockading Southern ports, the president had inadvertently recognized Confederate independence. Cantankerous old Thaddeus Stevens, a radical Republican congressman from Pennsylvania who had never been one of President Lincoln's more enthusiastic supporters, famously scolded the president by telling him, "If the rebel States were still in the Union, and only in treasonable revolt against the government, we were blockading ourselves"—a nation only imposed a blockade against another belligerent nation. As Congressman Stevens explained, President Lincoln had actually acknowledged the seceded states as a belligerent power and an independent country by issuing his proclamation. This was, he explained, "in accordance with the law of nations."[8]

But the president was not fazed by Thaddeus Stevens or by his opinion. "I see the point now, but I don't know anything about the law of nations, and I thought it was all right." Thad Stevens seemed surprised by this reply, as well as by the calmness of Lincoln's manner. "As a lawyer, Mr. Lincoln," he said, "I should have supposed you would have seen the difficulty at once."

"Mr. Lincoln" shrugged off this remark as well. "Oh, well," he replied, "I'm a good enough lawyer in a Western law court, I suppose, but we don't practise the law of nations up there, and I supposed Seward knew all about it, and I left it to him. But it's done now and can't be helped, so we must get along as well as we can." He had made up his mind and issued his proclamation, and coolly stated his case. Considering his agitated state of mind, the calmness of his reply probably surprised President Lincoln as much as Thaddeus Stevens.

After listening to what the president had to say, Thad Stevens concluded that "Mr. Lincoln was right . . . the rebel States were thenceforth an independent belligerent. Not an independent nation, of course, but an independent belligerent."[9]

The blockade would be a main factor in the coming war. Union warships reduced the number of merchant vessels entering Southern ports by about two-thirds, which dramatically hindered the South's war effort. Everything from gunpowder to sewing needles became scarce. After the war, a Confederate naval officer admitted that the US Navy's blockade "shut the Confederacy out from the world, deprived it of supplies, weakened its military and naval strength."[10] The president had taken a major step toward isolating the Confederacy—which he referred to as "the so-called Confederate States of America"—within a week of Fort Sumter.

Abraham Lincoln's state of mind at this point in time can best be described as uneasy. During the past week, he had endured the surrender of Fort Sumter, the secession of Virginia, the defection of some of the US Army's most accomplished and capable officers to the Confederacy, Jefferson Davis calling for privateers, and the Baltimore riot. It had been an unnerving week. When an acquaintance named Mary Darby Smith came to visit President Lincoln at the White House, he was not in a very receptive mood. Miss Smith asked the president to write something in her autograph book; he could not think of anything very congenial. The only thing he could manage was, "Whoever in later-times shall see this, and look at the date, will readily excuse the writer for not having indulged in sentiment, or poetry. With all kind regards for Miss Smith. A. LINCOLN."[11] He hoped the overall situation regarding the hostilities would improve, along with his own mood. And he especially hoped that Washington would not be occupied by secessionists during the week to come. But there was no guarantee that the state of affairs would get any better as far as the conflict with the South was concerned. And there was an excellent possibility that Washington might be in enemy hands within the next seven days. Given the current plight of the country, and in his existing frame of mind, there was no possibility of his thinking of anything cheerful or poetic to write in a girl's autograph album. He was too preoccupied with other, more discouraging, issues.

APRIL 20, 1861, SATURDAY
# "PRACTICAL AND PROPER" ADVICE

The Baltimore riot was still very much on President Lincoln's mind, along with the death of the four Massachusetts troops. He sent a letter, addressed jointly to Maryland governor Thomas Hicks and Baltimore mayor George W. Brown, on the subject of sending more soldiers through Baltimore to defend Washington. He began by thanking both "for your efforts to keep the peace in the trying situation in which you are placed" before getting to the point. "For the future, troops *must* be brought here," to Washington, President Lincoln wrote, "but I make no point of bringing them *through* Baltimore."[1]

He went on to say that he had no "military knowledge" himself. But he had spoken with General Winfield Scott at eight o'clock that morning, and the general had given him some "practical and proper" advice: "March them *around* Baltimore, and not through it." The president hoped that Governor Hicks and Mayor Brown agreed with the general's assessment, since "[b]y this, a collision of the people of Baltimore with the troops will be avoided, unless they go out of their way to seek it." He ended by saying emphatically, "I hope you will exert your influence to prevent this." In response to the president's letter, Mayor Brown sent a terse reply: he promised to preserve the peace provided that "no more troops will be brought through the city." It looked as though President Lincoln had managed to avert another confrontation, at least for the time being.[2]

But even though President Lincoln avoided further riots, the situation in Maryland still nagged at him. Governor Hicks was anything but a secessionist, but the president feared that he might be pressured into siding against the Union by pro-rebel members of the legislature. And

Mayor Brown was only a lukewarm Unionist, at best; his loyalty could not be relied upon, especially in a crisis. After thinking about the tense state of affairs in Baltimore and the alarming number—to Lincoln's way of thinking—of secessionists in the Maryland legislature, the president decided to ask Governor Hicks and Mayor Brown to come to the White House for a conference. He sent this telegram to both men at three o'clock in the morning: "Gov. Hicks, I desire to consult with you and the Mayor of Baltimore relative to preserving the peace of Maryland. Please come immediately by special train, which you can take at Baltimore, or if necessary one can be sent from hence. Answer forthwith."[3]

Governor Hicks was not in Baltimore at the time, but Mayor Brown received the president's telegram and wired back that he was "coming immediately."[4]

# DEFUSING AN AWKWARD SITUATION

**T**he mayor was as good as his word. Along with three *associates*, he took an early train and arrived in Washington at about 10:00 a.m. When they arrived at the White House, Mayor Brown and his companions were escorted to a meeting with President Lincoln, members of the cabinet, and General Winfield Scott. According to one source, "A long conversation and discussion ensued." During the course of this conversation, the president emphasized his desire to avoid another "collision with the people," but he also insisted on the "absolute necessity" of moving troops through Maryland for defense of Washington. He made it clear that the security of the capital was his chief concern. General Scott was also called upon to give his opinion, "which the General gave at length." He explained that troops could go through Maryland without going near Baltimore; they might be transported to Washington by way of Annapolis. The secretary of war, Simon Cameron, agreed that no troops would be sent through Baltimore if they were allowed to proceed by a different route.[1]

Mayor Brown assured President Lincoln that he would use "all lawful means" of preventing Baltimore residents from leaving the city to attack any federal troops, but he also stated that he could not guarantee anything more than his "best efforts." The citizens of Baltimore were restless and agitated. The "excitement was great," Brown told the president, and went on to say that it would be impossible for anyone to answer for the consequences of Northern troops "anywhere within our borders." Doing his best to be as diplomatic as possible, the president acknowledged the problems facing Mayor Brown and could only ask that Baltimore city officials did their best to "use their best efforts" to uphold the law. The interview ended with President Lincoln once again giving his assurances that no more troops would be sent through Baltimore. Mayor Brown seemed satisfied with what the president had to say; President Lincoln was relieved that Brown was content with the outcome of the meeting.[2]

Mayor Brown was just about the leave the White House with his associates when he received an alarming telegram from the president of the Baltimore and Ohio Railroad—a trainload of federal troops had just arrived at Cockeysville, about seventeen miles north of Baltimore. It looked as though these troops were headed straight for Baltimore, and the city was in a panic. The telegram read: "Three thousand Northern troops are reported to be at Cockeysville; intense excitement prevails; churches have been dismissed, and the people are arming in mass. To prevent terrific bloodshed, the result of your interview and arrangement is awaited."[3]

The mayor immediately showed the telegram to President Lincoln, which gave him "great surprise." He immediately reconvened the cabinet, recalled General Scott, and resumed the meeting with Mayor Brown. The president explained that he had no idea there were any troops at Cockeysville and, "in the most decided way," ordered them back either to York or Harrisburg. General Scott issued the order and was informed that the army units were not scheduled to be sent to Baltimore. They were on their way to Harrisburg and then to Philadelphia.[4] Mayor Brown was immediately given this information and, for the second time, was assured by the president that no troops would be sent through Baltimore. And for the second time, the mayor seemed satisfied by these assurances. When he returned to Baltimore, he reported what President Lincoln had to say.

This was a very clever move on President Lincoln's part. He not only had defused the Baltimore situation but also had strengthened his own position in Maryland with the state's pro-Union citizenry. "He did not expect to appease the Maryland rebels," according to one biography, but he very skillfully "made them clearly responsible for further bloodshed, should any occur, and thereby to hold the Maryland Unionists."[5] He might have been stressed and anxious, and constantly worried about defending Washington from secessionist attacks, but this did not interfere with his political skill or his ability to think while under pressure.

## APRIL 22, 1861, MONDAY

# THE PRESIDENT SPEAKS HIS MIND

**P**resident Lincoln's problems with defending Washington, and especially with moving troops through Maryland on their way to Washington, would not go away. Two days after promising both Mayor Brown and Governor Hicks—in writing—that he would send all army units around Baltimore instead of through it, Governor Hicks of Maryland wrote to ask the president "to send no more troops through that State."[1] The governor not only opposed soldiers going through Baltimore but also objected to Union troops traveling through any part of Maryland. In the same letter, Governor Hicks also suggested that Lord Lyons, the British ambassador residing in Washington, should be called upon "to act as mediator between the contending parties of our country."[2]

President Lincoln was not daunted by the governor's letter. He intended to send troops to Washington through Maryland, and did not give a damn whether Hicks liked it or not—he was determined to defend the capital. And he had no intention of allowing the representative of any foreign power, including Britain, to intervene in an American domestic dispute—especially not Lord Lyons, who made no secret of the fact that he despised Abraham Lincoln. Lord Lyons described President Lincoln as "a rough Westerner of the lowest origins" and a "rough farmer," among other unflattering things.[3] As far as he was concerned, Lincoln was nothing but an ignorant Midwestern peasant who had no business being president.

Probably because he did not trust himself, or his temper, to respond to Governor Hicks or his arrogant letter, President Lincoln asked Secretary of State William Seward to draft a reply. It turned out to be a

**200**

good and judicious decision. Secretary Seward's letter was to the point, but also was courteous and conciliatory. He explained that it was General Winfield Scott who had chosen to send Northern troops through Maryland "upon consultation with prominent magistrates and citizens of Maryland." Secretary Seward went on to say that any route used by army units in transit to Washington would be "further removed from the populous cities of the State, and with the expectation that it would, therefore, be the least objectionable one." As far as intervention by Lord Lyons was concerned, Seward said, "no domestic contention . . . ought in any case, to be referred to any foreign arbitrament [arbitration]."[4] (An editorial in a New York newspaper said the same thing about British intervention, but put it a bit more directly: "the people of the United States can settle their own differences without calling in a European monarchy to do it for them.")[5]

Secretary Seward spoke eloquently and persuasively to Governor Hicks, which President Lincoln appreciated. In his present state of mind, he knew that anything he said would have been offensive, and probably alienating. He realized that he would need the support of Governor Hicks if he was to keep Maryland from seceding from the Union. He also knew his own limitations, and that Secretary Seward would be much more diplomatic in his reply to Governor Hicks. With the help of his secretary of state, President Lincoln had defused a potentially confrontational situation—for the second time in three days.

But the day was not yet over; neither was President Lincoln's war of words with the City of Baltimore. The president received a group of young men, described as a "committee of fifty representing the Young Men's Christian Associations of Baltimore," shortly after reading Governor Hicks's letter. The committee came with a prepared statement for the president; the statement consisted of a number of peace terms for the government to follow. The visitors apparently thought their terms were reasonable and practical, but President Lincoln emphatically did not agree. As far as he was concerned, the conditions were completely one sided—he dismissed them as "peace on any terms," since they called for surrendering to the secessionists and for keeping all federal troops out of Maryland. They were certainly more unreasonable than the terms suggested by Governor Hicks and Mayor Brown.[6]

After listening in silence to what the group had to say, President Lincoln responded with a few well-chosen words of his own. All of his anger and pent-up frustrations toward Baltimore and its secessionist citizens came out in one long, bad-tempered burst. "You, gentlemen, come here to me and ask for peace on any terms, and yet have no word of condemnation for those who are making war on us," he began. "You express great horror of bloodshed, and yet would not lay a straw in the way of those who are organizing in Virginia and elsewhere to capture this city. The rebels attack Fort Sumter, and your citizens attack troops sent to the defense of the Government, and the lives and property in Washington, and yet you would have me break my oath and surrender the Government without a blow." Warming to his subject, he continued in the same manner and tone of voice: "There is no Washington in that—no Jackson in that—no manhood nor honor in that. I have no desire to invade the South; but I must have troops to defend this Capital. Geographically it lies surrounded by the soil of Maryland; and mathematically the necessity exists that they should come over her territory. Our men are not moles, and can't dig under the earth; they are not birds, and can't fly through the air. There is no way but to march across, and that they must do. But in doing this there is no need of collision. Keep your rowdies in Baltimore, and there will be no bloodshed. Go home and tell your people that if they will not attack us, we will not attack them; but if they do attack us, we will return it, and that severely."[7]

President Lincoln realized that he did not have to use any diplomacy with the members of the Baltimore committee, and did not even make an attempt at being tactful. He probably wished that he could have used the same language with Governor Hicks and Mayor Brown. The committee members must have been taken completely aback by the scolding, and just listened in stunned silence. The remarks did not have any effect on the fifty men but were highly therapeutic for the president, who had held his tongue concerning the Baltimore crisis up to that point. When his guests left the White House, President Lincoln would have had the pleasure of knowing that he finally had his say on the matter, especially since it had been delivered in a manner that was anything but diplomatic. He had finally spoken his mind.

# "WHY DON'T THEY COME!"

**P**resident Lincoln sent this memo to the secretary of the navy, Gideon Welles, sometime during the day this Tuesday: "Dear Sir: I think I saw three vessels go up to the Navy Yard just now. Will you please send down and learn what they are? Yours truly A. LINCOLN."[1] He was hoping that the ships were carrying troops to reinforce the undermanned Washington garrison, troops that he had been expecting for some time. The president never received a reply to his memo; at least there is no reply in the Lincoln papers.

No reinforcements reached Washington on Tuesday, which did not help soothe the president's jangled nerves. He paced the floor as he waited for news. For the past few days, newspapers had been reporting that troops had departed for the capital. The Seventh New York Regiment had already left for Washington, at least according to news accounts, and other units were also said to be on their way. But no troops ever arrived. Crowds gathered at the rail station every day to wait for a trainload of soldiers but always went home disappointed. President Lincoln was just as disappointed, and a lot more anxious. He paced back and forth for nearly a half hour on this Tuesday afternoon, stopping to look "long and wistfully out of the window down the Potomac in the direction of the expected ships." At one point he stopped and "broke out with irrepressible anguish in the repeated exclamation, 'Why don't they come! Why don't they come!'?"[2]

The president had good reason to be nervous. Washington faced "a degree of real peril such as had not menaced the capital since the British invasion in 1814."[3] If the capital was not actually under siege, it was at least surrounded by enemies. Attorney General Edward Bates made this alarming entry in his diary: "The People of Maryland and Virginia are in a ferment, a furore, regardless of law and common sense . . . both in Maryland and Virginia, they are in open arms against us, and by violence and terror they have silenced every friend of the Government."[4] President Lincoln later recalled that it had become necessary for him to choose whether "I should let the Government at once fall into ruin, or whether, availing myself of the broader powers conferred by the Constitution in cases of insurrection, I would make an effort to save it, with all its blessings, for the present age and for posterity."[5]

Residents of Washington were also becoming alarmed. Observers noted that "strangers, visitors, and transient sojourners in the city became possessed of an uncontrollable desire to get away." Clerks and government workers left the city in a panic, "by whatever chances of transportation offered themselves." Any number of army and navy officers also left the city, but for a different reason—they were going south to join the Confederate forces. The commander of Washington Navy Yard, Commodore Franklin Buchanan, left the service along with several of his subordinate officers and joined the Confederate navy. And Captain John B. Magruder, in charge of an artillery unit assigned to defend the capital, also left the city to join the Southern armed forces. Captain Magruder's defection hit President Lincoln particularly hard—only three days earlier, the captain had come to the White House and "repeated over and over again his asseverations and protestations of loyalty and fidelity" to the president.[6]

It seemed that everything and everyone was conspiring to put President Lincoln in a worse frame of mind than he was already in. The secession of Virginia, the riot in Baltimore, and the changing sides of Union officers all combined to lower his already shaky morale and add to his mental strain. He was beginning to think that he could not put his trust in anyone or anything. "His nerves played tricks on him, as the suspense was prolonged almost beyond endurance," one writer remarked.[7] If reinforcing troops would arrive soon, within the next day or so, this would certainly help calm him. Rumors and reports insisted that reinforcements were on their way, but none ever arrived.

# "THERE IS NO NORTH"

The president had two routine items to settle this Wednesday. He asked his postmaster, Montgomery Blair, if the appointment of postmaster general in Philadelphia had been made as yet, and went on to say that he had the appointment papers "laying by me" and would sign them "if you say so."[1] He also approved the retirement of two naval surgeons "as within recommended by the Secretary of the Navy."[2] Dealing with these two mundane bits of business probably put President Lincoln's mind at rest, at least for a little while, and gave him something else to think about besides defecting military officers and the defense of Washington. But he had another, much more serious, matter to deal with as well.

On the previous Monday, April 22, President Lincoln received a disturbing letter from former Maryland senator Reverdy Johnson. In his letter, Johnson wrote that "excitement and alarm" had spread throughout both Maryland and Virginia. The cause of this bad feeling, according to the former senator, was "an apprehension that it is your purpose to use the military force you are assembling in this District for the invasion of . . . these States."[3] The president did not answer this letter earlier "because of my aversion (which I thought you understood,) to getting on paper, and furnishing new grounds for misunderstanding."[4] In other words, he thought that anything he said would only make a bad situation even worse. But Johnson was not easily put off. On this Wednesday, Johnson sent another note to the president, in which he asked for a reply to his letter of April 22. He was planning to leave Washington, he explained, and would like some sort of answer before leaving.

President Lincoln obligingly replied to Reverdy Johnson's request—which was actually more of a demand than a request. In his reply, the president was not quite as brutally frank as he had been in his response to the Baltimore Committee two days earlier, but he did not pull any punches, either. He stated that his only purpose for bringing troops to the city was to defend the capital, and that he had no intention of invading Virginia. But he also made it clear that he did intend to be prepared in case Virginian forces invaded Washington—"In a word, if Virginia strikes us, are we not to strike back, and as effectively as we can?" In the last line of the letter the president forcefully summed up his position: "I have no objection to declare a thousand times that I have no purpose to invade Virginia or any other State, but I do not mean to let them invade us without striking back."[5] He neglected to mention the fact that the "military force" Johnson alluded to had not yet arrived in Washington, and that he had no real idea when these long-expected troops might arrive.

The president's anxiety over the failure of reinforcements to reach Washington was unmistakable when several wounded members of the Sixth Massachusetts Regiment came to visit the White House—an eyewitness called the president's nervousness an "additional manifestation of this bitterness of soul." These soldiers, including several officers, had been injured during the Baltimore riot of April 19. They seemed to be slightly embarrassed when they first met the president, but he quickly put them at ease "with sympathetic kindness" after a few minutes. President Lincoln thanked the men for their conduct during the riot, as well as for their prompt arrival in Washington, which he contrasted with "the unexplained delay which seemed to have befallen the regiments supposed to be somewhere on their way from the various States." He was clearly tense about the lack of promised troops as he addressed the soldiers, and "finally fell into a tone of irony to which only intense feeling ever drove him." At one point, he said, "I begin to believe that there is no North," and that the other troops who were supposed to be on their way were only a myth. "You are the only real thing."[6] The fact that he spoke to the men in this way shows how stressed and unhappy he was about the situation in Washington and the lack of troops to defend it.

APRIL 25, 1861, THURSDAY

# THE HAPPIEST MAN IN TOWN

E ven though no battles had been fought as yet, and President Lincoln continued to hope against hope that a civil war could be averted, or at least limited, he still had the war—and how to prepare for it—very much on his mind. Two days earlier, on April 23, Vice President Hannibal Hamlin wrote a memo on the subject of the army's unpreparedness for war. "We are sadly deficient, and we want and need and should have rifled cannon," he said. "Let me urge earnestly and frankly that the works at Chicopee [Massachusetts] be put in operation to their utmost capacity to furnish them."[1]

President Lincoln could not have agreed more. Activating the Chicopee cannon factory would certainly be a step in the right direction toward preparing the army for war. In response to the vice president's letter, Lincoln wrote this: "Let the suggestion of the Vice-President as to putting the Chicopee works into operation be duly considered by the War Department."[2] He knew that the armed forces were lacking in weapons and equipment, and had at least done something about solving the problem.

The meeting of the Maryland legislature, and especially the motives behind their meeting, also preoccupied President Lincoln on this Thursday. He wrote a worried letter to General Winfield Scott on that subject, informing the general that the legislature would gather at Annapolis on the following day "and, not improbably, will take action to arm the people of that State against the United States." But after consideration, he reached the conclusion that it would not be "justified" for General Scott "to arrest or disperse the members of that body." Using an attorney's logic, the president then went on to give two reasons why General Scott should not arrest them. First, "they have a clearly legal right to assemble; and, we can not know in advance, that their action will not be lawful, and peaceful."[3]

The second reason was not so much a legal motive as an exercise in cynicism, the result of a lifetime in politics. "If we arrest them, we can not long hold them as prisoners; and when liberated, they will immediately re-assemble, and take their action." And if the legislature were forbidden to convene in Annapolis, this would not have any effect, either, since they "will immediately re-assemble in some other place." It would be better simply to leave them alone and keep a close watch on them—which is exactly what President Lincoln instructed General Scott to do: he was "to watch, and await their action." And if the legislature did take action against the United States, "to arm their people against the United States," the president instructed General Scott "to adopt the most prompt, and efficient means to counteract, even, if necessary, to the bombardment of their cities—and in the extremest necessity, the suspension of the writ of habeas corpus."[4] Lincoln hoped that the legislators would not take steps to rebel against the US government, but he was fully prepared to act with force if they did attempt to provoke an armed conflict. He was hoping for the best but preparing for the worst.

Although the president still had any number of things that were bothering him, after this day was over he would have one less thing to worry about. The long-awaited reinforcements, which had been on their way to Washington for what seemed like forever, finally arrived. At around noon, the Seventh New York Regiment reached the rail depot; news of this event almost instantly spread throughout the city. "Immediately upon the fact of their arrival becoming known, large crowds made their way to the depot from every direction, until very soon the streets immediately surrounding the depot were almost entirely blocked up," an eyewitness reported.[5] The troops marched up Pennsylvania Avenue "in perfect step to the White House, with flags flying and bands playing," and "accepted the welcome of the Washington population as their rightful due."[6]

Everyone in town was happy and excited to see the New Yorkers, marching proudly in their "spick-and-span gray uniforms with pipe-clayed crossbelts,"[7] including Abraham Lincoln. As they made their way past the White House, accompanied by a marching band, the president came out and waved at the troops. He was visibly relieved to see them; according to one of the onlookers, he "smiled all over" and looked like the happiest man in town.[8] Within the next few days, thousands of troops from all over the North would continue to come. President Lincoln would be able to see tents and barracks surrounding the White House in all directions. The capital was no longer in danger. His mind could be at rest concerning one thing, at least.

## APRIL 26, 1861, FRIDAY

# UNPREPARED

**E**ven though Washington was now well defended and secure against any possible invasion, President Lincoln's busy mind would not let him relax. For one thing, he was concerned about his lack of experience with military matters and his shortcomings as a war leader. "Lincoln had no experience as a party leader or an executive officer, and was without knowledge of military affairs or acquaintance of military men," a major general in the Union army reflected. His state of mind was not improved any by the knowledge that his advisors were as unprepared as he was, including his secretary of war, Simon Cameron. "The talents of Simon Cameron, his first secretary of war, were political, not military . . . he had no knowledge of military affairs and could not give the President much assistance in assembling and organizing for war."[1]

On the other hand, his opposite number had an impressive military background and was surrounded by outstanding officers and military advisors. Jefferson Davis was a graduate of the United States Military Academy at West Point, had commanded troops during the Mexican War (as colonel of the Mississippi Rifles at the battle of Monterey), had served as secretary of war under President Franklin Pierce, and had been chairman of the Senate Military Committee until he resigned his senate seat to join the Confederacy. "He was not only well versed in everything relating to war, but was thoroughly informed concerning the character and capacity of prominent and promising officers of the army."[2] President Davis also had another advantage over President Lincoln: he "was blessed with a better pool of generals," most notably Robert E. Lee, while Lincoln was "cursed with lesser military leaders."[3] This disparity would cost the North dearly, especially early in the war, when the incompetence of undertrained and inexperienced Union officers would result in lost battles and unnecessary casualties.

An even more elementary problem also had to be taken into account—namely, the basic nature of the war itself. The South would be fighting a defensive war; its objective would be to protect its borders against attacks from the Northern armies. This meant that the Confederacy did not have to win the war. It only had to keep from losing it, to prevent the attacking Northern forces from occupying their home territory. A defensive campaign was much easier to conduct than a war of attack—which was what the North would have to conduct if it hoped to attain any sort of victory. British foreign secretary Lord John Russell was able to make this observation from the other side of the Atlantic Ocean. In a memo to his fellow members of the cabinet in London, he wrote, "as the war is aggressive on the part of the North and defensive on the part of the South, this result may be considered as favorable to the Southern cause."[4] Northern forces would have to take the offensive against the South; Southern defenders only had to keep beating back the Union army when it crossed into their territory. President Lincoln fully understood this.

Another cause for anxiety concerned the possibility of foreign intervention on the side of the Confederacy, particularly by the British government. Britain did not seem very friendly or sympathetic toward the Union. The British upper classes, including many members of the House of Lords, would have been more than happy to see the collapse of the American republic. The prime minister, Lord Palmerston, was openly hostile toward America; he referred to the country as "a dangerous power" and believed that the dissolution of the Union would be an enormous benefit to Britain and the British Empire. Palmerston made no secret of the fact that he sympathized with the Confederacy. A good many others in the government shared his sympathies.[5]

There was also the matter of a cotton shortage in Britain. The British textile industry was heavily dependent upon the South to supply its mills with raw cotton. Southerners were as aware of this as the British mill owners and the British government, as reporter William Russell found out during a dinner conversation in Charleston. Two locals bluntly informed him that the Southern states would stop delivering cotton unless Britain formally recognized the Confederate government. One of the dinner guests declared, "Why, sir, we have only to shut off your supply of cotton for a few weeks, and we can create a revolution in Great Britain. There are four millions of your people depending on us for their bread, not to speak of the many millions of dollars." He closed his argument with this ringing statement: "we know that England must recognize us."[6]

President Lincoln feared that the Charleston dinner guest was right; he also feared that British recognition and intervention would result in Confederate independence. After all, there was a precedent in American history—if the French had not intervened on the side of the American colonists during their War of Independence, the colonists would never have won the war against Britain. And if Britain interceded, France and other countries would be almost certain to follow suit.

To make matters even worse, the North was totally unprepared for the impending war. The majority of the US Army's small arms were obsolete—old smoothbore flintlocks that dated from the War of 1812. The army itself had nothing resembling a high command or a general staff; there was no overall strategic plan or even a planning committee to organize any sort of strategy or line of attack. The navy had its own set of problems. Their ships and equipment were more up to date, but there were not enough ships to maintain anything resembling an adequate blockade against Southern ports—there were only about twelve warships available to patrol the entire coastline between the Carolinas and Texas. President Lincoln knew how unprepared he was.

A group of men from Kansas, who called themselves the "Frontier Guard," came to visit President Lincoln at the White House during the afternoon. The Frontier Guard was a volunteer militia group under the leadership of Senator James H. Lane of Kansas, and it had been stationed "in and around the White House" as an unofficial security force for the past several days. Senator Lane heard a rumor that an attempt would be made to kidnap the president and overturn the government. Other

**213**

rumors began to circulate that President Lincoln and General Scott were in danger of assassination. The senator and his group set up a sort of informal headquarters at the Willard Hotel in mid-April, shortly before assuming their guard duty. The president invited the men to visit the White House and thanked them for their efforts.[7]

One of the leaders, a Colonel Vaughan, gave a short speech to inform President Lincoln that "when a dark cloud of peril" threatened Kansas, Senator Lane and the rest of the Kansas Guard drove Southern sympathizers from the state. Now they were in Washington to answer the country's call and support the Constitution and to "vindicate the majesty of the law." They had come to fight if necessary and were "ready for any emergency." Colonel Vaughan assured the president that he spoke for every man present when he said, *"No compromise with rebels"* (italics in original).[8]

President Lincoln listened to the fighting speech in silence. When it was over, he thanked the men for their sympathies as well as for their past services. He then made a short speech of his own. It was not quite as aggressive as Colonel Vaughan's address, but it said exactly what was on his mind—it was a mixture of belligerence and hope for peace. "I have desired as sincerely as any man—I sometimes think more than any other man—that our present difficulties might be settled without the shedding of blood," he told the gathering. "I will not say that all hope is yet gone." As was his usual custom, he saved the most important part of his speech until the end. "But if the alternative is presented, whether the Union is to be broken in fragments and the liberties of the people lost, or blood be shed, you will probably make the choice, with which I shall not be dissatisfied."[9] President Lincoln was still holding on to the slim chance that fighting could be averted; however, he was all but resigned to believing that war was unavoidable. He was in full agreement with Colonel Vaughan's promise to fight if necessary, as well as to give no compromise to the secessionists and their attempt to put an end to the union.

# A CONTROVERSIAL ORDER

P resident Lincoln took two more important steps toward organizing for war on this Saturday.

One of these was to amend his Proclamation of Blockade of April 19 by adding the ports of two additional states to his original list: Virginia and North Carolina. In his original draft he had also included Maryland, but to his immense relief, he decided that it was safe to cross out this strategic border state. ("Maryland, Virginia, North Carolina").[1] According to the Proclamation, both Virginia and North Carolina had been guilty of interfering with the collection of revenue and of seizing property belonging to the United States government, along with other offenses. Because of these offenses, "an efficient blockade of the ports of those States will also be established."[2] Because this was only an amendment to the April 19 decree, it did not produce the outpouring of comments and remarks, which were largely negative, of the original Proclamation.

The president's second communiqué was even more controversial than his blockade proclamation of April 19 had been. He sent a letter authorizing General Winfield Scott to suspend the writ of habeas corpus in certain sections of Maryland—"between the City of Philadelphia and the City of Washington, via Perryville, Annapolis City, and Annapolis Junction."[3] It probably did not come as any surprise to President Lincoln that the troublesome state of Maryland should be the subject of this order, as well as the center of still more controversy.

"You are engaged in repressing an insurrection against the laws of the United States," the president's order began. He continued in the same belligerent tone throughout the letter. "If at any point on or in the vicinity of the [any] military line, which is now [or which shall be] used between the City of Philadelphia and the City of Washington, via Perryville, Annapolis City, and Annapolis Junction, you find resistance which renders it necessary to suspend the writ of Habeas Corpus for the public safety, you, personally or through the officer in command at the point where the [at which] resistance occurs, are authorized to suspend that writ. ABRAHAM LINCOLN."[4]

President Lincoln was employing his authority as chief executive to arrest and to imprison anyone suspected of "disloyalty" or "disloyal practices" without trial and without pressing any formal charges. During the next four years, more than thirteen thousand people would be jailed and imprisoned indefinitely as a result of his proclamation. The majority of these individuals were Peace Democrats, members of the Democratic Party who opposed the war and openly supported an independent Confederate States of America. President Lincoln already had his hands full with a variety of other worries and complications. He did not need any political enemies making his life, and his attempts to prepare for war, more difficult. Having some of the more defiant antiwar Democrats behind bars would help to solve at least one of his problems.

Reaction to the president's order was not long in coming. In May, less than a month afterward, a state legislator from Maryland named John Merryman was arrested at his home without being charged with any crime. John Merryman was an outspoken secessionist and an advocate for Maryland to secede from the Union and join the Confederacy. He was also an officer in the Maryland State Militia who had destroyed railway bridges north of Baltimore to prevent federal troops from entering the city. President Lincoln was not happy about Merryman or his activities and decided to do something about them. He sent a detachment of soldiers to arrest Merryman. On May 25, he was duly apprehended and confined at Fort McHenry in Baltimore Harbor—the same Fort McHenry immortalized by Francis Scott Key in "The Star Spangled Banner"—where he was held without charges and denied legal counsel.

When the Merryman case came to the attention of Supreme Court justice Roger B. Taney, the eighty-four-year-old judge ordered that John

Merryman be brought before him to show cause for his arrest. The commanding officer of Fort McHenry refused, stating that by keeping his prisoner confined he was abiding by President Lincoln's orders. In response, an angry and frustrated Judge Taney challenged the president's authority to suspend habeas corpus on both legal and constitutional grounds. In *ex parte Merryman*, the judge wrote that President Lincoln had overstepped his authority, since no president had the authority to suspend habeas corpus. The president not only ignored this ruling but also issued a warrant for Judge Taney's arrest. Lincoln biographers generally dismiss the idea that any such warrant was ever issued. But the story, true or false, illustrates the fact that Honest Abe Lincoln could be ruthless and even brutal when the need arose. As one writer put it, "His supreme constitutional obligation was to preserve the nation by winning the war," even though no battle had been fought as yet. President Lincoln had no intention of complying with either Judge Taney or his ruling. John Merryman remained a prisoner in Fort McHenry, and the State of Maryland stayed in the Union.[5]

# APRIL 28, 1861, SUNDAY

# NO HOPE OF AN ARMISTICE

**T**his Sunday turned out to be relatively quiet for the president. The highlights of his day were a visit to a regiment stationed in Washington and a letter from a German diplomat.

During the afternoon, President Lincoln paid a visit to the Seventh New York Regiment, which was billeted in the House of Representatives chamber in the Capitol Building. The president was accompanied by Secretary of State William Seward "and other distinguished gentlemen." Both Lincoln and Seward made speeches that complimented the regiment for their military bearing and for their service to the country. The men were warned by their commanding officer that "[l]oud talking, whistling, singing, scuffling, or running will not be permitted within the building." The president seemed to enjoy himself during his visit, which certainly came as a nice change of pace from the usual White House routine.[1]

Later in the day, the president read a letter from Rudolph Schleiden, the ambassador from the German province of Bremen. With the knowledge of President Lincoln and the approval of Secretary Seward, Minister Schleiden had spoken with Confederate vice president Alexander Stephens in Richmond on April 25. The purpose of his meeting with Vice President Stephens was to ask if the Confederate government would consider an armistice and, if so, exactly what terms would be considered. Bremen was heavily dependent upon imports and exports for its income, and was also one of Europe's most active trading partners with the United States; he did not want to see Bremen's economy disrupted by a civil war. Secretary of State William H. Seward was all in favor of such a meeting, and he even arranged a pass for Schleiden to travel to Richmond, where Stephens happened to be. President Lincoln did not share Secretary Seward's enthusiasm. He only would agree to read and consider any terms that Vice President Stephens might propose.

On this Sunday, the German minister gave President Lincoln his report from Richmond. The report was not very encouraging. Vice President Stephens did not like the idea of a formal armistice but proposed a three-month truce instead—he called it a "de facto truce through tactful avoidance of an attack on both sides." He also insisted that Maryland be allowed to secede from the Union and join the Confederacy as a condition for any sort of peace agreement. Another condition was that President Lincoln should meet with Confederate officials and negotiate a settlement between North and South, a settlement that would result in Confederate independence. Vice President Stephens was realistic enough to see that President Lincoln would never agree to any such conditions. It was also fairly evident that he did not trust either Lincoln or his government, and he said that "it seems to be their policy to wage a war for the recapture of former possessions looking to the ultimate coercion and subjugation of the people of the Confederate States to their power and domain." He went on to argue, "With such an object on their part persevered in, no power on earth can arrest or prevent a most bloody conflict."[2]

Vice President Stephens was absolutely correct—President Lincoln had no intention of even considering these terms. The results of Minister Schleiden's meeting in Richmond—namely, that Stephens would not agree to any kind of armistice unless President Lincoln agreed to a separate Confederate States of America—did not come as any surprise to the president. In response, he informed Minister Schleiden that there would be no negotiations. Schleiden notified Stephens of the president's decision in a short letter: "It is only now and with deep regret that I can inform you that my attempt at contributing toward gaining time for reflection and if possible a favorable adjustment of the existing differences has failed."[3] Lincoln was not disappointed in the outcome of the Schleiden/Stephens talk, since he never expected anything to come out of it to begin with.

He had no idea how long the "bloody conflict" forecast by Vice President Stephens might last. Optimists were predicting a ninety-day war, but at this point in time President Lincoln was no longer optimistic. He decided not to accept any more ninety-day volunteers for the army; he would only accept recruits who would sign up for a three-year enlistment. On May 3, 1861, he would make this official: the president made a "call into the service of the United States of 42,034 volunteers to serve for the period of three years."[4] Some would insist that this was pessimistic and negative, but President Lincoln would have argued that this was only being realistic.

# THE TENSION THAT CAME WITH THE JOB

A mong the items President Lincoln had on his desk was the recommendation of a candidate for a diplomatic post in Russia, along with the request of an assignment for an administrative job in Nebraska. He wrote to Secretary of State William H. Seward that he had no objection to Timothy C. Smith being named for "one of the $2000 consulships remaining open in Russia." On the basis of this endorsement, Mr. Smith was appointed consul at Odessa. The president sent a similar memo to Interior Secretary Caleb B. Smith on the subject of appointing an agent for the Pawnee Indian Agency in the Nebraska Territory. President Lincoln endorsed Henry W. DuPuy for the position if it "has not already been disposed of."[1]

But President Lincoln's main concern was the impending war. He was still more than concerned with the possibility of an attack on Washington, especially with the chance of an artillery barrage directed against the White House. General Winfield Scott alerted the president to this danger three days earlier, in one of his daily reports. In response to General Scott's warning, President Lincoln sent a strongly, and somewhat awkwardly, worded communiqué to Navy Secretary Gideon Welles regarding the defense of the White House and its surrounding area. "You will please to have as strong a War Steamer as you can conveniently put on that duty, to cruise upon the Potomac, and to look in upon, and, if practicable, examine the Bluff and vicinity, at what is called the White House, once or twice per day." If an artillery battery should be discovered on the riverbank, the war steamer was directed to "drive away" its crew. Secretary Welles was also ordered "to report daily to your Department, and to me" regarding the situation.[2] Even though Maryland remained in the Union, the president continued to worry about secessionists creating mischief. Lincoln had been in office for eight weeks, and the tension that came with the job was taking its toll.

If President Lincoln had any idea of what people were saying about him since he had taken office, everything from malicious gossip to outright lies, the gossip might just have helped to relieve his overstretched nerves. Lincoln's homeliness and lack of formal education made him an easy target for ridicule. British reporter William Russell of the London *Times* managed to pick up a great deal of this talk during his time in Washington, and mentioned it in his diary. "The most terrible accounts are given of the state of things in Washington," he wrote on April 29. Among the terrible accounts Russell includes was this item: "Mr. Lincoln consoles himself for his miseries by drinking. Mr. Seward follows suit. The White House and capital are full of drunken border ruffians, headed by one Jim Lane, of Kansas."[3] (James Lane was a controversial US senator from Kansas, who was probably best known for killing a neighbor over a boundary dispute.) Hearing that he had consorted with drunken border ruffians in the company of his secretary of state, of all people, probably would have made President Lincoln laugh out loud, which would have been just what he needed to lighten the strain and tension he felt.

# APRIL 30, 1861, TUESDAY
# AN ENJOYABLE AFTERNOON

**P**resident Lincoln replied to a letter, dated April 23, from Stephen A. Hurlbut. Stephen Hurlbut, a friend of the president's from the time they both lived in Illinois, had gone on a fact-finding mission to Charleston in March. In his letter of April 23, Hurlbut complained that his entire company of volunteers had been rejected from joining any of the six Illinois regiments, on the grounds that all of the regiments "are more than full." His company was ready and willing for any kind of duty, he said, and requested that the men be given some sort of assignment as quickly as possible. "We will relieve the Regulars from the frontier," he told the president, "or act any where else, but we must act or spoil."[1] There was a fight coming, and Hurlbut and the hundred or so men of his company did not want to be left out of it.

President Lincoln was all sympathy. He sent young Mr. Hurlbut a memo to show his superiors back in Illinois, stating that Hurlbut "is especially worthy of attention. In anything further done for Illinois, let him not be neglected."[2] As usual, the president's word was as good as a command. Stephen A. Hurlbut received a commission as brigadier of volunteers on May 11, 1861.

The president also met with three leaders of the Potawatomi tribe, the native people of the Midwestern United States, at the White House. He did not seem very comfortable in his attempt to converse with his visitors. A witness to the meeting recalled that "[t]he President amused them greatly by airing the two or three Indian words he knew." His guests were also amused when Lincoln resorted to Pidgin English during the course of his conversation: "Where live now? When go back Iowa?"

When the visit finally ended, everyone concerned—especially President Lincoln—must have been greatly relieved.[3]

The president also had more official, as well as more comfortable and relaxed, conversations in the afternoon when he called upon several regiments that were stationed in Washington. Secretary of State William H. Seward came along with him. The regiments were billeted in buildings all throughout the city, including the Patent Office, where Lincoln and Seward made it a point to talk to several officers of the Rhode Island Regiment. "The companies were drawn up in a line in their quarters and received them in a hearty manner," one news reporter commented. Both the president and the secretary of state were greeted by "loud and repeated cheers" during their visit.[4] It was a cheerful and enjoyable afternoon, for both the troops and for President Lincoln. The cheerful days would be few and precious in the coming weeks and months.

# A THERAPEUTIC LETTER

**F**ort Sumter, specifically the capture of Fort Sumter on April 12, was the subject of two letters written by President Lincoln on this Wednesday. He sent a reassuring note to Captain Gustavus Fox, who was still fretting over the failure to reprovision the fortress a few weeks earlier. In his official report, dated April 19, 1861, Captain Fox expressed a good deal of resentment over the fact that USS *Powhatan* had been sent to Pensacola instead of Charleston. "I learned on the 13th instant that the *Powhatan* was withdrawn from duty off Charleston," he wrote with some anger and frustration, which meant "that the main portion—the fighting portion—of our expedition was taken away."[1]

In reply, President Lincoln wrote, "I sincerely regret that the failure of the late attempt to provision Fort-Sumpter, should be the source of any annoyance to you." Doing his best to be as supportive and encouraging as possible, he said, "I most cheerfully and truly declare that the failure of the undertaking has not lowered you a particle, while the qualities you developed in the effort, have greatly heightened you, in my estimation." He went on to say that he would not hesitate to select Captain Fox for any "daring and dangerous enterprize" that might arise anytime in the future. He signed his letter, "Very truly your friend A. LINCOLN."[2]

President Lincoln's second letter concerning Fort Sumter was written to Major Robert Anderson, who had commanded the Fort Sumter garrison. An "official" letter had been sent to Major Anderson on April 20, from the War Department, expressing the country's "appreciation and gratitude" for his services. But the president wanted to send a letter of his own, "a purely private and social letter," to thank the major for his "services and fidelity." Lincoln also invited him, along with "any of the officers who served with you at Fort Sumpter," to visit the White House "at your earliest convenience."[3] President Lincoln was fairly certain that he would be needing the major's services, as well as the services of Captain Fox, in the not too distant future.

The president also wrote another letter, of a completely different nature, to Governor Isham G. Harris of Tennessee. On April 28, Governor Harris sent a heated letter to President Lincoln protesting the seizure of the steamboat *C. E. Hillman* a few days earlier. The steamboat and its cargo, which was made up of weapons and ammunition, were owned by the citizens of Tennessee, Governor Harris insisted, and demanded to know if the seizure was carried out "by or under the instructions of the Federal Government, or is approved by said Government."[4]

This was the first time President Lincoln had ever heard of either the *C. E. Hillman* or of its seizure. He was not happy with the governor's letter, or with the tone of his letter, or with the governor himself. In his reply, he did not tell the governor to go straight to hell in so many words, but he came as close as possible without resorting to using that exact phrase.

In his opening paragraph, President Lincoln sarcastically advised Governor Harris that his letter "claiming that the said boat and its cargo are the property of the State of Tennessee and her citizens; and demanding to know whether the seizure was made by the authority of this Government, or is approved by it, is duly received." As he continued, the president's sarcasm turned to anger. He explained that the US government had no "official" information regarding the seizure or who authorized it (the order was given by Governor Richard Yates of Illinois), but he went on to say that "assuming that the seizure was made," and that the cargo consisted of munitions that were owned by the State of Tennessee under "the control of its Governor," "the Government avows the seizure."[5]

President Lincoln carried on in the same vein, giving Governor Harris a few well-chosen words regarding his actions and attitudes. He did not come right out and call the governor a traitor, but he certainly implied his disloyalty. "A legal call was recently made upon the said Governor of Tennessee" to furnish a quota of militia "to suppress an insurrection against the United States," the president reminded Governor Harris. The only response received was a refusal, "couched in disrespectful and malicious language."[6] What Governor Harris actually said was "Tennessee will not furnish a single man for purpose of coercion, but 50,000, if necessary, for the defense of our rights and those of our Southern brethren."[7]

The president then came to his main point. "This Government therefore infers that munitions of War passing into the hands of said Governor, are intended to be used against the United States." In addition, "the government will not indulge the weakness of allowing it, so long as it is in its power to prevent." He ends his invective by informing Governor Harris that the majority of Tennessee's citizens remain loyal to the Union, and that the State of Tennessee "holds itself responsible in damages for all injuries it may do to any who may prove to be such."[8]

The letter probably had no effect at all on Governor Harris, especially since President Lincoln's claim that the majority of Tennessee's citizens were loyal to the Union turned out to be pure wishful thinking—on June 8, 1861, the state's residents would vote by an overwhelming majority, of more than two to one, to secede from the Union and join the Confederacy. But it must have been a highly therapeutic experience for the president. He finally had the opportunity to tell a Southern governor exactly what he thought of him, and probably enjoyed himself hugely.

President Lincoln also enjoyed himself that evening, when he attended a performance by the band of the Seventh New York Regiment. The band concert was given in the grounds adjacent to the White House. The president did his best to attend concerts, as well as the theater, whenever he had the opportunity. These events not only brought him some much needed entertainment but also helped calm his nerves. On this particular occasion, President Lincoln became the main attraction; the audience paid more attention to him than to the band. When he stepped out on the balcony, "the band was deserted at once, and everyone rushed up to get a glimpse of the new president." He made a few "pleasant remarks" but could not be heard very well because of the high wind. Only when the president went back inside did the crowd go back to "its position around the band."[9]

## MAY 2, 1861, THURSDAY
# THE PRESIDENT RECEIVES A WARNING

**"O**ur Chicago detective has arrived," President Lincoln wrote to Secretary of State William H. Seward from the White House, "and I have promised to have you meet him and me here at 8 O'clock this evening." The "Chicago detective" was Allan J. Pinkerton, who offered his services in a letter to the president on April 21. Pinkerton also enclosed a secret code in his letter, which he would use in any future communication with the president. "In the present disturbed state of affairs I dare not trust this to the mails so send by one of my force who was with me at Baltimore," Pinkerton informed President Lincoln. He was referring to the meeting he had with Lincoln during the president-elect's journey to Washington before the inauguration, when Pinkerton warned Lincoln of a planned assassination attempt on his way through Baltimore. Since then, there had been other assassination threats as well. Allan Pinkerton's letter would not be the last time that the president would receive an assassination warning.[1]

## MAY 3, 1861, FRIDAY
# A TACIT ADMISSION


**P**resident Lincoln made a decision to expand his April 15 call for volunteers into federal service. He issued a call, a proclamation, for 42,034 additional volunteers to serve for a period of three years. The original 75,000 signed on for only ninety days. In his proclamation, the president also increased the size of the regular army by the addition of eight regiments of infantry, one regiment of cavalry, and one regiment of artillery, for a grand total of 22,714 men. The navy was also expanded by adding 18,000 men. All this was being done "for the protection of the National Constitution and the preservation of the National Union by the suppression of the insurrectionary combinations now existing in several States."[1]

If President Lincoln still held any remaining shred of hope that the coming of war could be avoided, or that the war would be relatively short, this proclamation served as a tacit admission that he had finally given up any such hope. His call for the expansion of both the army and the navy confirm that he now expected that the coming war would be a long and bloody affair—although no one, including the president, had any real idea of just how long and bloody it would turn out to be. (The prevailing view throughout the North was that any fighting would last only three months, at most.) He also declared that he hoped for "the speediest possible restoration of peace and order and, with these, of happiness and prosperity throughout our country."[2] But President Lincoln made it clear that none of this would take place until the country first endured an extended period of violence and destruction. There is a note of sadness in the proclamation, but its overall tone is of determination and resolution—the war might go on for three or four years, or possibly longer, but in the long run the Constitution and the Union would prevail.

# "THEIR DEAD EXTENDED FOR MILES"

**P**resident Lincoln attended Sunday church services, but his mind probably was not on that morning's sermon. He had just sent a federal army to attack a Confederate force defending the key railroad junction at Manassas, Virginia. The federal force had begun its advance during the early morning hours, just a few hours past. The president could be forgiven if his thoughts were elsewhere—Manassas is about thirty-five miles to the south of Washington—as the preacher spoke.

The Union forces were under the command of forty-two-year-old Irvin McDowell, who had been promoted to the rank of brigadier general in May, only two months before. General McDowell was a professional soldier, a graduate of West Point, a veteran of the Mexican War, and highly thought of by General Winfield Scott. His plan was to force the Confederates from their defensive position and "if possible, destroy the railroad leading from Manassas to the Valley of Virginia, where the enemy has a large force."[1] He was well aware that the troops he commanded were undertrained and totally inexperienced. In a report on the situation, the general stated his thoughts on his new command straightforwardly: "For the most part our regiments are exceedingly raw and the best of them, with few exceptions, not over steady in line."[2] Before going into battle for the first time, he would like to have had more training for his men. But President Lincoln could not afford the time for additional training and preparation—the enlistments of his ninety-day volunteer force of seventy-five thousand men would soon be expiring. He informed General McDowell that the enemy's troops were just as raw

At the first battle of Bull Run / Manassas, Union forces were under the command of forty-two-year-old Irvin McDowell. He was well aware that the troops he commanded were undertrained and totally inexperienced.

and untrained as his own; he famously said that both sides, North and South, were all green alike.

Despite their lack of experience, General McDowell's men gave a good account of themselves. They managed to push the Confederates out of their positions and chased them toward the rear in full retreat. Telegrams from General McDowell's headquarters at the front reported that the enemy was being driven from the field. Congressmen and senators had driven out from Washington to watch the battle and were amazed at what they were seeing. President Lincoln was amazed as well. He followed the progress of the fighting from the War Office telegraph office, which was adjacent to the White House. "Lincoln hardly left his seat in our office and waited with deep anxiety for each succeeding dispatch," in the words of an observer. "All the morning and well along into the afternoon, McDowell's telegrams were more or less encouraging, and Lincoln and his advisers waited with eager hope."[3] From the reports, it looked as though General McDowell's troops were on the verge of a decisive success.

But the center of the Confederate line held firm. A brigade of Virginians commanded by Thomas J. Jackson stood their ground "like a stone wall," according to legend, and stopped the Union advance. Because of this incident, Stonewall Jackson became a legend in his own right. This proved to be the turning point of the battle. Confederate replacements arrived; Union forces began retreating, and their entire line eventually broke. Federal troops ran from the field in a panic, and the retreat degenerated into a rout. Union losses were prohibitive. "The loss of Regiment in this disastrous affair was ninety-three killed, wounded and missing," wrote a private in the Second Rhode Island Volunteers.[4] Other regiments suffered similar losses. Overall, it was a very harsh debut for Union forces.

An officer with a Confederate regiment gave a Southern view of the battle and its outcome. A lieutenant with the Thirtieth Virginia Volunteers, Charles Minor Blackford, had been in line of battle nearly all day but did not take part in the heaviest part of the day's fighting. His unit, company B, lost only one officer, a captain named Winston Radford. "Beyond this," the lieutenant wrote, "our loss was very small and my company had only one or two wounded slightly." But the Union forces were not nearly as fortunate. Lieutenant Blackford recalled that the enemy suffered "a terrible rout;" he was astonished by the carnage. "The actual loss of the enemy I do not know but their dead extended for miles and their wounded filled every house and shed in the neighborhood."[5]

President Lincoln was astonished, as well, when he read the telegram reports from Manassas. To the bewilderment of everyone in the room, the dispatches came to an abrupt stop during the afternoon hours. The eerie silence was broken by the shocking announcement, "Our army is

A unit of federal cavalry at Sudley Springs, Virginia, roughly ten miles north of Manassas, in a photo taken shortly after the Battle of Bull Run / Manassas. The first full-scale battle of the Civil War turned into a rout when Northern soldiers broke ranks and ran from the field.

retreating," followed by details of the retreat. A sixteen-year-old operator later wrote, "I told the War Department office of the retreat of the Union Army, saying that those who passed my office first, were wounded soldiers, a few at a time, then squads of soldiers, followed later by companies and regiments."[6] A US senator from Michigan, Zachariah Chandler, had actually seen the battle and drove to the White House a few hours after the fighting ended. The senator "found Mr. Lincoln despondent, exhausted with his labors, and greatly depressed by the defeat and the loss of life involved." He gave the president what amounted to a pep talk, urging him to call for more troops and advising him not to be discouraged by the defeat. His talk apparently had its intended effect; when Senator Chandler departed the White House a few hours later, "he left Mr. Lincoln cheered, encouraged and resolute."[7]

The Battle of Bull Run / Manassas showed the population of the North a bitter reality, a reality President Lincoln had already seen and been forced to accept: the war would not be a ninety-day fight but, instead, would go on for years. After reading news accounts of the battle, a soldier from New Jersey was moved to remark, "The theory entertained by the National authorities that the rebellion would be crushed out in three months' time soon proved erroneous."[8]

# LINCOLN'S FIRST INAUGURAL ADDRESS— FINAL TEXT, MARCH 4, 1861

F ellow-citizens of the United States:[1]
    In compliance with a custom as old as the government itself, I appear before you to address you briefly, and to take, in your presence, the oath prescribed by the Constitution of the United States, to be taken by the President "before he enters on the execution of this office."

I do not consider it necessary at present for me to discuss those matters of administration about which there is no special anxiety or excitement.

Apprehension seems to exist among the people of the Southern States, that by the accession of a Republican Administration, their property, and their peace, and personal security, are to be endangered. There has never been any reasonable cause for such apprehension. Indeed, the most ample evidence to the contrary has all the while existed, and been open to their inspection. It is found in nearly all the published speeches of him who now addresses you. I do but quote from one of those speeches when I declare that "I have no purpose, directly or indirectly, to interfere with the institution of slavery in the States where it exists. I believe I have no lawful right to do so, and I have no inclination to do so." Those who nominated and elected me did so with full knowledge that I had made this, and many similar declarations, and had never recanted them. And more than this, they placed in the platform, for my acceptance, and as a law to themselves, and to me, the clear and emphatic resolution which I now read:

*Resolved,* That the maintenance inviolate of the rights of the States, and especially the right of each State to order and control its own domestic institutions according to its own judgment exclusively, is essential to that balance of power on which the perfection and endurance of our political fabric depend; and we denounce the lawless invasion by armed force of the soil of any State or Territory, no matter what pretext, as among the gravest of crimes."

I now reiterate these sentiments; and in doing so, I only press upon the public attention the most conclusive evidence of which the case is susceptible, that the property, peace and security of no section are to be in any wise endangered by the now incoming Administration. I add too, that all the protection which, consistently with the Constitution and the laws, can be given, will be cheerfully given to all the States when lawfully demanded, for whatever cause—as cheerfully to one section as to another.

There is much controversy about the delivering up of fugitives from service or labor. The clause I now read is as plainly written in the Constitution as any other of its provisions:

"No person held to service or labor in one State, under the laws thereof, escaping into another, shall, in consequence of any law or regulation therein, be discharged from such service or labor, but shall be delivered up on claim of the party to whom such service or labor may be due."

It is scarcely questioned that this provision was intended by those who made it, for the reclaiming of what we call fugitive slaves; and the intention of the law-giver is the law. All members of Congress swear their support to the whole Constitution—to this provision as much as to any other. To the proposition, then, that slaves whose cases come within the terms of this clause, "shall be delivered," their oaths are unanimous. Now, if they would make the effort in good temper, could they not, with nearly equal unanimity, frame and pass a law, by means of which to keep good that unanimous oath?

There is some difference of opinion whether this clause should be enforced by national or by state authority; but surely that difference is not a very material one. If the slave is to be surrendered, it can be of but little consequence to him, or to others, by which authority it is done.

And should any one, in any case, be content that his oath shall go unkept, on a merely unsubstantial controversy as to *how* it shall be kept?

Again, in any law upon this subject, ought not all the safeguards of liberty known in civilized and humane jurisprudence to be introduced, so that a free man be not, in any case, surrendered as a slave? And might it not be well, at the same time to provide by law for the enforcement of that clause in the Constitution which guarantees that "the citizens of each State shall be entitled to all privileges and immunities of citizens in the several States"?

I take the official oath to-day, with no mental reservations, and with no purpose to construe the Constitution or laws, by any hypercritical rules. And while I do not choose now to specify particular acts of Congress as proper to be enforced, I do suggest that it will be much safer for all, both in official and private stations, to conform to, and abide by, all those acts which stand unrepealed, than to violate any of them, trusting to find impunity in having them held to be unconstitutional.

It is seventy-two years since the first inauguration of a President under our national Constitution. During that period fifteen different and greatly distinguished citizens, have, in succession, administered the executive branch of the government. They have conducted it through many perils; and, generally, with great success. Yet, with all this scope for [of] precedent, I now enter upon the same task for the brief constitutional term of four years, under great and peculiar difficulty. A disruption of the Federal Union, heretofore only menaced, is now formidably attempted.

I hold, that in contemplation of universal law, and of the Constitution, the Union of these States is perpetual. Perpetuity is implied, if not expressed, in the fundamental law of all national governments. It is safe to assert that no government proper, ever had a provision in its organic law for its own termination. Continue to execute all the express provisions of our national Constitution, and the Union will endure forever— it being impossible to destroy it, except by some action not provided for in the instrument itself.

Again, if the United States be not a government proper, but an association of States in the nature of contract merely, can it, as a contract, be peaceably unmade, by less than all the parties who made it? One party to a contract may violate it—break it, so to speak; but does it not require all to lawfully rescind it?

Descending from these general principles, we find the proposition that, in legal contemplation, the Union is perpetual, confirmed by the history of the Union itself. The Union is much older than the Constitution. It was formed in fact, by the Articles of Association in 1774. It was matured and continued by the Declaration of Independence in 1776. It was further matured and the faith of all the then thirteen States expressly plighted and engaged that it should be perpetual, by the Articles of Confederation in 1778. And finally, in 1787, one of the declared objects for ordaining and establishing the Constitution, was *"to form a more perfect Union."* But if [the] destruction of the Union, by one, or by a part only, of the States, be lawfully possible, the Union is *less* perfect than before the Constitution, having lost the vital element of perpetuity.

It follows from these views that no State, upon its own mere motion, can lawfully get out of the Union,—that *resolves* and *ordinances* to that effect are legally void, and that acts of violence, within any State or States, against the authority of the United States, are insurrectionary or revolutionary, according to circumstances.

I therefore consider that in view of the Constitution and the laws, the Union is unbroken; and to the extent of my ability I shall take care, as the Constitution itself expressly enjoins upon me, that the laws of the Union be faithfully executed in all the States. Doing this I deem to be only a simple duty on my part; and I shall perform it, so far as practicable, unless my rightful masters, the American people, shall withhold the requisite means, or in some authoritative manner, direct the contrary. I trust this will not be regarded as a menace, but only as the declared purpose of the Union that will constitutionally defend and maintain itself.

In doing this there needs to be no bloodshed or violence; and there shall be none, unless it be forced upon the national authority. The power confided to me will be used to hold, occupy, and possess the property and places belonging to the government, and to collect the duties and imposts; but beyond what may be necessary for these objects, there will be no invasion—no using of force against or among the people anywhere. Where hostility to the United States in any interior locality, shall be so great and so universal, as to prevent competent resident citizens from holding the Federal offices, there will be no attempt to force obnoxious strangers among the people for that object. While the strict legal right may exist in the government to enforce the exercise of these offices, the attempt to do so would be so irritating, and so nearly impracticable with all, that I deem it better to forego, for the time, the uses of such offices.

The mails, unless repelled, will continue to be furnished in all parts of the Union. So far as possible, the people everywhere shall have that sense of perfect security which is most favorable to calm thought and reflection. The course here indicated will be followed, unless current events and experience shall show a modification or change to be proper; and in every case and exigency my best discretion will be exercised according to circumstances actually existing, and with a view and a hope of a peaceful solution of the national troubles, and the restoration of fraternal sympathies and affections.

That there are persons in one section or another who seek to destroy the Union at all events, and are glad of any pretext to do it, I will neither affirm nor deny; but if there be such, I need address no word to them. To those, however, who really love the Union may I not speak?

Before entering upon so grave a matter as the destruction of our national fabric, with all its benefits, its memories, and its hopes, would it not be wise to ascertain precisely why we do it? Will you hazard so desperate a step, while there is any possibility that any portion of the ills you fly from have no real existence? Will you, while the certain ills you fly to, are greater than all the real ones you fly from? Will you risk the commission of so fearful a mistake?

All profess to be content in the Union, if all constitutional rights can be maintained. Is it true, then, that any right, plainly written in the

Constitution, has been denied? I think not. Happily the human mind is so constituted, that no party can reach to the audacity of doing this. Think, if you can, of a single instance in which a plainly written provision of the Constitution has ever been denied. If by the mere force of numbers, a majority should deprive a minority of any clearly written constitutional right, it might, in a moral point of view, justify revolution—certainly would, if such right were a vital one. But such is not our case. All the vital rights of minorities, and of individuals, are so plainly assured to them, by affirmations and negations, guaranties and prohibitions, in the Constitution, that controversies never arise concerning them. But no organic law can ever be framed with a provision specifically applicable to every question which may occur in practical administration. No foresight can anticipate, nor any document of reasonable length contain express provisions for all possible questions. Shall fugitives from labor be surrendered by national or by State authority? The Constitution does not expressly say. *May* Congress prohibit slavery in the territories? The Constitution does not expressly say. *Must* Congress protect slavery in the territories? The Constitution does not expressly say.

From questions of this class spring all our constitutional controversies, and we divide upon them into majorities and minorities. If the minority will not acquiesce, the majority must, or the government must cease. There is no other alternative; for continuing the government, is acquiescence on one side or the other. If a minority, in such case, will secede rather than acquiesce, they make a precedent which, in turn, will divide and ruin them; for a minority of their own will secede from them whenever a majority refuses to be controlled by such minority. For instance, why may not any portion of a new confederacy, a year or two hence, arbitrarily secede again, precisely as portions of the present Union now claim to secede from it? All who cherish disunion sentiments, are now being educated to the exact temper of doing this.

Is there such perfect identity of interests among the States to compose a new Union, as to produce harmony only, and prevent renewed secession?

Plainly, the central idea of secession, is the essence of anarchy. A majority, held in restraint by constitutional checks and limitations, and always changing easily with deliberate changes of popular opinions and sentiments, is the only true sovereign of a free people. Whoever rejects it, does, of necessity, fly to anarchy or to despotism. Unanimity is impossible; the rule of a minority, as a permanent arrangement, is wholly inadmissible; so that, rejecting the majority principle, anarchy or despotism in some form is all that is left.

I do not forget the position assumed by some, that constitutional questions are to be decided by the Supreme Court; nor do I deny that such decisions must be binding in any case, upon the parties to a suit; as to the object of that suit, while they are also entitled to very high respect and consideration in all parallel cases by all other departments of the government. And while it is obviously possible that such decision may be erroneous in any given case, still the evil effect following it, being limited to that particular case, with the chance that it may be over-ruled, and never become a precedent for other cases, can better be borne than could the evils of a different practice. At the same time, the candid citizen must confess that if the policy of the government upon vital questions, affecting the whole people, is to be irrevocably fixed by decisions of the Supreme Court, the instant they are made, in ordinary litigation between parties, in personal actions, the people will have ceased to be their own rulers, having to that extent practically resigned their government into the hands of that eminent tribunal. Nor is there in this view any assault upon the court or the judges. It is a duty from which they may not shrink, to decide cases properly brought before them; and it is no fault of theirs if others seek to turn their decisions to political purposes.

One section of our country believes slavery is *right*, and ought to be extended, while the other believes it is *wrong*, and ought not to be extended. This is the only substantial dispute. The fugitive slave clause of the Constitution, and the law for the suppression of the foreign slave trade, are each as well enforced, perhaps, as any law can ever be in a community where the moral sense of the people imperfectly supports

the law itself. The great body of the people abide by the dry legal obligation in both cases, and a few break over in each. This, I think, cannot be
perfectly cured, and it would be worse in both cases *after* the separation
of the sections, than before. The foreign slave trade, now imperfectly
suppressed, would be ultimately revived without restriction, in one section; while fugitive slaves, now only partially surrendered, would not be
surrendered at all, by the other.

Physically speaking, we cannot separate. We can not remove our
respective sections from each other, nor build an impassable wall
between them. A husband and wife may be divorced, and go out of the
presence, and beyond the reach of each other; but the different parts of
our country cannot do this. They cannot but remain face to face; and
intercourse, either amicable or hostile, must continue between them. Is
it possible, then, to make that intercourse more advantageous or more
satisfactory, *after* separation than *before*? Can aliens make treaties easier
than friends can make laws? Can treaties be more faithfully enforced
between aliens than laws can among friends? Suppose you go to war, you
cannot fight always; and when, after much loss on both sides, and no gain
on either, you cease fighting, the identical old questions, as to terms of
intercourse, are again upon you.

This country, with its institutions, belongs to the people who
inhabit it. Whenever they shall grow weary of the existing Government, they can exercise their *constitutional* right of amending it, or
their *revolutionary* right to dismember or overthrow it. I cannot be
ignorant of the fact that many worthy and patriotic citizens are desirous of having the national Constitution amended. While I make no
recommendation of amendments, I fully recognize the rightful authority of the people over the whole subject to be exercised in either of the
modes prescribed in the instrument itself; and I should, under existing circumstances, favor rather than oppose a fair opportunity being
afforded the people to act upon it.

I will venture to add that to me the Convention mode seems pref-
erable, in that it allows amendments to originate with the people them-

selves, instead of only permitting them to take or reject propositions, originated by others, not especially chosen for the purpose, and which might not be precisely such as they would wish to either accept or refuse. I understand a proposed amendment to the Constitution, which amendment, however, I have not seen, has passed Congress, to the effect that the federal government shall never interfere with the domestic institutions of the States, including that of persons held to service. To avoid misconstruction of what I have said, I depart from my purpose not to speak of particular amendments, so far as to say that holding such a provision to now be implied constitutional law, I have no objection to its being made express and irrevocable.

The Chief Magistrate derives all his authority from the people, and they have referred none upon him to fix terms for the separation of the States. The people themselves can do this if also they choose; but the executive, as such, has nothing to do with it. His duty is to administer the present government, as it came to his hands, and to transmit it, unimpaired by him, to his successor.

Why should there not be a patient confidence in the ultimate justice of the people? Is there any better or equal hope, in the world? In our present differences, is either party without faith of being in the right? If the Almighty Ruler of nations, with his eternal truth and justice, be on your side of the North, or on yours of the South, that truth, and that justice, will surely prevail, by the judgment of this great tribunal of the American people.

By the frame of the government under which we live, this same people have wisely given their public servants but little power for mischief; and have, with equal wisdom, provided for the return of that little to their own hands at very short intervals.

While the people retain their virtue and vigilance, no administration, by any extreme of wickedness or folly, can very seriously injure the government in the short space of four years.

My countrymen, one and all, think calmly and *well*, upon this whole subject. Nothing valuable can be lost by taking time. If there be an object to *hurry* any of you, in hot haste, to a step which you would never take *deliberately*, that object will be frustrated by taking time; but no good object can be frustrated by it. Such of you as are now dissatisfied still have the old Constitution unimpaired, and, on the sensitive point, the laws of your own framing under it; while the new administration will have no immediate power, if it would, to change either. If it were admitted that you who are dissatisfied, hold the right side in the dispute, there still is no single good reason for precipitate action. Intelligence, patriotism, Christianity, and a firm reliance on Him, who has never yet forsaken this favored land, are still competent to adjust, in the best way, all our present difficulty.

In *your* hands, my dissatisfied fellow countrymen, and not in *mine*, is the momentous issue of civil war. The government will not assail *you*. You can have no conflict without being yourselves the aggressors. *You* have no oath registered in Heaven to destroy the government, while *I* shall have the most solemn one to "preserve, protect, and defend it."

I am loath to close. We are not enemies, but friends. We must not be enemies. Though passion may have strained, it must not break our bonds of affection. The mystic chords of memory, stretching from every battle-field, and patriot grave, to every living heart and hearth-stone, all over this broad land, will yet swell the chorus of the Union, when again touched, as surely they will be, by the better angels of our nature.

# NOTES

## March 4, 1861, Monday: The Most Widely Anticipated Speech

1. William H. Herndon and Jesse W. Weik, *Herndon's Life of Lincoln* (New York: World, 1949), 386.

2. "Liberty and Union, Now and Forever, One and Inseparable," Last Best Hope of Earth, May 2, 2016, https://lastbesthopeofearth.com/2016/05/02/liberty-and -union-now-and-forever-one-and-inseparable/.

3. Marquis James, *The Life of Andrew Jackson* (New York: Bobbs-Merrill, 1938), 610.

4. Herndon and Weik, *Herndon's Life of Lincoln*, 386.

5. Jean H. Baker, "Learning from Buchanan," *New York Times*, February 26, 2011.

6. *Evening Star* (Washington, DC), March 4, 1861.

7. Herndon and Weik, *Herndon's Life of Lincoln*, 400.

8. Allen Thorndike Rice, "The Diary of a Public Man," *North American Review* (1879): 382–85.

9. Herndon and Weik, *Herndon's Life of Lincoln*, 400–401.

10. Herndon and Weik, *Herndon's Life of Lincoln*, 401.

11. "An Incident of the Inauguration," *Cincinnati Commercial*, March 11, 1861, quoted in Allan Nevins, "He Did Hold Lincoln's Hat: Senator Douglas' Act Is Verified, at Last, by First-Hand Testimony," *American Heritage*, February 1959.

12. Herndon and Weik, *Herndon's Life of Lincoln*, 401.

13. All passages from the final draft of the inaugural address are from Abraham Lincoln, *The Collected Works of Abraham Lincoln*, ed. Roy P. Basler (New Brunswick, NJ: Rutgers University Press, 1953), 4:262–71. The text of the entire speech is given in the appendix.

14. Herndon and Weik, *Herndon's Life of Lincoln*, 401.

15. *New York Herald*, March 5, 1861.

16. *New York Herald*, March 5, 1861.

17. Herndon and Weik, *Herndon's Life of Lincoln*, 401.

18. *New York Herald*, March 5, 1861.

19. Lincoln, *Collected Works*, 4:145.

20. Walter Stahr, *Seward: Lincoln's Indispensable Man* (New York: Simon & Schuster, 2012), 228.

21. Lincoln, *Collected Works*, 4:273.

22. Lincoln, *Collected Works*, 4:273.

23. David Herbert Donald, *Lincoln* (New York: Simon & Schuster, 1995), 282.
24. Donald, *Lincoln*, 282.
25. Donald, *Lincoln*, 282.
26. Stahr, *Seward*, 518.
27. Glyndon G. Van Deusen, *William Henry Seward* (New York: Oxford University Press, 1967), 336.
28. *New York Times*, March 5, 1861.
29. *Evening Star* (Washington, DC), March 5, 1861.
30. Jean H. Baker, *Mary Todd Lincoln: A Biography* (New York: Norton, 1987), 85.
31. *Evening Star* (Washington, DC), March 5, 1861.
32. *New York Herald*, March 6, 1861.
33. Henry Adams, *The Education of Henry Adams* (Boston: Houghton Mifflin, 1918), 105.

## March 5, 1861, Tuesday: Crisis on the First Day

1. *Richmond Enquirer*, March 5, 1861.
2. *Charleston Mercury*, March 5, 1861.
3. *Wilmington Herald*, March 7, 1861.
4. *Richmond Enquirer*, March 5, 1861.
5. *New York Times*, March 5, 1861.
6. Joseph Holt and Winfield Scott to Abraham Lincoln, March 5, 1861, Abraham Lincoln Papers, Library of Congress, Washington, DC.
7. Charles Francis Adams Sr., diary entry, March 10, 1861, in *The Civil War Diaries*, by Charles Francis Adams Sr. (Unverified Transcriptions) (Boston: Massachusetts Historical Society, 2015), http://www.masshist.org/publications/cfa-civil-war/view?id=DCA61d069.
8. Henry Adams, *The Education of Henry Adams* (Boston: Houghton Mifflin, 1918), 106.
9. Abraham Lincoln, *The Collected Works of Abraham Lincoln*, ed. Roy P. Basler (New Brunswick, NJ: Rutgers University Press, 1953), 4:274.
10. Lincoln, *Collected Works*, 4:274–75.
11. Lincoln, *Collected Works*, 4:275.
12. Joseph Holt and Winfield Scott to Abraham Lincoln, March 5, 1861, Abraham Lincoln Papers, Library of Congress, Washington, DC.
13. Lincoln, *Collected Works*, 4:267.
14. George W. Hazzard to Abraham Lincoln, October 21, 1860, Abraham Lincoln Papers, Library of Congress, Washington, DC.
15. William Howard Russell, *My Diary North and South* (Boston: Burnham, 1863), 71.
16. Lincoln, *Collected Works*, 4:215–16.

17. Orville Hickman Browning, *The Diary of Orville Hickman Browning* (Springfield: Illinois State Historical Library, 1925), 1:47. Note: Lincoln used the spelling "Sumpter" (not Sumter) in his writings.

### March 6, 1861, Wednesday: First Cabinet Meeting

1. Abraham Lincoln, *The Collected Works of Abraham Lincoln*, ed. Roy P. Basler (New Brunswick, NJ: Rutgers University Press, 1953), 4:276.
2. Lincoln, *Collected Works*, 4:276.
3. Salmon P. Chase to Abraham Lincoln, March 6, 1861, Abraham Lincoln Papers, Library of Congress, Washington, DC.
4. Lincoln, *Collected Works*, 4:276.
5. *"The Soldiers' Home," President Lincoln's Cottage*, March 10, 2013, https://www.lincolncottage.org/the-soldiers-home.
6. William O. Stoddard, *Inside the White House in War Times* (New York: Webster, 1890), 13.
7. *"Upstairs* at the White House, Mr. Lincoln's Office," Mr. Lincoln's White House, n.d., https://www.mrlincolnswhitehouse.org/the-white-house/upstairs-at-the-white-house/upstairs-white-house-mr-lincolns-office/index.html.
8. Edward Bates, *The Diary of Edward Bates, 1859–1866*, ed. Howard K. Beale (Washington, DC: US Government Printing Office, 1933), 177.

### March 7, 1861, Thursday: Encouraging News from Virginia

1. Abraham Lincoln, *The Collected Works of Abraham Lincoln*, ed. Roy P. Basler (New Brunswick, NJ: Rutgers University Press, 1953), 4:277.
2. Lincoln, *Collected Works*, 4:277.
3. Lincoln, *Collected Works*, 4:277.
4. Francis Fessenden, *Life and Public Services of William Pitt Fessenden* (Boston: Houghton Mifflin, 1907), 1:127.
5. "Upstairs at the White House, Mr. Lincoln's Office," Mr. Lincoln's White House, n.d., https://www.mrlincolnswhitehouse.org/the-white-house/upstairs-at-the-white-house/upstairs-white-house mr-lincolns-office/index.html.
6. *New York Times*, March 6, 1861.

### March 8, 1861, Friday: In a Quandary

1. *New York Times*, March 7, 1861.
2. *New York Herald*, March 7, 1861; *New York Times*, March 7, 1861.
3. Jefferson Davis, *The Rise and Fall of the Confederate Government* (Richmond, VA: Garrett and Massie, 1938), 1:49.

4. Davis, *Rise and Fall of the Confederate Government*, 1:48.

5. Ron Soodalter, "The Day New York Tried to Secede," HistoryNet, October 26, 2011, https://www.historynet.com/the-day-new-york-tried-to-secede.htm.

6. *Evening Star* (Washington, DC), March 9, 1861.

7. William O. Stoddard, *Inside the White House in War Times* (New York: Webster, 1890), 52.

8. Stoddard, *Inside the White House*, 52.

9. *Evening Star* (Washington, DC), March 9, 1861.

10. *New York Herald*, March 13, 1861.

11. *Evening Star* (Washington, DC), March 9, 1861.

12. *New York Herald*, March 13, 1861.

13. *Evening Star* (Washington, DC), March 9, 1861.

14. *New York Herald*, March 13, 1861.

15. *Evening Star* (Washington, DC), March 9, 1861.

## March 9, 1861, Saturday: A Tense Cabinet Meeting

1. Abraham Lincoln, *The Collected Works of Abraham Lincoln*, ed. Roy P. Basler (New Brunswick, NJ: Rutgers University Press, 1953), 4:281.

2. Lina Mann, "Spies, Lies and Disguise: Abraham Lincoln and the Baltimore Plot," White House Historical Association, n.d., https://www.whitehousehistory.org/spies-lies-and-disguise-abraham-lincoln-and-the-baltimore-plot.

3. Lincoln, *Collected Works*, 4:280.

4. Lincoln, *Collected Works*, 4:278.

5. Lincoln, *Collected Works*, 4:280.

6. Edward Bates, *The Diary of Edward Bates, 1859–1866*, ed. Howard K. Beale (Washington, DC: US Government Printing Office, 1933), 177.

7. Bates, *Diary of Edward Bates*, 177.

8. Bates, *Diary of Edward Bates*, 177–78. Fort Moultrie and Fort Cummings' Point were smaller installations in Charleston Harbor, close by Fort Sumter.

9. Gideon Welles, *Diary of Gideon Welles* (Boston: Houghton Mifflin, 1911), 1:9.

10. Welles, *Diary of Gideon Welles*, 1:10.

11. Lincoln, *Collected Works*, 4:274.

12. Lincoln, *Collected Works*, 4:275.

13. Lincoln, *Collected Works*, 4:266.

## March 10, 1861, Sunday: A Rare Day of Peace and Quiet

1. William E. Barton, *The Life of Abraham Lincoln: Two Volumes in One* (New York and Boston: Books, 1943), 2:42.

2. Abraham Lincoln, *The Collected Works of Abraham Lincoln*, ed. Roy P. Basler (New Brunswick, NJ: Rutgers University Press, 1953), 1:383.

3. Lincoln, *Collected Works*, 4:191.
4. Lincoln, *Collected Works*, 7:542.
5. *New York Times*, March 10, 1861.

### March 11, 1861, Monday: Secret Negotiations

1. Abraham Lincoln, *The Collected Works of Abraham Lincoln*, ed. Roy P. Basler (New Brunswick, NJ: Rutgers University Press, 1953), 4:281.
2. Lincoln, *Collected Works*, 4:281.
3. Lincoln, *Collected Works*, 4:281. President Lincoln appointed John C. Fremont to the rank of major general in the US Army on May 15, 1861.
4. Lincoln, *Collected Works*, 4:279.
5. Gideon Welles, *Diary of Gideon Welles* (Boston: Houghton Mifflin, 1911), 1:12. In his memoirs, Jefferson Davis wrote that the delegates arrived in Washington "two or three days before the expiration of Mr. Buchanan's term of office as President of the United States." Jefferson Davis, *The Rise and Fall of the Confederate Government* (Richmond, VA: Garrett and Massie, 1938), 264.
6. Davis, *Rise and Fall of the Confederate Government*, 12.

### March 12, 1861, Tuesday: The Pressures of Office

1. Abraham Lincoln, *The Collected Works of Abraham Lincoln*, ed. Roy P. Basler (New Brunswick, NJ: Rutgers University Press, 1953), 4:282.
2. Lincoln, *Collected Works*, 4:282.
3. Lincoln, *Collected Works*, 4:284.
4. "Confederate States of America—Confederate Commissioners to Secretary Seward March 12, 1861," Yale Law School, n.d., https://avalon.law.yale.edu/19th_century/csa_c031261.asp.
5. William O. Stoddard, *Abraham Lincoln: The Life and Times of a Great Life* (New York: Fords, Howard & Hulbert, 1884), 217.
6. "Confederate States of America—Confederate Commissioners to Secretary Seward March 12, 1861."
7. *New York Herald*, March 14, 1861.
8. Frederic Bancroft, *The Life of William H. Seward* (New York: Harper, 1900), 2:103.
9. Stoddard, *Abraham Lincoln*, 217.
10. *Evening Star* (Washington, DC), March 12, 1861.

### March 13, 1861, Wednesday: A New Plan

1. Abraham Lincoln, *The Collected Works of Abraham Lincoln*, ed. Roy P. Basler (New Brunswick, NJ: Rutgers University Press, 1953), 4:282.

2. Henry J. Raymond, *The Life and Public Services of Abraham Lincoln* (New York: Derby and Miller, 1865), 170.

## March 14, 1861, Thursday: Almost Unbearable Tension

1. *New York Herald*, March 15, 1861.
2. Edward Bates, *The Diary of Edward Bates, 1859–1866*, ed. Howard K. Beale (Washington, DC: US Government Printing Office, 1933), 177–78.
3. Richard N. Current, *Lincoln and the First Shot* (Philadelphia: Lippincott, 1963), 64.
4. Current, *Lincoln and the First Shot*, 64.
5. *New York Herald*, March 15, 1861.

## March 15, 1861, Friday: Lincoln Sends a Memo

1. Abraham Lincoln, *The Collected Works of Abraham Lincoln*, ed. Roy P. Basler (New Brunswick, NJ: Rutgers University Press, 1953),4:284.
2. Lincoln, *Collected Works*, 4:285.
3. Lincoln, *Collected Works*, 4:385.
4. Lincoln, *Collected Works*, 4:385.
5. Lincoln, *Collected Works*, 4:385.
6. Lincoln, *Collected Works*, 4:385.
7. Lincoln, *Collected Works*, 4:385.
8. Lincoln, *Collected Works*, 4:385.
9. *New York Tribune*, November 9, 1860.
10. Edward Bates, *The Diary of Edward Bates, 1859–1866*, ed. Howard K. Beale (Washington, DC: US Government Printing Office, 1933), 179.

## March 16 and 17, 1861, Saturday and Sunday: A Quiet Weekend

1. Abraham Lincoln, *The Collected Works of Abraham Lincoln*, ed. Roy P. Basler (New Brunswick, NJ: Rutgers University Press, 1953), 4:286.
2. Lincoln, *Collected Works*, 4:286.
3. Lincoln, *Collected Works*, 4:287.
4. Horace Porter, *Campaigning with Grant* (Secaucus, NJ: Blue and Grey, 1984), 426.
5. Lincoln, *Collected Works*, 4:287–88.
6. George Cornewall Lewis, *Letters of the Right Hon. Sir George Cornewall Lewis, Bart., to Various Friends*, ed. G. F. Lewis (London: Longmans, Green, 1870), 395.
7. *New York Herald*, March 18, 1861.

## March 18, 1861, Monday: Tariffs, Appointments, and a Memo

1. Abraham Lincoln, *The Collected Works of Abraham Lincoln*, ed. Roy P. Basler (New Brunswick, NJ: Rutgers University Press, 1953), 4:288.
2. Lincoln, *Collected Works*, 4:288–90.
3. Lincoln, *Collected Works*, 4:288–90.
4. "The Collection of Revenue," *New York Herald*, March 18, 1861.
5. Lincoln, *Collected Works*, 4:292.
6. Lincoln, *Collected Works*, 4:292.
7. Lincoln, *Collected Works*, 4:293.
8. Lincoln, *Collected Works*, 4:290.
9. "Reciprocal Trade Agreement Act (1934)," Living New Deal, accessed April 1, 2019, https://livingnewdeal.org/glossary/reciprocal-trade-agreement-act-1934.
10. *Lincoln, Collected Works*, 4:293.
11. Henry Adams, *The Education of Henry Adams* (Boston: Houghton Mifflin, 1918), 115.

## March 19, 1861, Tuesday: An Order for Captain Fox

1. Abraham Lincoln, *The Collected Works of Abraham Lincoln*, ed. Roy P. Basler (New Brunswick, NJ: Rutgers University Press, 1953), 4:294.
2. Gustavus V. Fox, *Correspondence of Gustavus Vasa Fox*, ed. Robert Means Thompson and Richard Wainwright (New York: De Vinne, 1920), 1:9–10.
3. John G. Nicolay and John Hay, *Abraham Lincoln: A History* (New York: Century, 1890), 3:389.
4. Fox, *Correspondence of Gustavus Vasa Fox*, 1:10.

## March 20, 1861, Wednesday: White House Activities

1. Abraham Lincoln, *The Collected Works of Abraham Lincoln*, ed. Roy P. Basler (New Brunswick, NJ: Rutgers University Press, 1953), 4:296–97.
2. Lincoln, *Collected Works*, 4:296.
3. Lincoln, *Collected Works*, 4:296.

## March 21, 1861, Thursday: Conflicting Opinions

1. Abraham Lincoln, *The Collected Works of Abraham Lincoln*, ed. Roy P. Basler (New Brunswick, NJ: Rutgers University Press, 1953), 4:297.
2. Lincoln, *Collected Works*, 4:297.
3. John G. Nicolay and John Hay, *Abraham Lincoln: A History* (New York: Century, 1890), 3:389.

4. *Albany Evening Journal*, March 27, 1861.
5. Nicolay and Hay, *Abraham Lincoln*, 3:389–90.
6. Nicolay and Hay, *Abraham Lincoln*, 3:388.

## March 22, 1861, Friday: A Cabinet Meeting and a Reception

1. *Evening Star* (Washington, DC), March 4, 1861.
2. Edward Bates, *The Diary of Edward Bates, 1859–1866*, ed. Howard K. Beale (Washington, DC: US Government Printing Office, 1933), 177.
3. *Evening Star* (Washington, DC), March 4, 1861.
4. *Evening Star* (Washington, DC), March 4, 1861.
5. *Evening Star* (Washington, DC), March 4, 1861.
6. *Evening Star* (Washington, DC), March 4, 1861.

## March 23 and 24, 1861, Saturday and Sunday: A Much-Needed Rest

1. Daniel Mark Epstein, *The Lincolns: Portrait of a Marriage* (New York: Ballantine Books, 2009), 320.
2. A. L. Lang, *Memoirs of Robert E. Lee* (Secaucus, NJ: Blue and Gray, 1983), 89.
3. U. S. Grant, *Personal Memoirs of U. S. Grant* (Old Saybrook, CT: Konecky & Konecky, 1886), 134.
4. James Longstreet, *From Manassas to Appomattox* (New York: Konecky & Konecky, 1992), 29.
5. Asia Booth Clarke, *The Unlocked Book: A Memoir of John Wilkes Booth by His Sister Asia Booth Clarke*, ed. Eleanor Farjeon (New York: Putnam, 1938), 202–4.
6. William Tecumseh Sherman, *Memoirs of General William T. Sherman* (New York: Appleton, 1889), 184.
7. Sherman, *Memoirs*, 196.
8. Sherman, *Memoirs*, 196.

## March 25, 1861, Monday: Waiting for News

1. Abraham Lincoln, *The Collected Works of Abraham Lincoln*, ed. Roy P. Basler (New Brunswick, NJ: Rutgers University Press, 1953), 4:298.
2. Lincoln, *Collected Works*, 4:298.
3. Lincoln, *Collected Works*, 4:298.
4. *Post and Courier* (Charleston, SC), February 12, 2010.
5. Ward Hill Lamon, *Recollections of Abraham Lincoln, 1847–1865*, ed. Dorothy Lamon Teillard (Washington, DC: published by the editor, 1911), 71.

## March 26, 1861, Tuesday: Denying a Request

1. Abraham Lincoln, *The Collected Works of Abraham Lincoln*, ed. Roy P. Basler (New Brunswick, NJ: Rutgers University Press, 1953), 4:299.
2. *New York Times*, March 26, 1861.
3. *New York Herald*, March 24, 1861.

## March 27, 1861, Wednesday: An Upsetting Report

1. Abraham Lincoln, *The Collected Works of Abraham Lincoln*, ed. Roy P. Basler (New Brunswick, NJ: Rutgers University Press, 1953), 4:300.
2. Lincoln, *Collected Works*, 4:300.
3. Stephen Hurlbut to Abraham Lincoln, March 27, 1861, Abraham Lincoln Papers, Library of Congress, Washington, DC, https://www.loc.gov/item/mal 0838800.
4. Hurlbut to Lincoln, March 27, 1861.
5. Lincoln, *Collected Works*, 4:95.
6. Hurlbut to Lincoln, March 27, 1861.
7. Hurlbut to Lincoln, March 27, 1861.
8. Ward Hill Lamon, *Recollections of Abraham Lincoln, 1847–1865*, ed. Dorothy Lamon Teillard (Washington, DC: published by the editor, 1911), 74.
9. William Howard Russell, *My Diary North and South* (Boston: Burnham, 1863), 37.
10. Russell, *My Diary North and South*, 37.
11. Russell, *My Diary North and South*, 38.
12. Russell, *My Diary North and South*, 39.
13. Russell, *My Diary North and South*, 39.

## March 28, 1861, Thursday: A Memo from General Scott

1. John G. Nicolay and John Hay, *Abraham Lincoln: A History* (New York: Century, 1890), 3:394.
2. *Evening Star* (Washington, DC), March 30, 1861.
3. William Howard Russell, *My Diary North and South* (Boston: Burnham, 1863), 43.
4. Russell, *My Diary North and South*, 44.
5. Russell, *My Diary North and South*, 45.
6. Russell, *My Diary North and South*, 41–42.
7. Nicolay and Hay, *Abraham Lincoln*, 3:394.
8. Nicolay and Hay, *Abraham Lincoln*, 3:394–95.
9. Nicolay and Hay, *Abraham Lincoln*, 3:395.

## March 29, 1861, Good Friday: The President Orders an Expedition

1. David Herbert Donald, *Lincoln* (New York: Simon & Schuster, 1995), 288.
2. Abraham Lincoln, *The Collected Works of Abraham Lincoln*, ed. Roy P. Basler (New Brunswick, NJ: Rutgers University Press, 1953), 4:300–301.
3. Edward Bates, *The Diary of Edward Bates: 1859–1866* (Washington, DC: US Government Printing Office, 1933), 180.
4. Bates, *Diary of Edward Bates*, 180.
5. Lincoln, *Collected Works*, 4:301.
6. Lincoln, *Collected Works*, 4:301.
7. Richard N. Current, *Lincoln and the First Shot* (Philadelphia: Lippincott, 1963), 81.

## March 30, 1861, Saturday: Political Appointments

1. Abraham Lincoln, *The Collected Works of Abraham Lincoln*, ed. Roy P. Basler (New Brunswick, NJ: Rutgers University Press, 1953), 4:288, 4:302.
2. Lincoln, *Collected Works*, 4:302.
3. Lincoln, *Collected Works*, 4:303.
4. William Howard Russell, *My Diary North and South* (Boston: Burnham, 1863), 53.
5. Russell, *My Diary North and South*, 54.

## March 31, 1861, Easter Sunday: A Vital Decision

1. James Cooley, "The Relief of Fort Pickens," *American Heritage Magazine*, February 1974, https://www.americanheritage.com/relief-fort-pickens?issue=53100.
2. Frederick W. Seward, *Seward at Washington as Senator and Secretary of State* (Albany, NY: Weed Parsons, 1890), 538–39.
3. Cooley, "The Relief of Fort Pickens."

## April 1, 1861, Monday: "I Must Do It"

1. Abraham Lincoln, *The Collected Works of Abraham Lincoln*, ed. Roy P. Basler (New Brunswick, NJ: Rutgers University Press, 1953), 4:314.
2. Lincoln, *Collected Works*, 4:314.
3. Lincoln, *Collected Works*, 4:315.
4. Lincoln, *Collected Works*, 4:315.
5. Lincoln, *Collected Works*, 4:315.
6. Lincoln, *Collected Works*, 4:318.
7. Lincoln, *Collected Works*, 4:316.

8. Lincoln, *Collected Works*, 4:317.
9. Lincoln, *Collected Works*, 4:317.
10. Lincoln, *Collected Works*, 4:317.
11. Lincoln, *Collected Works*, 4:317–18.
12. Lincoln, *Collected Works*, 4:318.
13. Jefferson Davis, *The Rise and Fall of the Confederate Government* (Richmond, VA: Garrett and Massie, 1938), 1:59.
14. Lincoln, *Collected Works*, 4:316.
15. Lincoln, *Collected Works*, 4:316.
16. Lincoln, *Collected Works*, 4:316.
17. Lincoln, *Collected Works*, 4:318.
18. Lincoln, *Collected Works*, 4:317.
19. Lincoln, *Collected Works*, 4:317.
20. Stephen B. Oates, *With Malice toward None: The Life of Abraham Lincoln* (New York: Harper & Row, 1977), 243.

## April 2, 1861, Tuesday: An Unplanned Visit

1. Abraham Lincoln, *The Collected Works of Abraham Lincoln*, ed. Roy P. Basler (New Brunswick, NJ: Rutgers University Press, 1953), 4:319.
2. Lincoln, *Collected Works*, 4:319.
3. Lincoln, *Collected Works*, 4:320.
4. Lincoln, *Collected Works*, 4:320.
5. *Evening Star* (Washington, DC), April 3, 1861.
6. *Evening Star* (Washington, DC), April 3, 1861.

## April 3, 1861, Wednesday: Increasing War Nerves

1. Abraham Lincoln, *The Collected Works of Abraham Lincoln*, ed. Roy P. Basler (New Brunswick, NJ: Rutgers University Press, 1953), 4:321.
2. Lincoln, *Collected Works*, 4:321.
3. Lincoln, *Collected Works*, 4:320.
4. James Cooley, "The Relief of Fort Pickens," *American Heritage Magazine*, February 1974, https://www.americanheritage.com/relief-fort-pickens?issue=53100.
5. Erasmus D. Keyes, *Fifty Years' Observation of Men and Events, Civil and Military* (New York: Scribner, 1884), 387.
6. Cooley, "The Relief of Fort Pickens."
7. Lincoln, *Collected Works*, 4:321.
8. *New York Times*, April 3, 1861.

## April 4, 1861, Thursday: A Disappointing Meeting

1. Abraham Lincoln, *The Collected Works of Abraham Lincoln*, ed. Roy P. Basler (New Brunswick, NJ: Rutgers University Press, 1953), 4:322.
2. Lincoln, *Collected Works*, 4:321–22.
3. *Interview between President Lincoln and Col. John B. Baldwin, April 4, 1861, Statements & Evidence* (Staunton, VA: "Spectator" Job Office; Strasburg, Printer, 1864), 9–13.
4. *Interview between President Lincoln and Col. John B. Baldwin*, 13.
5. Frederick W. Seward, *Seward at Washington as Senator and Secretary of State* (Albany, NY: Weed Parsons, 1890), 536.
6. Gustavus Fox, *Confidential Correspondence of Gustavus Vasa Fox, Assistant Secretary of the Navy, 1861–1865*, ed. Robert Means Thompson and Richard Wainwright (New York: Naval History Society, 1920), 1:21–22.

## April 5, 1861, Friday: The President Signs Two Sets of Orders

1. Abraham Lincoln, *The Collected Works of Abraham Lincoln*, ed. Roy P. Basler (New Brunswick, NJ: Rutgers University Press, 1953), 4:322.
2. Lincoln, *Collected Works*, 4:323.
3. "Abraham Lincoln Corrects His Presidential Salary Payment, Which Credits Him with Days Not Worked," Shapell, April 5, 1861, http://www.shapell.org/manu script/honest-abe/.
4. *Evening Star* (Washington, DC), April 6, 1861.
5. John G. Nicolay and John Hay, *Abraham Lincoln: A History* (New York: Century, 1890), 3:433.
6. Gideon Welles, *Diary of Gideon Welles* (Boston: Houghton Mifflin, 1911), 1:23.
7. Charles M. Segal, *Conversations with Lincoln* (New York: Putnam, 1961), 107.

## April 6, 1861, Saturday: "The Rebellion Was Rapidly Culminating"

1. Stephen Hurlbut to Abraham Lincoln, March 27, 1861, Abraham Lincoln Papers, Library of Congress, Washington, DC, https://www.loc.gov/item/mal0838800.
2. Abner Doubleday, *Reminiscences of Forts Sumter and Moultrie in 1860–'61* (New York: Harper, 1876), 135–36.
3. *Daily Times* (Columbus, GA), April 6, 1861.
4. Doubleday, *Reminiscences of Forts Sumter and Moultrie*, 136.
5. Abraham Lincoln, *The Collected Works of Abraham Lincoln*, ed. Roy P. Basler (New Brunswick, NJ: Rutgers University Press, 1953), 4:323–24.
6. James M. McPherson, *Tried by War: Abraham Lincoln as Commander in Chief* (New York: Penguin, 2008), 20.

7. Gideon Welles, *Diary of Gideon Welles* (Boston: Houghton Mifflin, 1911), 1:29.

8. Welles, *Diary of Gideon Welles*, 1:30.

9. Welles, *Diary of Gideon Welles*, 1:30.

10. Eleven months later, John L. Worden commanded the ironclad USS *Monitor* during its battle with CSS *Virginia* (formerly USS *Merrimack*) at Hampton Roads, Virginia.

11. Welles, *Diary of Gideon Welles*, 1:24.

12. John G. Nicolay and John Hay, *Abraham Lincoln: A History* (New York: Century, 1890), 3:440.

13. Welles, *Diary of Gideon Welles*, 1:24.

14. Welles, *Diary of Gideon Welles*, 1:25.

15. Welles, *Diary of Gideon Welles*, 1:25.

16. Welles, *Diary of Gideon Welles*, 1:25.

## April 7, 1861, Sunday: A Bleak Day

1. US Congress, Joint Committee on Reconstruction, Report of the Joint Committee on Reconstruction, 39th Cong., First Session (Washington, DC: US Government Printing Office, 1866), pt. 2, 114.

2. US Congress, Joint Committee on Reconstruction, Report of the Joint Committee, 114.

3. "Abraham Lincoln and Virginia," Abraham Lincoln's Classroom, n.d., https://www.abrahamlincolnsclassroom.org/abraham-lincoln-state-by-state/abraham-lincoln-and-virginia/index.html.

4. US Congress, Joint Committee on Reconstruction, Report of the Joint Committee, 115.

5. John Minor Botts, *The Great Rebellion: Its Secret History, Rise, Progress, and Disastrous Failure* (New York: Harper, 1866), 196.

## April 8, 1861, Monday: Growing Tensions

1. Abraham Lincoln, *The Collected Works of Abraham Lincoln*, ed. Roy P. Basler (New Brunswick, NJ: Rutgers University Press, 1953), 4:324.

2. Jefferson Davis, *The Rise and Fall of the Confederate Government* (Richmond, VA: Garrett and Massie, 1938), 1:284–85.

3. Lincoln, *Collected Works*, 4:324.

4. Lincoln, *Collected Works*, 4:324.

## April 9, 1861, Tuesday: Deceptive Calm

1. Gustavus Fox, *Confidential Correspondence of Gustavus Vasa Fox, Assistant Secretary of the Navy, 1861–1865*, ed. Robert Means Thompson and Richard Wainwright (New York: Naval History Society, 1920), 1:31–32.

2. Fox, *Confidential Correspondence of Gustavus Vasa Fox*, 1:31.
3. *Evening Star* (Washington, DC), April 9, 1861.

## April 10, 1861, Wednesday: Waiting for News

1. Abraham Lincoln, *The Collected Works of Abraham Lincoln*, ed. Roy P. Basler (New Brunswick, NJ: Rutgers University Press, 1953), 4:326.
2. *New York Herald*, April 10, 1861.
3. Jefferson Davis, *The Rise and Fall of the Confederate Government* (Richmond, VA: Garrett and Massie, 1938), 1:239.
4. Davis, *Rise and Fall of the Confederate Government*, 1:239.

## April 11, 1861, Thursday: An Unacceptable Demand

1. Abraham Lincoln, *The Collected Works of Abraham Lincoln*, ed. Roy P. Basler (New Brunswick, NJ: Rutgers University Press, 1953), 4:327.
2. Lincoln, *Collected Works*, 4:327.
3. Lincoln, *Collected Works*, 4:328.
4. Abraham Lincoln Papers, April 11, 1861, Library of Congress, Washington, DC.
5. *Evening Star* (Washington, DC), April 15, 1861.
6. Jefferson Davis, *The Rise and Fall of the Confederate Government* (Richmond, VA: Garrett and Massie, 1938), 1:246.
7. Davis, *Rise and Fall of the Confederate Government*, 1:250.
8. Davis, *Rise and Fall of the Confederate Government*, 1:254.
9. Davis, *Rise and Fall of the Confederate Government*, 1:247.
10. Davis, *Rise and Fall of the Confederate Government*, 1:247.
11. Davis, *Rise and Fall of the Confederate Government*, 1:247–48.
12. Davis, *Rise and Fall of the Confederate Government*, 1:248.
13. Gustavus Fox, *Confidential Correspondence of Gustavus Vasa Fox, Assistant Secretary of the Navy, 1861–1865*, ed. Robert Means Thompson and Richard Wainwright (New York: Naval History Society, 1920), 1:32.
14. *New York Herald*, April 12, 1861.

## April 12, 1861, Friday: The Crisis Reaches a Climax—A Last Peaceful Day at the White House

1. Jefferson Davis, *The Rise and Fall of the Confederate Government* (Richmond, VA: Garrett and Massie, 1938), 1:252.
2. Mary Boykin Chesnut, *A Diary from Dixie*, ed. Isabella D. Martin and Myrta Lockett Avary (New York: Appleton, 1906), 35.

3. Gustavus Fox, *Confidential Correspondence of Gustavus Vasa Fox, Assistant Secretary of the Navy, 1861–1865*, ed. Robert Means Thompson and Richard Wainwright (New York: Naval History Society, 1920), 1:32.

4. Edward Bates, *The Diary of Edward Bates, 1859–1866*, ed. Howard K. Beale (Washington, DC: US Government Printing Office, 1933), 182.

5. Bates, *Diary of Edward Bates*, 182.

6. William Howard Russell, *My Diary North and South* (Boston: Burnham, 1863), 77.

7. Richard N. Current, *Lincoln and the First Shot* (Philadelphia: Lippincott, 1963), 154.

8. Jan Morris, *Lincoln: A Foreigner's Quest* (New York: Thorndike, 2000), 141.

## April 13, 1861, Saturday: Visitors

1. *Daily News* (New York), April 13, 1861.

2. *New York Times*, April 13, 1861.

3. *New York Herald*, April 13, 1861.

4. Winston S. Churchill, *A History of the English-Speaking Peoples: The Great Democracies* (New York: Dodd, Mead, 1958), 168.

5. *New York World*, April 19, 1861.

6. Elisha Hunt Rhodes, *All for the Union* (New York: Vintage, 1992), 3.

7. Samuel Toombs, *New Jersey Troops in the Gettysburg Campaign* (Orange, NJ: Evening Mail Publishing House, 1888), 1.

8. Alistair Cooke, *Alistair Cooke's America* (New York: Knopf, 1974) , 206.

9. Jefferson Davis, *The Rise and Fall of the Confederate Government* (Richmond, VA: Garrett and Massie, 1938), 1:vii.

10. *Nashville Union & American*, June 5, 1861.

11. Abraham Lincoln, *The Collected Works of Abraham Lincoln*, ed. Roy P. Basler (New Brunswick, NJ: Rutgers University Press, 1953), 4:327.

12. Lincoln, *Collected Works*, 4:330.

13. *Baltimore Sun*, April 15, 1861.

14. Lincoln, *Collected Works*, 4:330–31.

15. Lincoln, *Collected Works*, 4:331.

16. *Evening Star* (Washington, DC), April 13, 1861.

17. Gustavus Fox, *Confidential Correspondence of Gustavus Vasa Fox, Assistant Secretary of the Navy, 1861–1865* (New York: Naval History Society, 1920), 33.

18. *Baltimore Sun*, April 15, 1861.

19. James R. Gilmore, *Personal Recollections of Abraham Lincoln and the Civil War* (London: Macqueen, 1899), 15.

20. Gilmore, *Personal Recollections*, 15–16.

21. Gilmore, *Personal Recollections*, 17–18.
22. Gilmore, *Personal Recollections*, 18.
23. Gilmore, *Personal Recollections*, 18–19.
24. James M. McPherson, *Battle Cry of Freedom: The Civil War Era* (New York: Oxford University Press, 1988), 312.
25. Gilmore, *Personal Recollections*, 20.
26. Gilmore, *Personal Recollections*, 20.
27. Gilmore, *Personal Recollections*, 21.
28. Gilmore, *Personal Recollections*, 21–22.

## April 14, 1861, Sunday: More Visitors

1. John A. O'Brien, "Seeking God's Will: President Lincoln and Rev. Dr. Gurley," *Journal of the Abraham Lincoln Association* 39, no. 2 (Summer 2018): 33.
2. John G. Nicolay and John Hay, *Abraham Lincoln: A History* (New York: Century, 1890), 4:77.
3. Abraham Lincoln, *The Collected Works of Abraham Lincoln*, ed. Roy P. Basler (New Brunswick, NJ: Rutgers University Press, 1953), 4:331–32.
4. Nicolay and Hay, *Abraham Lincoln*, 4:79.
5. Abner Doubleday, "I Aimed the First Gun," in *Battles and Leaders of the Civil War*, ed. Ned Bradford (New York: Grammercy Books, 1956), 9.
6. Union Battle Reports, 1874–1899; Records of the Adjutant General's Office, Record Group 94; National Archives, Washington, DC.
7. Nicolay and Hay, *Abraham Lincoln*, 4:79.
8. *Evening Star* (Washington, DC), April 15, 1861.
9. Carl Sandburg, *Abraham Lincoln: The Prairie Years and the War Years, One Volume Edition* (New York: Harcourt, Brace & World, 1954), 231.
10. Sandburg, *Abraham Lincoln*, 231.

## April 15, 1861, Monday: A Depressing Meeting

1. *Evening Star* (Washington, DC), April 15, 1861.
2. *New York Herald*, April 15, 1861.
3. *Philadelphia Inquirer*, April 15, 1861.
4. Abraham Lincoln, *The Collected Works of Abraham Lincoln*, ed. Roy P. Basler (New Brunswick, NJ: Rutgers University Press, 1953), 4:331–32.
5. Frederick W. Seward, *Reminiscences of a War-Time Statesman and Diplomat, 1830–1915* (New York: Putnam, 1915), 153–54.
6. James M. McPherson, *Battle Cry of Freedom: The Civil War Era* (New York: Oxford University Press, 1988), 276.
7. McPherson, *Battle Cry of Freedom*, 277.

8. *New York Times*, April 15, 1861.
9. The Seventh New York Regiment had departed in a storm of cheers.
10. Joshua Wolf Shenk, *Lincoln's Melancholy: How Depression Challenged a President and Fueled His Greatness* (Boston: Houghton Mifflin, 2005), 175.

## April 16, 1861, Tuesday: An Uneventful Day

1. *New York Herald*, April 16, 1861.
2. U. S. Grant, *Personal Memoirs of U. S. Grant* (Old Saybrook, CT: Konecky & Konecky, 1886), 137–38.
3. James Longstreet, *From Manassas to Appomattox* (New York: Konecky & Konecky, 1992), 29–30.
4. William Tecumseh Sherman, *Memoirs of General William T. Sherman* (New York: Appleton, 1889), 203.
5. Sherman, *Memoirs*, 200–203.

## April 17, 1861, Wednesday: Increasing Anxieties

1. Abraham Lincoln, *The Collected Works of Abraham Lincoln*, ed. Roy P. Basler (New Brunswick, NJ: Rutgers University Press, 1953), 4:336–37.
2. Stephen B. Oates, *With Malice toward None: The Life of Abraham Lincoln* (New York: Harper & Row, 1977), 227.
3. "Confederate States of America—Proclamation of April 17, 1861," Yale Law School, n.d., https://avalon.law.yale.edu/19th_century/csa_p041761.asp. See also *New York Times*, April 18, 1861.
4. "Confederate States of America—Proclamation of April 17, 1861."
5. Winfield Scott to Abraham Lincoln, April 17, 1861, Abraham Lincoln Papers, Library of Congress, Washington, DC, https://www.loc.gov/resource/mal.0916800/.

## April 18, 1861, Thursday: A Regretted Loss

1. Abraham Lincoln, *The Collected Works of Abraham Lincoln*, ed. Roy P. Basler (New Brunswick, NJ: Rutgers University Press, 1953), 4:337.
2. Robert E. Lee, *The Wartime Papers of Robert E. Lee*, ed. Clifford Dowdey (Boston: Little, Brown, 1961), 4.
3. Lee, *Wartime Papers*, 4.
4. A. L. Long, *Memoirs of Robert E. Lee* (Secaucus, NJ: Blue and Gray, 1983), 89.
5. Lee, *Wartime Papers*, 8.
6. Emory M. Thomas, *Robert E. Lee: A Biography* (New York: Norton, 1995), 189.
7. Lee, *Wartime Papers*, 8–9.
8. Lee, *Wartime Papers*, 8.

9. Stephen B. Oates, *With Malice toward None: The Life of Abraham Lincoln* (New York: Harper & Row, 1977), 232.

10. James M. McPherson, *Battle Cry of Freedom: The Civil War Era* (New York: Oxford University Press, 1988), 280.

11. Margaret Leech, *Reveille in Washington 1860–1865* (New York: Harper, 1941), 59–60.

## April 19, 1861, Friday: A Controversial Proclamation

1. Frederick W. Seward, *Reminiscences of a War-Time Statesman and Diplomat, 1830–1915* (New York: Putnam, 1916), 155.

2. *New York Herald*, April 20, 1861.

3. Abraham Lincoln, *The Collected Works of Abraham Lincoln*, ed. Roy P. Basler (New Brunswick, NJ: Rutgers University Press, 1953), 4:340.

4. Lincoln, *Collected Works*, 4:340.

5. Jefferson Davis, *The Rise and Fall of the Confederate Government* (Richmond, VA: Garrett and Massie, 1938), 1:260.

6. *Richmond Examiner*, April 23, 1861.

7. Lincoln, *Collected Works*, 4:339.

8. *New York Herald*, July 8, 1867.

9. *New York Herald*, July 8, 1867.

10. James M. McPherson, *Battle Cry of Freedom: The Civil War Era* (New York: Oxford University Press, 1988), 381.

11. Lincoln, *Collected Works*, 4:339.

## April 20, 1861, Saturday: "Practical and Proper" Advice

1. Abraham Lincoln, *The Collected Works of Abraham Lincoln*, ed. Roy P. Basler (New Brunswick, NJ: Rutgers University Press, 1953), 4:340.

2. Lincoln, *Collected Works*, 4:340.

3. Lincoln, *Collected Works*, 4:341.

4. Lincoln, *Collected Works*, 4:341.

## April 21, 1861, Sunday: Defusing an Awkward Situation

1. *National Republican* (Washington, DC), April 23, 1861.

2. *National Republican* (Washington, DC), April 23, 1861.

3. John G. Nicolay and John Hay, *Abraham Lincoln: A History* (New York: Century, 1890), 4:131.

4. *National Republican* (Washington, DC), April 23, 1861.

5. Nicolay and Hay, *Abraham Lincoln*, 4:132.

## April 22, 1861, Monday: The President Speaks His Mind

1. *New York Daily Tribune*, April 24, 1861.
2. Abraham Lincoln, *The Collected Works of Abraham Lincoln*, ed. Roy P. Basler (New Brunswick, NJ: Rutgers University Press, 1953), 4:341.
3. Dean B. Mahin, *One War at a Time: The International Dimensions of the American Civil War* (Washington, DC: Brassey's, 1999), 41.
4. Lincoln, *Collected Works*, 4:341.
5. *New York Daily Tribune*, April 24, 1861.
6. Lincoln, *Collected Works*, 4:342.
7. Lincoln, *Collected Works*, 4:342.

## April 23, 1861, Tuesday: "Why Don't They Come!"

1. Abraham Lincoln, *The Collected Works of Abraham Lincoln*, ed. Roy P. Basler (New Brunswick, NJ: Rutgers University Press, 1953), 4:341.
2. John G. Nicolay and John Hay, *Abraham Lincoln: A History* (New York: Century, 1890), 4:152.
3. Nicolay and Hay, *Abraham Lincoln*, 4:137.
4. Edward Bates, *The Diary of Edward Bates, 1859–1866*, ed. Howard K. Beale (Washington, DC: US Government Printing Office, 1933), 185.
5. Nicolay and Hay, *Abraham Lincoln*, 4:137.
6. Nicolay and Hay, *Abraham Lincoln*, 4:141–42.
7. Margaret Leech, *Reveille in Washington 1860–1865* (New York: Harper, 1941), 65.

## April 24, 1861, Wednesday: "There Is No North"

1. Abraham Lincoln, *The Collected Works of Abraham Lincoln*, ed. Roy P. Basler (New Brunswick, NJ: Rutgers University Press, 1953), 4:342.
2. Lincoln, *Collected Works*, 4:343.
3. Lincoln, *Collected Works*, 4:343.
4. Lincoln, *Collected Works*, 4:342.
5. Lincoln, *Collected Works*, 4:343.
6. John G. Nicolay and John Hay, *Abraham Lincoln: A History* (New York: Century, 1890), 4:152–53.

## April 25, 1861, Thursday: The Happiest Man in Town

1. Abraham Lincoln, *The Collected Works of Abraham Lincoln*, ed. Roy P. Basler (New Brunswick, NJ: Rutgers University Press, 1953), 4:344.

2. Lincoln, *Collected Works*, 4:343.

3. Lincoln, *Collected Works*, 4:344.

4. Lincoln, *Collected Works*, 4:344.

5. *National Republican* (Washington, DC), April 26, 1861.

6. Margaret Leech, *Reveille in Washington 1860–1865* (New York: Harper, 1941), 66.

7. Leech, *Reveille in Washington*, 66.

8. Richard N. Current, *Lincoln and the First Shot* (Philadelphia: Lippincott, 1963), 167.

### April 26, 1861, Friday: Unprepared

1. James B. Fry, "The South Triumphant, the North Disappointed," in *Battles and Leaders of the Civil War*, ed. Ned Bradford (New York: Grammercy Books, 1956), 25–26.

2. Fry, "The South Triumphant," 26.

3. Tom Wheeler, *Mr. Lincoln's T-Mails* (New York: Collins, 2008), 43.

4. Dean B. Mahin, *One War at a Time: The International Dimensions of the American Civil War* (Washington, DC: Brassey's, 1999), 133.

5. Henry Adams, *The Education of Henry Adams* (Boston: Houghton Mifflin, 1918), 105.

6. William Howard Russell, *My Diary North and South* (Boston: Burnham, 1863), 118.

7. *National Republican* (Washington, DC), April 27, 1861.

8. *National Republican* (Washington, DC), April 27, 1861.

9. Abraham Lincoln, *The Collected Works of Abraham Lincoln*, ed. Roy P. Basler (New Brunswick, NJ: Rutgers University Press, 1953), 4:345.

### April 27, 1861, Saturday: A Controversial Order

1. "Lincoln, Abraham. Lincoln Extends the Blockade of Southern Ports to Virginia and North Carolina (April 27, 1861)," Sotheby's, n.d., https://www.sothebys .com/en/buy/auction/2020/fine-books-and-manuscripts-including-americana/lin coln-abraham-lincoln-extends-the-blockade-of.

2. Abraham Lincoln, *The Collected Works of Abraham Lincoln*, ed. Roy P. Basler (New Brunswick, NJ: Rutgers University Press, 1953), 4:346–47.

3. Lincoln, *Collected Works*, 4:347.

4. Lincoln, *Collected Works*, 4:347.

5. James M. McPherson, "As Commander-in-Chief I Have a Right to Take Any Measure Which May Best Subdue the Enemy," in *This Mighty Scourge: Perspectives on the Civil War* (New York: Oxford University Press, 2007), 214.

## April 28, 1861, Sunday: No Hope of an Armistice

1. William Swinton, *History of the Seventh Regiment, National Guard, State of New York, during the War of Rebellion* (New York: Fields, Osgood, 1870), 134.
2. Ralph Haswell Lutz, *Rudolph Schleiden and the Visit to Richmond, April 25, 1861* (Washington, DC: Library of Congress, 1917), 211–13.
3. Lutz, *Rudolph Schleiden*, 213.
4. "United States Volunteers in the Civil War," Global Security, n.d., https://www.globalsecurity.org/military/agency/army/usv-civil-war.htm#google_vignette.

## April 29, 1861, Monday: The Tension That Came with the Job

1. Abraham Lincoln, *The Collected Works of Abraham Lincoln*, ed. Roy P. Basler (New Brunswick, NJ: Rutgers University Press, 1953), 4:348.
2. Lincoln, *Collected Works*, 4:348.
3. William Howard Russell, *My Diary North and South* (Boston: Burnham, 1863), 151.

## April 30, 1861, Tuesday: An Enjoyable Afternoon

1. Abraham Lincoln, *The Collected Works of Abraham Lincoln*, ed. Roy P. Basler (New Brunswick, NJ: Rutgers University Press, 1953), 4:349.
2. Lincoln, *Collected Works*, 4:349.
3. John Hay, *Letters of John Hay and Extracts from Diary* (Washington, DC: printed [but not published] by Clara Stone Hay, 1908), 1:28.
4. *National Republican* (Washington, DC), May 1, 1861.

## May 1, 1861, Wednesday: A Therapeutic Letter

1. Abraham Lincoln, *The Collected Works of Abraham Lincoln*, ed. Roy P. Basler (New Brunswick, NJ: Rutgers University Press, 1953), 4:351.
2. Lincoln, *Collected Works*, 4:350–51.
3. Lincoln, *Collected Works*, 4:350.
4. Lincoln, *Collected Works*, 4:352.
5. Lincoln, *Collected Works*, 4:351.
6. Lincoln, *Collected Works*, 4:351.
7. Lincoln, *Collected Works*, 4:352.
8. Lincoln, *Collected Works*, 4:351–52.
9. *Evening Star* (Washington, DC), May 2, 1861.

## May 2, 1861, Thursday: The President Receives a Warning

1. Abraham Lincoln, *The Collected Works of Abraham Lincoln*, ed. Roy P. Basler (New Brunswick, NJ: Rutgers University Press, 1953), 4:353.

## May 3, 1861, Friday: A Tacit Admission

1. Abraham Lincoln, *The Collected Works of Abraham Lincoln*, ed. Roy P. Basler (New Brunswick, NJ: Rutgers University Press, 1953), 4:353.
2. Lincoln, *Collected Works*, 4:354.

## Epilogue, July 21, 1861, Sunday: "Their Dead Extended for Miles"

1. James B. Fry, "The South Triumphant, the North Disappointed," in *Battles and Leaders of the Civil War*, ed. Ned Bradford (New York: Grammercy Books, 1956), 29.
2. Fry, "The South Triumphant," 33.
3. David Homer Bates, *Lincoln in the Telegraph Office: Recollections of the United States Military Telegraph Corps during the Civil War* (New York: Century, 1907), 88–91.
4. Elisha Hunt Rhodes, *All for the Union* (New York: Vintage Books, 1985), 22.
5. Charles Minor Blackford, from "Letters from Lee's Army," in *The Civil War: The First Year Told by Those Who Lived It*, ed. Brooks D. Simpson, Stephen W. Sears, and Sheehan-Dean Aaron (New York: Library of America, 2011), 459–61.
6. Bates, *Lincoln in the Telegraph Office*, 91–93.
7. Arthur T. Pierson, *Zachariah Chandler: An Outline Sketch of His Life and Public Services* (Detroit: Post and Tribune, 1880), 211.
8. Samuel Toombs, *New Jersey Troops in the Gettysburg Campaign* (Orange, NJ: Evening Mail Publishing House, 1888), 2.

## Appendix: Lincoln's First Inaugural Address—Final Text, March 4, 1861

1. Abraham Lincoln, *The Collected Works of Abraham Lincoln*, ed. Roy P. Basler (New Brunswick, NJ: Rutgers University Press, 1953), 4:262–71.

# INDEX

www.ingramcontent.com/pod-product-compliance
Lightning Source LLC
Chambersburg PA
CBHW021957090426
42811CB00001B/68